AF856127

CONSULAR AUTHORITY OVER SEAMEN FROM THE UNITED STATES POINT OF VIEW

CONSULAR AUTHORITY OVER SEAMEN FROM THE UNITED STATES POINT OF VIEW

by

GEORGE C. GARBESI
Professor of Law, Loyola Universtiy at Los Angeles

Springer-Science+Business Media, B.V. 1968

ISBN 978-94-017-5822-2 ISBN 978-94-017-6267-0 (eBook)
DOI 10.1007/978-94-017-6267-0

Originally published by Martinus Nijhoff, The Hague, Netherlands in 1968.
Softcover reprint of the hardcover 1st edition 1968

TABLE OF CONTENTS

CHAPTER I

INTRODUCTION

In any situation in which two or more states contend for authority over the same event or person, there is invariably conflict between them as to whether the claim of one or the other is valid or, if both are concededly valid, as to which, if either, has priority. This entire work is devoted to an attempt to define the United States' position in situations where potential conflict arises out of the fact that seamen of one state are physically present within another state, usually on a vessel of the first state.

Ordinarily, for historic reasons, the power of a state within its own territory is presumed to be supreme. If aliens come within the geographic confines of a state, they are, while there, subject to the immediate control of the local authorities.[1] It may be that a state occasionally exercises its authority over aliens within its borders in such a manner as to create an international claim in the state of which an injured alien is a national. However, it is clear that ordinarily no state may exercise any sovereign authority within another state.[2]

There are certain exceptions recognized in international law to the rule that a state may not exercise jurisdiction within the territory of another state. For example, a state is entitled to exercise control over its own naval vessels abroad, even within the confines of another state.[3] The same is true of foreign embassies and homes of foreign diplomats.[4] In each case where international law recognizes some degree of state competence within the territory of other states, there is some strong

[1] I *Oppenheim's International law* 255–256 (6th ed. by Lauterpacht, N.Y., Longmans, Green and Co., 1940).

[2] *Id.* at 256–257; *Restatement, The Foreign Relations Law of the United States* (Proposed Official Draft, The American Law Institute, 1962) § 47. (1), hereinafter referred to simply as *Restatement*.

[3] *Id.* at 764; *Restatement* § 52.

[4] *Id.* at 417; *Restatement* § 82.

mutual interest which is protected by the permissive rule. In the case of naval vessels and embassies, the interest protected is the historic sensitivity of states to insults to their dignity. From the point of view of most states, any interference with either would be intolerable. Additionally, and doubtlessly even more significant, is the fact that any interference would constitute an unjustifiable burden upon the efficient functioning of the embassy or vessel.[5]

Historically, there has been recognized an international community interest in encouragement of the flow of international commerce.[6] One of the most effective ways of pursuing that policy was and is the imposition of only those minimal restrictions on international navigation which are essential to protect some other vital state interest. Each state may be presumed to desire, and therefore pursue, the policies which least detrimentally affect the movements of her own vessels in international trade. Therefore, the least restriction upon all vessels is likely to result from subjecting each to the control of the authorities of its own state, no matter where it happens to be. As a result, a somewhat ill-defined jurisdiction in the flag state has been recognized on board its vessels while in foreign waters. It is the aim herein to attempt to clarify the situation thus created.

Because these problems are generally resolved with a minimum of publicity, there is a tendency to feel that no problem exists. In fact, the writer has discussed the matter with various people in the foreign service of the United States who have stated that consuls have no authority over seamen abroad. Perhaps one reason for the declining interest in the United States in the subject is the increasingly comprehensive administrative role which the seamen's unions are playing in the resolution of disputes between seamen *inter se* and between them and their employers. The writer has been informed by one major unlicensed seamen's union that the consul is not involved in employment contract disputes, that the union policy is that grievances of this nature which cannot be settled while the ship is abroad must be de-

[5] See I *Oppenheim's International Law* 792–793 (8th ed. by Lauterpacht, David McKay, N.Y., 1955.), Engelke v. Mussmann, [1928] A.C. 433, [1928] All E.R. 18, 23; *cf.* Art. 23, "Harvard Research Draft Convention on Diplomatic Privileges and Immunities," 26 *A.J.I.L.* Supp. 89 (1932).

[6] For a good discussion of this interest and its promotion by transnational private organizations, see White, L. C., *International Non-Governmental Organizations* 19, 61, 206, 207 (Rutgers, New Brunswick, 1951). For a conflict of laws approach to the same problem, see Savigny, Friedrich Carl von, *Private International Law, and the Retrospective Operation of Statutes, A Treatise on the Conflict of Laws, and the Limits of their Operation in respect of Place and Time* 59, 69, 70 (Wm. Guthrie, trans., T. & T. Clark, Edinburgh, 1880).

ferred until her return to a United States port, and that any intervention by a consul in such a matter would be protested by the union. Although the unions and employers cannot avoid the effect of law defining consular authority, as a practical matter, a substantial percentage of potential problem situations will be withdrawn from consular consideration in this manner. There is no doubt that since the days when Nathaniel Hawthorne was United States consul in Liverpool, the nature and severity of the consular officer's problems with seamen has changed. An excerpt from his works will illustrate the extreme nature of the problem at that time:

> All the matters that I have been treating of, however, were merely incidental, and quite distinct from the real business of the office. A great part of the wear and tear of mind and temper resulted from the bad relations between the seamen and officers of American ships. Scarcely a morning passed, but that some sailor came to show the marks of his ill-usage on shipboard. Often, it was a whole crew of them, each with his broken head or lived bruise, and all testifying with one voice to a constant series of savage outrages during the voyage; or, it might be, they laid an accusation of actual murder, perpetrated by the first or second officers, with many blows of steel-knuckles, a rope's end, or a marlin-spike, or by the captain, in the twinkling of an eye, with a shot of his pistol. Taking the seamen's view of the case, you would suppose that the gibbet was hungry for the murderers. Listening to the captain's defence, you would seem to discover that he and his officers were the humanest of mortals, but were driven to a wholesome severity by the mutinous conduct of the crew, who, moreover, had themselves slain their comrade in the drunken riot and confusion of the first day or two after they were shipped. Looked at judiciously, there appeared to be no right side to the matter, nor any right side possible in so thoroughly vicious a system as that of the American mercantile marine. The Consul could do little, except to take depositions, hold forth the greasy Testament to be profaned anew with perjured kisses, and in a few instances of murder or manslaughter, carry the case before an English magistrate, who generally decided that the evidence was too contradictory to authorize the transmission of the accused for trial in America.[7]

However, in the nature of maritime affairs, there will still be many situations which require some administrative or judicial action while the vessel is abroad. Under these circumstances, the action will either have to be taken by the local authorities or by some official of the flag state. To the extent that applicable law admits it and is effective, the master of the vessel may handle these problems. There will be, however, many situations in which the master is one of the adversaries in the dispute or in which his authority is not effective for some

[7] *Hawthorne's Works*, Vol. VII, "Our Old Home English Note-Books," Vol. I, p. 48. (Boston, Cambridge, Houghton, Mifflin, 1870).

reason. Then, if the flag state is to exercise authority at all, it will have to be through its duly appointed official, the consul.[8]

As an illustration that these are not problems of purely historic interest: On May 19, 1964, the S.S. Pomona, a Liberian flag freighter, put into Honolulu shortly after the axe murder of her master on the high seas. The master was Norwegian as was part of the crew. The rest of the crew were Spanish, Swedish, Dutch, Argentinian and Colombian. Both local police and the Federal Bureau of Investigation indicated that they had no jurisdiction because of the location of the act which caused the death. However, as an accommodation to the Norwegian consul, Honolulu police did investigate the matter. Ultimately, at the request of the Norwegian consul, a crew member, also Norwegian, who had been detained by his orders, was deported to Norway by the United States authorities.[9]

The statistics alone tend to illustrate the importance of this inquiry. In 1956 more than one million seamen were employed on ships of more than 100 gross tons.[10] These seamen are constantly moving with their ships to all ports of the world, and of course carry their conflicts and problems with them.

The policy considerations too, which dictate leaving as much authority as possible in the officials of the flag state, have continued up to the present. This policy was well formulated by the United States Supreme Court in *Wildenhus's Case*

> From experience, however, it was found long ago that it would be beneficial to commerce if the local government would abstain from interfering with the internal discipline of the ship, and the general regulation of the rights and duties of the officers and crew towards the vessel or among themselves.[11]

[8] For general discussion, see Childs, J. Rives, *American Foreign Service* (N.Y. 1948), pp. 108 *et sec.*

[9] *The Sydney Morning Herald*, May 20, 21, 22, 1964. Note: This incident is not referred to to demonstrate the legal result. There is serious question whether the Norwegian consul had any legal authority, in view of the fact that the vessel flew the Liberian flag. The writer has been informed that the vessel belonged to a Liberian corporation (Namdal Shipping and Trading Co.), the beneficial interest in which was held by two expatriate Norwegians resident for many years in Brazil. Perhaps the very diversity of contacts in this case with such a variety of different states would justify some easily applied rule as to jurisdiction – such as the flag state having authority in all cases. In the instant case, the writer is informed that a Liberian governmental official actually went to Honolulu to investigate the matter in conjunction with the Norwegian police, and that he concurred in the voluntary return of the man to Norway, where he was not prosecuted because of lack of evidence.

[10] *I.L.O. Conference Documents*, 41st Session, 1958, Report I, p. 8.

[11] 120 U.S. 1, 12 (1886).

Sixty-six years later, the same Court said:

> Respondent places great stress upon the assertion that petitioner's commerce and contacts with the ports of the United States are frequent and regular, as basis for applying our statutes to incidents aboard his ships. But the virtue and utility of sea-borne commerce lies in its frequent contacts with more than one country. If, to serve some immediate interest, the courts of each were to exploit every such contact to the limit of its power, it is not difficult to see that a multiplicity of conflicting and overlapping burdens would blight international carriage by sea. Hence, courts of this and other commercial nations have generally deferred to a non-national or international maritime law of impressive maturity and universality.[12]

L. S. Woolf, in his *International Government,* describes the nationalism psychosis which tends to counteract the interest in freedom of commerce by insistence that each country administer every incident of its national life fully and without interference or cooperation from any other country.[13] Thereafter, he demonstrates how the inclusive interest of all nations in encouraging commerce has resulted in various attempts at international maritime legislation.[14] All international conventions the purpose of which is to regulate international maritime commerce reflect the desire of the signatory states to stimulate that commerce. However, in some the policy is more clearly formulated than in others. In the treaty which established the Intergovernmental Maritime Consultative Organization, one of the purposes of the organization is stated to be "to encourage the removal of discriminatory action and unnecessary restrictions by Governments affecting shipping engaged in international trade so as to promote the availability of shipping services to the commerce of the world without discrimination." [15]

Another example of an attempt in a convention to disrupt as little as possible, consistently with the primary purpose of the convention, international maritime trade by application of local authority over foreign ships will be found in the World Health Organization's International Sanitary Regulations. It precludes application of any sanitary measure to any foreign ship passing through the territorial sea unless

[12] Lauritzen v. Larsen, 345 U.S. 571, 581 (1952). For an early writer's views, see Savigny, Friedrich Carl von, *Private International Law, and the Retrospective Operation of Statutes. A Treatise on the Conflict of Laws, and the Limits of their Operation in Respect of Place and Time* (Wm. Guthrie, trans., T. & T. Clark, Edinburgh 1880), pp. 59, 69, 70. Savigny's thesis was that application of conflict of laws rules to produce equivalent results regardless of forum would encourage the flow of commerce.

[13] (London 1916), p. 113.

[14] *Id.* at 169 *et sec.*

[15] 1948, TIAS 4044, Art. 1 (b), 9 USTIAS 621, 623.

the vessel is to call at a port of that state.[16] It further proscribes any measure other than a medical examination on board foreign vessels passing through canals or waterways to ports in other states unless there is a reasonable probability that the vessel is carrying a contagious disease from an infected area, in which case a guard may be stationed on board to prevent contact with the shore.[17] There is also a general proscription of any measure other than medical examination on board a healthy ship in port, provided the passengers and crew do not disembark.[18] Finally, a vessel is given the option of departing rather than submitting to any sanitary measures in port. Such a vessel is given a right to bunker and take on stores and water in quarantine before leaving.[19] All of these provisions reflect an attempt by the parties to reconcile the primary purpose of the convention with the desire to permit vessels to come and go without restriction.

The General Agreement on Tariffs and Trade includes a clause clearly dedicated to serving the interest of all states in maintaining an unimpeded flow of traffic.[20]

The International Labor Organization convention on officers' competency certificates also seeks to protect the international interest in unimpeded maritime traffic, while at the same time attempting to insure that competent officers will be in charge of merchant ships. Only national authorities of the flag state are authorized to take any steps for its enforcement or punishment for its violation. Authorities of another state where the vessel happens to be, having knowledge of a violation, may only notify a consular officer of the state of registration of the facts.[21] That state is then obligated to investigate and take any steps dictated by the facts.

The convention for the protection of submarine cables too attempts to protect submarine cables from damage by merchant vessels, without unduly burdening their movements. Although, as a matter of administrative necessity, naval vessels of any party are authorized to apprehend the offending ship and make the investigation, the vessel and its people may only be tried in the courts of the state to which it belongs.[22] A somewhat similar regime has been established as recently

16 1951, TIAS 3625, Art. 32, 7 USTIAS 2255, 2271.
17 Art. 33, *id.*
18 Art. 34, *id.* at 2272.
19 Art. 44, *id.* at 2274.
20 Art. V, 61 Stat. Pt. 5, A21.
21 Art. 5, 6, 54 Stat. 1683, 1686, 1687.
22 1884, Art. VIII, X, 24 Stat. 989, 995, 996. See the discussion of this treaty in Woolf, L. S., *International Government* 132 *et sec.* (1916).

as 1961 in the convention for the prevention of oil pollution of the sea.[23] The authorities of any state party to the convention are empowered to investigate a suspected violation on board a vessel of any other in its ports. This action must be taken "expeditiously ... and the ship shall not be delayed." [24] Any enforcement or punishment activity is reserved for the flag state,[25] and it would presumably be deferred until the vessel returned there, any necessary interim action being taken by the consul.

There are other treaties which in a similar manner recognize a need to protect maritime commerce from unjustifiable interference by non-flag state authorities abroad. The International Labor Organization has adopted other conventions not referred to here which accommodate that interest. The ones used here are sufficiently indicative, and the United States is a party to each. Since it is the United States' practice and law with which this work deals, those treaties are particularly useful.[26]

For the purpose of this study, of course, treaty provisions alone would be wholly inadequate as the sole source material from which draw conclusions. It is true that treaties are important evidence of the attitude of the Department of State on problems of international law with which they deal, in addition to constituting rules binding upon the United States *vis-à-vis* the other parties. However, there are other sources which aid in defining the attitude of the Executive, the primary being diplomatic correspondence dealing with the same problems.

It is not only the attitudes and responses of the executive branch of government to international legal problems which constitute the complete picture of the United States' position on the subject. Although the executive branch is constitutionally endowed with control of international relations of the United States, both Congress and the judiciary, in the exercise of their normal function, necessarily encroach from time to time on the conduct of foreign relations.[27] This action must be considered both because of its direct effect in defining the official position of the United States and for its effect upon the executive in the exercise of its primary obligation in the field.

The inquiry will be restricted to the immediate question of consular

[23] TIAS 4900, 12 USTIAS 2989.

[24] Art. IX (2), *id.* at 2996–2997.

[25] Art. III (3), X, *id.* at 2992–2994, 2998.

[26] The fact that the United States is not a party to a treaty does not necessarily mean that the treaty represents law not binding on the United States. It may be a codification of existing general international law and therefore binding on the United States.

[27] For a treatment of one aspect of this problem, see *Ambassadors and Other Public Ministers*, 7 Atty. Gen. 186.

authority, and no effort will be made to go into such pertinent but collateral questions as the enforcement of foreign judgments, *resjudicata*, collateral estoppel, double jeopardy and extradition. Choice of laws problems will be considered only to the extent necessary to give a complete picture of the consul's position. Finally, since public vessels are subjected to a completely different regime not specifically involving consuls, their legal position will not be considered.[28] The entire discourse is predicated upon the assumption that we are dealing with vessels engaged in non-governmental commercial operations. Thus, in the case of United States vessels, all military, Coast Guard, hydrographic and governmental research vessels are excluded from consideration. Included, however, are state owned vessels engaged in commerce.

The arrangement is as follows: Chapter II is devoted to an analysis of the history of consular jurisdiction over seamen specifically, starting with a discussion of the medieval antecedents of the consular institution and its development among the ruins of the Roman Empire. It continues through the period of the capitulations and up to World War I. The reason for choosing World War I as the terminal point for the historic chapter is that United States policy concerning consular authority deviated markedly at about that time, the Seamen's Act of 1915 being one manifestation of the change.

Chapter III is devoted to a discussion of the general problems inherent in determining the seamen over whom the consul may exercise authority. This involves, of course, the question of which vessels may be considered vessels of the United States for jurisdictional purposes. It also deals with the dichotomy between the executive and legislative branches on that subject. At this point, also, is considered briefly the legal effect of international legal rules within the United States.

Chapter IV deals with general jurisdictional problems. First, it is necessary to fix the status of the consul in matters involving ships and shipping. Basically, the discussion identifies him as the official of the flag state who applies the law of that state, where possible, to controversies affecting the seamen on board. Thereafter, the discussion focuses upon general considerations which affect conflict of jurisdiction controversies between the state of the vessel's nationality and other states into which the vessel comes from time to time. The major factors considered here are the type of act involved, the effect of the act and

[28] See I *Oppenheim's International Law* 461, *supra* note 5, and *Restatement* § 52.

the location of the vessel at the time of the act. The United Nations Conventions on the law of the Sea are considered in some detail at this point. The purpose of the chapter is to draw in broad outlines those areas where the local authorities may be expected to have primary jurisdiction and those where they are precluded from acting. In the latter situations, and in those where local authorities do not act for some other reason, the flag state will have jurisdiction and will exercise it through one of its consular officers if he decides that some immediate action is indicated.

The final chapter takes up the problems dealt with in chapter IV in a more refined form, the idea being to determine how the general jurisdictional principles developed in earlier chapters are applied in practice to concrete fact situations. Civil and criminal jurisdictional questions are first dealt with together, primarily for convenience in analyzing the treaty provisions which deal with the subject in a general manner. Thereafter, the specific problems incidental to criminal acts are considered, and finally, civil and administrative jurisdictional problems.

CHAPTER II

HISTORY OF THE JURISDICTION OF THE CONSULAR OFFICER

From a historical point of view, the consular authority may be traced back to certain functionaries of the ancient Greek city-states, known as *prostates* and *proxeni*. These officials exercised jurisdiction and applied a special body of law to foreigners residing for the purpose of trade within their territory, but, different from the modern consul, exercised authority derived from the local sovereign rather than from the state of those over whom they exercised jurisdiction. Their position as precursor of the present day consular officer lies in the fact that they were appointed for the purpose of deciding disputes involving foreigners according to a body of law distinct from that governing the local inhabitants and of a nature more nearly approximating that to which they were accustomed in their native lands.

With this establishment in their own law, it is not surprising that the Greeks sought to, and were successful in convincing the Egyptian government during the sixth century, B.C., to permit the Greek settlers to select *prostates* from amongst their own number to administer Greek law in the resolution of controversies among members of the Greek community.[1]

This official, then, would be the true forebear of modern consular officers. He, like they, administered a body of law personal to its subjects derived from their own society,[2] rather than from the mores of the people there residing. Also, he owed his position of authority not to the local sovereign – although it was exercised with his license – but to the consent of the persons over whom it was exercised. Modern consuls, of course, derive their authority from such consent only in-

[1] See I Phillipson, *The International Law and Custom of Ancient Creece and Rome* 147–156 (1911).

[2] See E. R. Adair, *The Exterritoriality of Ambassadors in the Sixteenth and Seventeenth Centuries* 6, 11, 125 ,259 (1929).

directly, being uniformly appointed to their positions by the government of a foreign state rather than by any group of individuals in their private capacity. This development did not come about until much later. The institution of personal law administered by and for foreign communities funtioned also for the Jewish community in Egypt.[3]

Among the various legal institutions of the Greeks which had an effect upon the handling of similar problems in early Rome was that of the application of a special body of law to foreign merchants there. Although it was not originally related to that subject, it is to the Romans that we owe the term "consul" itself. As used by the Romans, it denoted an official of the Roman government. When the monarchy came to an end, in 510 B.C., the king was replaced by two annually appointed officers originally designated "praetors," and later "consuls." [4] The Digests of Justinian attribute the name "consul" to a derivation from the fact that they "consulted" the interest of the state above all else.[5] Apparently, these officers performed judicial as well as executive functions. Thereafter, the term consul became commonly applied to high judicial officers generally.[6]

The actual official who applied this special body of law to disputes involving foreigners was known as the *praetor peregrinus*, and he derived his authority from the consuls.[7] The term "praetor" described an official with general judicial functions, one class of whom were designated *peregrinus* because their special function was the administration of justice to the "peregrini" or foreigners.[8]

The body of law administered by the *praetor peregrinus* was not "personal" in the same sense as was the law administered in the Greek

[3] See Goodenough, Erwin Ramsdell, *Jewish Courts in Egypt* (1929) The author attributes this to a belief in personal law current at that time. p. 18. For a discussion of personal law amongst the Germanic peoples in the Roman Empire of the Middle Ages, see Savigny, *The History of the Roman Law during the Middle Ages* ch. III, LXXI, *et seq.* (1829). In chapter III, there is also an excellent discussion of the process whereby the personal law system gradually grew into a territorial legal community.

[4] Lee, *Elements of Roman Law* 4 (1949); D. 1, 2, 2, § 16, I Monro, *The Digest of Justinian* 10 (1904); I Sherman & Robinson, *Roman Readings in Roman Law* § 557 (1933). For a complete discussion of "consular" jurisdiction within the Roman Empire during the Middle Ages, see I Savigny, *The History of the Roman Empire during the Middle Ages* 29 *et seq.*, and 353 *et seq.* (1829).

[5] *Id.*

[6] D. 1, 10 and D. 1, 17, I Monro, *The Digest of Justinian* 45, 49–56 (1904). "Consul" described as a judge and "proconsul" as the highest judicial official of a province.

[7] Amos, *Roman Civil Law* 45 (1883); Lee, *Elements of Roman Law* 12 (1949).

[8] D. I, 3, 27, I Monro, *The Digest of Justinian* 12 (1904); I Strachan-Davidson, *Problems of the Roman Criminal Law* (MDCCCXII) 216; Sherman & Robinson, *Roman Readings in Roman Law* § 567 (1933).

and Jewish communities in Egypt. However, it was a special body of law applicable only to foreigners residing within the jurisdiction of Rome.

The application of a special body of law to foreign merchants in Rome bound them together in a legal community in much the same manner that personal law bound people of a common nationality. Being assured of the consistent application of such a body of law encouraged them to enter into the Roman community for the purpose of performing a desirable social function.[9]

The Roman jurisprudential theory was that all private law could be classified into three basic subdivisions: 1.) that derived from the rules of natural law, which was conceived to be those common sense rules dictated by man's existence as an animal, and having force over all animals, including man; [10] 2.) the civil law, which was that body of rules peculiar to a particular people and dependent upon the course of their own particular social mores but not inconsistent with the first category; and 3.) *jus gentium*, which was a body of rules not inconsistent with natural law but also not identical with it. *Jus gentium*, the law which was applied by the *praetor peregrinus* to foreigners residing in Rome, was conceived of as that body of rules which is dictated by necessity arising out of man's existence as a social being, as distinguished from his biological nature.[11] This *jus gentium* was the Roman equivalent of the personal law applied in the various foreign communities in Egypt – it constituted a recognition and attempted legal solution of the problems implicit in the presence of foreign merchants

[9] Savigny compares this legal community with the legal community defined by the personal law of the nomadic German tribes which invaded and settled in the old Roman Empire and that of the theologico-legal community of the Jews in Europe up until the 19th Century. *Private International Law, and the Retrospective Operation of Statutes* 58–59 (1880). See also Savigny, *The History of the Roman Law during the Middle Ages* 3 *et seq.* (1829).

[10] The biological function of mating was used as an example, and all the derivative institutions of matrimony and family.

[11] D. 1, 1, 1, I Monro, *the Digest of Justinian* 1–5 (1904); Lee, *Elements of Roman Law* 48 (1949); *Radin on Roman Law* 35 (1927). Examples of rules in this category were the duty of submission to parents and government and the right to repel violence. A means of determining the rules in this category, presumably, would have been to examine many municipal law systems and finding common provisions – similarly to the use of common principles of municipal law systems as evidence of a rule of international law by the International Court of Justice. The Court is required to apply "the general principles of law recognized by civilised nations." Art. 38 (1.) (c.) of the Statute of the International Court of Justice; Lauterpacht, "Decisions of Municipal Courts as a Source of International Law," 29 *Brit. Y. B. Int. L.* 65; S.S. "Lotus" (France v. Turkey) *P.C.I.J.*, Ser. A, No. 10, pp. 28, 74. Of course, it might be doubted whether the Roman *praetor peregrinus* would have had available to him any source from which he could examine any other municipal law system which may have existed concurrently with his own, and was probably, therefore, required to reason from general principles to arrive at the precise content of the *jus gentium*.

within the community. Commerce was deemed to be of sufficient importance to justify encouraging it by providing its foreign agents with a familiar legal climate not likely to alienate them. Both the application of personal law in Egypt and *jus gentium* in Rome were attempts to foster commerce by providing as little friction as possible. There is some body of thought that the belief in personal law was the real basis for the earlier capitulations [12] and not fear of the diversity between Christian and non-Christian cultures as suggested by some writers.[13]

During the time that the Roman Empire encompassed all the known civilized world, the application of the special, primarily commercial, body of law known as *jus gentium* was all that was deemed necessary to encourage commerce. During that time, the Mediterranean was a "Roman lake" binding the Empire into an economic unit,[14] and it was the function of the *jus gentium* to integrate the empire and foreign commercial communities into a single legal community. There were no political frontiers known to the Romans with which they had to be concerned, as a result of which questions of conflicts of jurisdiction between states did not arise. Therefore, there was no occasion to take the next step, namely not only application of a special body of law to "foreigners," but also its application by a special official of a foreign state.

From the time that Rome was occupied by the Germanic forces in 476 A.D., there was still formally a Roman Empire, since the conquering general was constituted viceroy of the Roman Emperor in Constantinople,[15] and thereafter the invaders merely settled in a new part of the Empire and became Romanised. This situation prevailed until the year 800 A.D., when Charlemagne was constituted Holy Roman Emperor by Pope Leo, thus converting the *de facto* division, camouflaged by the formal recognition of the authority of the Eastern emperor, into an open cleavage between the governments of the two divisions, each claiming dominion over the whole, but neither being in a position to enforce its will upon the other. During this period, two processes made it necessary to reassess commerce, including its legal foundation. The sudden expansion and lightning conquests by the adherants of Islam destroyed the commercial and political unity of

[12] Discussed *infra* at p. 39.
[13] Schuyler, *American Diplomacy* 59 (1886); Walker, *A History of the Law of Nations* 230 (1899).
[14] Pirenne, *Mohammed and Charlemagne* ch. I (1956).
[15] Bryce, *The Holy Roman Empire* 23 *et seq.* (1889).

the Mediterranean, and the political unity of the Western Empire began to disintegrate.

From 634 to 712 A.D., the Arabic forces overran practically all of the Near East (not including Constantinople) and the entire African provinces of Rome, in addition to Spain.[16] By the year 916, this expansion had terminated,[17] leaving a completely changed condition of world affairs. No longer was the Mediterranean a body of water which served to unify commerce; it was now the frontier between two hostile and fundamentally different peoples. The Arabs, unlike the Germanic peoples, did not become Romanised; they "Arabised" the conquered territories, including the people. Where the German occupation ended in continuity of the unity of the west, the Arabic destroyed it. If commerce was to be encouraged, it would have to be by a set of rules consonant with this new state of affairs. Ultimately, in 1453, the Turks were successful in capturing Constantinople, and thereafter pushing into south-eastern and central Europe before being turned back at the gates of Vienna. In the sixth century and continuing to the tenth, began the development of the autonomous, commercially oriented Italian city-states such as Venice, Genoa and Amalfi.[18] The prosperity and even existence of these embryonic states depended almost exclusively upon their commerce, so that the only thing consistent about their political activity was that it always tended to foster that activity, at least in their view. It was this singleness of purpose which caused them to make war on one another and upon the empire, and even to ally themselves from time to time with the Arabs, who were continually attacking and pillaging various parts of Italy after having conquered Sicily.[19] It was fully consistent with that purpose that special maritime and commercial codes should have been created by them as the legal tool to effectuate the policy of protection and encouragement of commerce.

In the year 987 A.D., with the accession of Hugh Capet, France became formally detached from the empire.[20] By this time, the Empire had evolved into a loose federation of the many Germanic states linked rather insignificantly with the Italian territories. This was the period when the commercial cities of Germany were coming into existence and assuming autonomy in a manner similar to that of the development

[16] *Supra* note 14, at p. 149 *et seq.*
[17] *Id.*
[18] *Id.* at 174–185.
[19] *Id.*
[20] *Supra* note 15, at 136.

of the Italian city-states. During the thirteenth and fourteenth centuries, these cities, known as the Hanseatic League, came into a position of power and prosperity, also substantially dependent upon their commerce to the exclusion of other factors.[21] Here too, for similar reasons, one might expect to find the adoption of special legal codes to foster commercial activity.

In view of the fact that there were now other sovereign jurisdictions which could influence the commercial-legal climate, it was necessary to conclude agreements which would prevent or minimize any adverse effect. Sir Travers Twiss, in his introduction to the *Black Book of Admiralty*, asserts that there were two conditions precedent to the establishment of an international commerce on any substantial scale. One was "the permission on the part of the local authorities for the foreign merchants and mariners to settle their controversies according to their own laws." [22] Since nationalism had not yet become a potent force, and since both parties recognized the desirability of encouraging the growth of commerce, such agreements were not difficult to conclude. In fact, it has been suggested that during the reign of the Latin Kings in Jerusalem, during the limited period during which the Mohammedan rule in that area of the world was suspended, they found it not only desirable, but necessary to insist that merchants from abroad should settle their own disputes by their own law applied by judges of their own selection who understood it.[23] The special maritime codes were the municipal law descendants of the Roman *jus gentium*, whereas the agreements among the newly emerging states were the natural development in the new international arena.

It appears that the governmental development of municipal codes and inter-state agreements to deal with the legal problems of commerce was superimposed upon a private institution devised for the same purpose. The merchants had associated themselves in occupational guilds and adopted rules designed to compel the settlement of commercial disputes without the interposition of any governmental authority. These disputes were to be settled by application of a special body of largely customary law applicable exclusively to commercial disputes, and which ultimately developed into what became known as the law

[21] *Id.* at 214.

[22] Vol. 4, 1876, p. LXXIX. The other condition was the renunciation by territorial authorities of the "right of wreck." The "right of wreck" was the right, practised nearly universally, of the local authorities appropriating the property in any wreck within their territory and selling the surviving mariners into slavery.

[23] *Id.* at XVIII.

merchant in England. Local governments were persuaded to go so far as to set aside certain areas such as fairs, markets and port areas as exempt from central governmental jurisdiction, thus giving free scope to the development, through the guilds, of a body of peculiarly commercial law. The highest officer of the guild was charged with its administration, and enforced his judgments with the aid of duly constituted magistrates. Ultimately, he was himself invested with the magistrates' authority. The Italian merchants, dispersing throughout the Mediterranean and Europe in large numbers, carried this system with them into foreign lands,[24] and the person charged with the settlement of disputes there had an official capacity conferred upon him by the city from where they came. He was known as a consul.[25] The law applied by him was, to some limited extent, codified.

Apparently, the earliest of the maritime and commercial codes known to historians was the Amalfitan Table.[26] In it, the official in whom authority is vested is consistently referred to as "consul," [27] and he is invested with rather broad judicial power. For instance, he had discretion to grant maintenance to seamen ashore for the benefit of the enterprise at a higher rate than that provided by the code if the sojourn was in barren country; [28] he could permit a ship to sail with imperfect tackle and gear if he was satisfied that such action was justified by the circumstances; [29] In case of contract for sale of a ship, where the parties could not agree as to the time of passing title, he

[24] See the discussion of "factories" in Piggott, *Exterritoriality* 174 (1907).

[25] Mitchell, *An Essay on the Early History of the Law Merchant* ch. I–III (1904).

[26] Sir Travers Twiss, in his introduction to Volume four of the *Black Book of Admiralty*, attributes its origin to the tenth century. (1876) at XI On the other hand, L. A. Senigallia places the earliest date of a written record at just prior to 1131. *Tabula De Amalpha* (1934). There is substantial evidence that there was at a much earlier date a set of special rules pertaining to maritime affairs known as the *Rhodian Sea Law* because of its source in the Island of Rhodes. It is referred to in the Code of Justinian and in the Digests as being controlling law in absense of contra special enactments. D. 14, 2, 9, Scott, *The Civil Law* (1932). Thus, it would be of much earlier origin than the tenth century. However, no written document setting it forth in whole or in part is known to exist, and there is no evidence of contents bearing on the question being considered here. It may be that the Romans derived their notions of a *jus gentium*, and its content, from the Rhodian Sea Law, which apparently was a restatement of a common law of the sea widely adhered to beyond Rhodes. *The Rhodian Sea Law* CXXIII (1909). However, there is no reason to suppose that the international flavor of the later codes would have existed at that early date.

[27] *E.g.* §§ 13, 22, 34, 39, 50, 4 *Black Book of Admiralty* 11, 17, 25, 27, 37 (1876). In his introduction to volume 3 of the *Black Book of Admiralty*, Sir Travers Twiss says, "Thus the most ancient extant source of Modern Maritime Law are the Decisions of the Consuls of the Sea of the city of Trani on the shores of the Adriatic Gulf. They purport to be of the date of A.D. 1063 ...." p. XLIII. It seems that there was a parallel development of maritime law in Trani to that in Amalphi.

[28] § 13, *id.* at 11.

[29] § 22, *id.* at 17.

was empowered to fix the time and be present when the agreement was executed; [30] and he was even authorized to supervise the end of the voyage accounting and to bind all interested parties by his determination as to the details of the account.[31] Finally, he was vested with at least some criminal jurisdiction, having the power to levy fines for disobedience of lawful commands.[32]

Although it is not expressly so stated, apparently the consul was a judicial officer in a court having exclusive jurisdiction over maritime affairs. There is a reference in section 34 [33] to the "Maritime Court of the noble city of Amalfi," coupled with a requirement that a ship sale, which must be approved by the court, is subject to the authority of the consul. Section 39 [34] requires the accounting to be "in the court and in the presence of the consuls," who are authorized to determine and validate the final account. Sections 23 and 25 refer to certain procedural judicial duties.[35]

It seems to have been contemplated by the originators of the Amalfitan Table that the consul might, under some circumstances at least, function in his judicial capacity outside the territory of the city. Section 39 [36] provides that the terminal voyage accounting should be conducted before the consul whether the voyage terminate and the ship therefore be located beyond the confines, as well as within the city. In fact, it is a fair interpretation of the whole code that it was contemplated that it would have extraterritorial effect.

Another of these codes, the Maritime Ordinances of Trani,[37] refers in each article to its promulgators as "the consuls of the sea." This code too ascribes the judicial authority in maritime disputes to the consuls.[38]

Complementing their municipal legal approach to the protection of

[30] § 34, *id.* at 25.
[31] § 39, *id.* at 27.
[32] § 50, *id.* at 37.
[33] *Id.* at 25.
[34] *Id.* at 27.
[35] *Id.* at 17–18.
[36] *Id.* at 27.
[37] *Id.* at 522–543.
[38] Section XXV was designed to resolve the problem which arises out of a dispute between merchant charterer and owner of a ship concerning dispatch of the vessel. If the merchants unreasonably delay dispatching her, she becomes at their risk and they must pay for the detention as and in the amount determined by the consuls. *Id.* at 539. Section XXVIII implicitly gives the consul power to determine whether a mariner was justified in killing the master and therefore should not be banished. *Id.* at 541. This latter provision is almost universally duplicated in the other early maritime codes. See *e.g.* Art. 26 and 28 of the *Gotland Sea-Laws*, Art. XXIV of the *Laws of Wisby*, Art. 26 of *The Purple Book of Bruges*. Id. at 83, 85–86, 272, 317, 319.

vital commercial interests with moves in the international arena, Amalfi obtained from the King of Jerusalem, in 1178 A.D., an exemption of its merchants from the exercise of local jurisdiction over disputes among themselves, which were to be settled by them according to their own customs. In 1190, the same privilege was granted by Naples to all Amalfitan subjects. Trani obtained similar privileges within the territory of the King of Jerusalem in the same year.[39] Indeed, either by specific agreement or by tacit acceptance of an almost universal custom, the practise of foreigners having their disputes resolved by judges of their own nationality applying their own law became widespread.[40]

The development of a special maritime and commercial law, at least partially in codified form, proceeded in the north German cities in a manner which paralleled its evolution in the Italian city-states. The commercial codes of these cities reflected the general belief that commerce would best be encouraged by applying a body of familiar law to the dealings of merchants. For example, actions by mariners against their employers were limited by the "Maritime Law of the Osterlings" to proceedings before a local alderman, upon pain of a ten mark fine.[41] These codes were also attempts in other ways to prevent interference with the natural flow of commerce. Mariners on vessels about to depart for sea were protected against arrest for debt for this reason.[42] In fact, it appeared that the same problem was being resolved in the same way wherever it arose. In 1368, The Kiing of Sweden granted permission to the merchants of Amsterdam and Enchuysen to form commercial establishments in Swedish cities and to have their controversies settled by their own judges and according to their own law.[43] In France, an ordinance of the kings and a statute of Marseilles required the carrying on board French vessels of a judicial officer to resolve disputes which arose pertaining to the venture.[44]

Except for the codes of Trani and Amalfi, the oldest source of maritime law is the *Judgments of Oleron*. Apparently, there was an autonomous establishment there prior to 1199 when Queen Elinor of Aquitaine legalized it by granting a charter.[45] In 1314, a special court functioned there administering general maritime law; and its judgments

[39] *Id.* at XI, XV.

[40] *Supra* note 25, at 50–51.

[41] Art. XL and XLI, IV *Black Book of Admiralty* 381, 383 (1876).

[42] *E.g.*, Art. 6, *The Gotland Sea-Laws, id.* at 59; Art. VI, *The Laws of Wisby,id.* at 267; Art. 6, *Code of the Teutonic Order of Livonia, id.* at 291.

[43] *Id.* at XXXVII.

[44] This law dates from 1246 A.D. III *Black Book of Admiralty* 183 (1874).

[45] II *Black Book of Admiralty* XXVII (1873).

were recorded for future use as precedents.[46] The judgments, along with *The Customs of Oleron*, were reduced to writing, constituting the foundation of maritime law in Spain, England and Jerusalem. Although there were some differences of detail to be found in those three jurisdictions, which were the result of their acquiring the law of Oleron through different channels,[47] they all show unmistakably a common source and reflect the common policy of protecting and encouraging commerce.

In Barcelona, the adoption of this special body of maritime law dates from 1258 A.D., when King James I of Aragon published an ordinance establishing a special maritime tribunal.[48] Consuls of the sea were first appointed in Barcelona in 1279, and Peter III of Aragon established a special consular jurisdiction in Valencia in 1283, providing that all maritime disputes should be decided according to the custom of the sea which prevailed at Barcelona.[49] In cases of controversies between merchants and mariners there, the consuls consulted first the merchants' guild to ascertain the controlling law, and then the navigators' guild. In cases of conflict, the rule espoused by the navigators' guild was enforced.[50] In the Kingdom of Aragon, as in France, from 1258, a special consul was appointed to accompany each ship sailing out of the kingdom, who would have authority to adjudicate all disputes, both aboard the ship and on shore between members of the ship's company.[51] This official was required to apply the same law, namely that body of law adopted from Oleron, as was his shoreside counterpart.

Both the jurisdiction of the consul and the governing body of law were superimposed upon the guild system of private autonomous regulation. By article XL of the *Customs of the Sea*, disputes between owners and charterers concerning where the vessel is to load were referred to two officials of the navigators' guild for final decision,[52] as were disputes between owners and merchants as to the value of the ship for purposes of general average contribution.[53] The consuls themselves were elected annually by the membership of the navigators' guild, as was one of their number who served as an appellate

[46] *Id.* at XXXVII.
[47] I *Black Book of Admiralty* LXIV–LXIX (1871).
[48] II *Black Book of Admiralty* LXVI–LXVII (1873).
[49] *Id.* at LXVI.
[50] IV *Black Book of the Admiralty* XCL (1876).
[51] III *Black Book of the Admiralty* 181–183 (1874).
[52] *Id.* at 115–118.
[53] *Id.* at 265–271.

tribunal from decisions of the consuls.[54] These consuls were given the broadest of jurisdiction in matters maritime, as will be seen from the following excerpts from the *Judicial Order of the Courts of the Consuls of the Sea:*

> The consuls determine all questions which concern freight, damage to cargo laden on board ship, mariners' wages, partnerships in ship-building, sales of ships, jetison, commissions entrusted to masters or to mariners, debts contracted by the master who has borrowed money for the wants or necessities of his vessel, promises made by the master to a merchant, or by a merchant to a master, goods found upon the open sea or on the beach, the fitting out of ships, galleys, or other vessels, and generally all other contracts which are set forth in the Customs of the Sea.[55]
>
> The consuls of the sea have all ordinary jurisdiction over all the contracts, which have to be determined according to the usage and custom of the sea, and which are declared, stated, and specified in the Customs of the Sea.[56]

The apparent desire was to create a legal community among mariners and merchants, ashore and afloat, for the purpose of assuring certainty and continuity in legal relations within that community.

In England during the early Middle Ages, a recognition was beginning to develop that commercial matters should be dealt with in a manner consistent with international standards, regardless of how similar problems might be handled locally. Pollack and Maitland say that the "law merchant" was conceived as a body of rules distinct from the common law during the thirteenth century,[57] but undoubtedly the practise itself was long in the making before it became formally recognized.[58] The so-called "Customaries" of the early English boroughs were the repositories of the rules applicable to international marine commerce, commonly referred to as the "Law Merchant." This body of law was applied by a local tribunal to all controversies of a commercial or maritime nature wherein a foreigner was involved as a party. Special courts to administer the "Law Marine" to passing mariners were provided for in the "Domsday book of the borough of Ipswich" as early as the year 1200 A.D. A similar practise was recorded in the official documents of other English boroughs. This is the earliest record of an exclusively maritime and commercial jurisdiction and law

[54] The Judicial Order of the Courts of the Consuls of the Sea, IV *Black Book of the Admiralty* 451 (1876).

[55] Ch. XXII, *id.* at 473–474.

[56] Ch. XXXI, *id.* at 483.

[57] *The History of English Law Before the Time of Edward I,* 450 (1895).

[58] See Potter, *An Historical Introduction to English law and its Institutions* 90, 160–162 (1943).

in operation in England.[59] Article XL of *The Domes Day of Gippeswich* provided for a special simplified procedure in cases between merchants, and Article L provided for the application of the law merchant to such controversies.[60] England, then, had embarked upon a legal program, similar to that found in other growing commercial centers of Europe, of keeping alive the legacy from Rome, namely the policy of providing for a prompt, competent adjudication of maritime cases according to a universal law of the sea. In the year 1100, King Henry I reorganized the system, but only for the purpose of rendering it even more expeditious and favorable to the growing commerce.[61]

The *Judgments of the Sea* of Oleron were adopted as controlling law in admiralty and commercial matters in England as early as the reign of Richard I, when he returned from the Holy Land, but were apparently in use before then.[62] England thereby came to share a body of substantive commercial law in common with other major centers of commerce. The statute of 12 Edward III formally adopted the whole body of the maritime law of Oleron as controlling in England.[63] These same laws were adopted in Flanders in the middle of the 14th century.[64] Lubeck had a similar code in the year 1240, and Wisby a similar body of law at least as early as 1505.[65] The entire European civilization, then, was bound together in a commercial legal community from the Baltic through the Atlantic and Mediterranean to its easternmost end.

Those entities which grew out of the Roman Empire admitted among themselves the extraterritorial effect of their laws pertaining to maritime affairs. However, the other great power in the commercial world at that time, namely Turkey, had a different legal history and would not automatically recognize the effect of those laws. Therefore, in order to carry out their commercial policies effectlively, it was necessary for the western European countries to conclude agreements with Turkey extending the community into its territory. In 1453 and 1454 respectively, Genoa and Venice concluded treaties with Turkey which conferred upon their consuls both civil and criminal jurisdiction over their nationals while in Turkey.[66] In 1535, France also concluded

[59] II *Black Book of the Admiralty* VII–VIII (1873).
[60] *Id.* at 127, 137.
[61] *Id.* at VIII. Among other changes, he made the law of wreck applicable only in cases where there were no survivors. I *Black Book of the Admiralty* XLV (1871).
[62] III *Black Book of the Admiralty* XIV (1874).
[63] I *Black Book of the Admiralty* LXI (1871).
[64] IV *Black Book of the Admiralty* XLVII (1876).
[65] *Id.* at XXIV, XXVII.
[66] Lee, *Consular Law and Practise* 5 (1961).

such a treaty with the Ottoman Porte.[67] It was upon the features of this treaty that all the subsequent capitulations were based.[68] Apparently, Poland too had concluded such a treaty sometime prior to 1675.[69] Great Britain concluded a comprehensive treaty on the subject with the Ottoman Porte in 1675.[70] This treaty, being the basis of the subsequent treaties concluded by the United States with both Turkey and other states, will be considered here in some detail.

Articles I and II dealt generally with the right of British subjects to be free of any restraint upon their persons or property.[71] Article VII gave the same assurance to men of commerce.[72] Article VIII relieved all British subjects of the threat of imprisonment for debt, or apparently even of demands being made upon them for payment of claimed debts.[73] By article X, the British ambassador was given sole jurisdiction to decide complaints made against a British subject.[74] It would seem to follow from that article that a dispute between two British subjects would be resolved by the ambassador. At any rate, it was specifically so stated in article XVI.[75]

Although there are obviously some difficulties of reconciling apparently inconsistent provisions in this treaty, at least the minimum extent to which British subjects were removed from local jurisdiction by it can be determined. In civil controversies solely involving British subjects, the parties were subject to the exclusive jurisdiction of the British sovereign representative. If a subject of any other state, including Turkey, were involved in a civil controversy with a British subject, the cause had to be heard at a particular location and in the presence of the British representative.[76] If a British subject were charged with a criminal act, he could only be tried by a court consisting

[67] I *Dictionnaire Diplomatique* 398 (1933).

[68] *Id.;* 4 *Encyclopaedia Britannica* 812 (1950).

[69] See the reference to that agreement, in addition to those with Venice and France, in the preamble to the treaty between Turkey and Britain of 1675. Treaties, etc. of Commerce and Navigation between Great Britain and Foreign Powers Wholly or Partially in Force on January 1, 1907, 9035 (1907); II *Hertslett's Commercial Treaties* 347 (1840).

[70] *Id.*

[71] II *Hertslett's Commercial Treaties* 347–348.

[72] *Id.* at 348.

[73] *Id.* at 348–349.

[74] *Id.* at 349. Article XXIV appears inconsistent with this in that it requires that the ambassador or his representative merely be present at any time that litigation is heard involving a British subject and a subject of some other nation. p. 352. Article XLII gives joint jurisdiction to the local judges and the ambassador in criminal matters involving British subjects. p. 357.

[75] *Id.* at 350.

[76] This is, of course, far less than the British subject's rights under article X. *Id.* at 349.

of the local judge and the British representative conjointly.[77] These provisions should be compared with the section on the capitulations entered into by the United States with various Arabic and Oriental countries.[78]

THE UNITED STATES HISTORY OF CONSULAR JURISDICTION

Although prior to that time the United States had sent representatives overseas for the purpose of performing consular functions, it was by the treaty of amity and commerce concluded with France in February, 1778, that formal recognition was first given to the right of consular representation. Article XXIX of that treaty says: "The two contracting parties grant mutually the liberty of having each in the ports of the other, consuls, vice-consuls, agents and commissaries, whose functions shall be regulated by a particular agreement." [79] The functions of these representatives was made subject to further agreement between the parties. However, France almost immediately availed herself of the right accorded by the treaty, and established consular offices within the United States. The United States continued to rely upon their commercial and political representatives abroad to perform consular functions.[80] It was not until January, 1781, that the United States finally appointed a vice-consul to serve in France.[81] Similar general provisions permitting mutual consular representation were contained in treaties concluded between the United States and The Netherlands in 1782,[82] Sweden in 1783,[83] and Prussia in 1785.[84]

[77] Article XLII, *id.* at 357. This article could have been construed as being limited to cases involving British seamen, since it says "or other persons navigating under their flag," thus leaving all other British subjects responsive only to the British representative under Art. X. *Id.* at 349.

[78] See *post* at p. 38 *et seq.*

[79] 8 Stat. 12, 28. This treaty was annulled by Act of Congress of 7 July, 1798, 1 Stat. 578, and was mutually abrogated by the convention with France of Sep. 30, 1800, Art. II (b), 8 Stat. 178.

[80] Carr, "The American Consular Service," 1 *A.J.I.L.* 891, 892 (1907).

[81] A consul had been appointed in 1780, but had been killed at sea on his way to take up his duties. *Id.* at 783.

[82] Art. XXI, 8 Stat. 32, 44. A further treaty was concluded with The Netherlands in 1839 wherein continued consular representation was recognized and specific reference made to deserters in the same article. Art. III, 8 Stat. 523, 524.

[83] Art. XXVI, *id.* at 60, 74.

[84] Art. XXV, *id.* at 84, 98. This article, unlike the ones contained in the treaties with France, The Netherlands and Sweden, expressly made the consul subject to local law in the same manner as any private citizen of his country. Additionally, it contained a most-favored-nation clause with regard to consular authority, so that when the United States thereafter concluded its consular convention with France, the same consular powers redounded to the Prussian consul. Art. XXVI, *id.*

In 1784, pursuant to the treaty clause of 1778,[85] Benjamin Franklin signed a treaty with France which was to regulate consular functions as between the two countries. However, that treaty was never ratified by the United States because it conferred more extraterritorial consular jurisdiction over ships and seaman than considered desirable.[86] However, a consular convention was concluded by Thomas Jefferson in 1788,[87] and this one was duly ratified in the following year.[88]

In the treaty of 1788, consular functions were carefully delineated. It delegated rather broad civil and criminal authority over ships and mariners. Article VI [89] gave him the authority to adjust average losses sustained elsewhere than within local territorial waters, provided that only nationals of his own sovereign had an interest in the adjustment. Article VII [90] gave him exclusive authority to deal with wrecked vessels of his state, the local authorities being pledged to assist in these activities but enjoined from interfering without request. By Article VIII, it was provided:

> The consuls or vice-consuls shall exercise police over all the vessels of their respective nations, and shall have on board the said vessels all power and jurisdiction in civil matters, in all the disputes which may there arise; they shall have an entire inspection over said vessels, their crew, and the changes and substitutions there to be made; for which purpose they may go on board the said vessels whenever they may judge it necessary. Well understood that the functions hereby allowed shall be confined to the interior of the vessels, and that they shall not take place in any case which shall have any interference with the police of the ports where the said vessels shall be.[91]

This article conferred upon the consul, in the clearest terms, a complete civil and criminal jurisdiction over matters pertaining to the internal economy of national ships. The only problem would be the determination of whether a particular matter reached beyond the vessel, its resolution being therefore reserved primarily to the local authorities. No attempt will be made to analyze in terms of concrete

[85] *Supra* note 79.
[86] *Supra* note 80, at 894.
[87] 8 Stat. 106.
[88] It was nullified by Act of Congress of 7 July, 1798, and mutually abrogated by the Convention with France of September 30, 1800. *Supra* note 79. A new treaty was concluded in 1822, but it only contained reference to consular handling, with judicial assistance, of deserters from his country's vessels. Art. 6., 8 Stat. 278, 280. The parties seem to have assumed a mutual right to consular representation, notwithstanding the abrogation of the treaties of 1778 and 1788.
[89] *Supra* note 87, at 110.
[90] *Id.*
[91] *Id.* at 112.

fact situations the boundaries of his authority under this article. For the purposes of a historical treatment of the question, a general formulation of the limits should surfice. However, Articles X and XI [92] expressly place acts committed ashore by members of the ship's company outside consular authority, and provide him with a right only of notification upon an arrest subsequently being made on board. Thereafter, he was entitled to have the man delivered to him for his discretionary deportation on ships of his state instead of being set at at liberty. Consular criminal authority was expanded by Article IX,[93] which gave him authority to demand assistance from local authorities in arresting, detaining in prison and transporting deserters back to their respective countries.[94] Both civil and criminal jurisdiction were further clarified by Article XII, which applied by its terms not only to mariners, but also to any dispute involving only citizens of one of the contracting parties in the territory of the other:

> All differences and suits between the subjects of the Most Christian King, in the United States, or [vice-versa] ..., and particularly all disputes relative to the wages and terms of agreement of the crews of the respective vessels, and all differences of whatever nature they be, which may arise between the privates of the said crews, or between any of them and their captains, or between the captains of different vessels of their nation, shall be determined by the respective consuls and vice-consuls, either by a reference to arbitrators or by a summary judgment, and without costs. No officer of the country, civil or military, shall interfere therein, or take any part whatever in the matter; and the appeals from the said consular sentences shall be carried before the tribunals of France or of the United States, to whom it may appertain to take cognizance thereof.[95]

Apparently, no thought was given to the problem presented by a dispute between a national of one party serving on a vessel of the other and another member of the ship's company. If it were not for the first part of the Article, which defines disputes between subjects of the consul's country within the territory of the other, coupled with "and particularly," one would have concluded that the seaman acquired the nationality of his ship for the purposes of that article.

[92] *Id.*

[93] *Id.*

[94] It should be noted that this particular power of consuls of the United States and of foreign consuls in the United States has been expressly mullified by an Act of Congress known as the Seamen's Act of 1915. See *post* at p. 50.

[95] *Id.* at 114.

This problem will be treated elsewhere.[96] A most-favored-nation clause was included.[97]

The treaties with France which have been examined were typical of the United States' approach to consular relations with states of the European cultural and legal posture. There was an underlying assumption of legal equality, all rights and duties being reciprocal, and neither party getting a legal advantage not common to both. A French consul had the same authority to deal with matters maritime concerning French interests in the United States as did his American counterpart in France. The same is true of the treaties with The Netherlands, Sweden and Prussia.[98] In both the treaty with France and the one with the The Netherlands, there were provisions requiring the other party to aid the United States in its efforts to establish a favorable regime with the Barbary Powers of North Africa.[99] In neither of these instruments was a like obligation imposed regarding any European state. These provisions disclose an implicit assumption that the two groupings of states should, for the purposes of international relations, be treated differently. There is no doubt that that assumption was justified, in view of the then existing practise of the Barbary States' financing governmental operations by the proceeds of piracy, or tribute in lieu thereof, in the Mediterranean.[100] This practise constituted an insufferable burden on commerce, and it was the intention of the United States to eliminate it.

The first of the so-called "capitulations" was negotiated by Thomas Barclay with Morocco, and was signed by John Adams and Thomas Jefferson in 1787.[101] As might be expected, this treaty could almost be described as a unilateral assumption of obligations by Morocco *vis-*

[96] *Post* at p. 90. It is interesting to note the language of Article XIII, which refers to the policy of facilitating commerce by establishment of special commercial-legal tribunals: "The general utility of commerce having caused to be established within the dominions of the Most Christian King, particular tribunals and forms for expediting the decision of commercial affairs, the merchants of the United States shall enjoy the benefit of these establishments; and the Congress of the United States will provide in the manner the most conformable to its laws, for the establishment of equivalent advantages in favour of the French merchants, for the prompt dispatch and decision of affairs of the same nature." *Id.*

[97] Article XV, *id.* This clause specifically mentions the "powers, authority and privileges" of consuls. The significance of this type of clause will be considered in one of the succeeding chapters. *Post* at pp. 132 *et seq.* In the treaty with Great Britain of 1794, which settled outstanding problems which arose out of the war of independence, there was provision for consular representation, but no definition of function. Art. XVI, 8 Stat. 116, 125. That provision was renewed in the Convention of July 3, 1815, Art. 4, 8 Stat. 228, 230.

[98] 1782, 1783, 1785, 8 Stat. 32, 60, 84.

[99] France, Art. VIII, 8 Stat. 12, 16. The Netherlands, Art. XXIII, 8 Stat. 32, 44.

[100] See 5 Moore, *Digest of International Law* 391–397.

[101] 8 Stat. 100.

à-vis the United States, rather than an agreement between two equals. The whole tone of the compact is that of assurance to the United States of certain rights, most of which were modelled after earlier similar grants to European powers. Article XXIII provides:

> The consuls of the United States of America shall reside in any seaport of our dominions that they shall think proper; and they shall be respected, and enjoy all the privileges which the consuls of any other nation enjoy ....[102]

Article XX reads:

> If any citizen of the United States, or any person under their protection, shall have any disputes with each other, the consul shall decide between the parties, and whenever the consul shall require any aid or assistance from our government, to enforce his decision, it shall be immediately granted to him.[103]

By its terms, then, it applied to all disputes between members of the group including citizens and persons under the protection of the United States. It was general enough to include any civil or criminal dispute which involved only members of a United States ship's company, including passengers, and whether or not citizens of the United States, since they would in any case be under the diplomatic protection of the flag state. Its scope was somewhat restricted by the next article, which made any act resulting in killing or wounding cognizable in the local courts if there was diversity of citizenship, the consul being entitled to assist as the trial.[104]

Similar treaties were concluded with Algiers in 1795,[105] with Tripoli in 1796,[106] and with Tunis in 1797.[107] The treaty with Tripoli included a most-favored-nation clause which produced the desired extraterritorial jurisdiction which was secured in the other three by express provision.[108]

[102] *Id.* at 103.

[103] *Id.*

[104] Art. XXI, *id.* A substantially similar substitute treaty was concluded in 1836, the provisions concerning consuls remaining the same. 8 Stat. 484.

[105] Art. XV, 8 Stat. 133, 135. A new treaty was concluded with Algiers in 1815, which placed commerce, including consular jurisdiction, on a most-favored-nation basis and expressly gave the United States consuls the same extra territorial jurisdiction as had been granted by Morocco. Art. 12, 19, 8 Stat. 224, 225–226, 227. Another treaty containing similar provisions was signed in December, 1816. 8 Stat. 244.

[106] Art. IX, 8 Stat. 154, 155.

[107] Art. XX, 8 Stat. 157, 160. This treaty was modified by the treaty of February 24, 1824, but not in any way significant to this inquiry. 8 Stat. 298.

[108] This provision was duplicated in the Treaty of Peace and Amity with Tripoli of June 4, 1805. Art. 11th, 8 Stat. 214, 215. In addition, express provisions concerning the litigation of criminal and civil actions, similar to those in the treaty with Morocco, were included. Art. 18th, 19th, *id.* at 216, 217. It is not pertinent to this inquiry to discuss the political and military pressures utilized by the United States to induce the conclusion of these treaties. See 5 Moore, *Digest of International Law*, 391–397.

Thomas Jefferson became Secretary of State in 1790, at a time when United States policy concerning the status of consuls was in confusion. He undertook to organize the system, and it was largely due to his efforts that Congress passed the first legislation defining consular functions.[109] The immediate purpose of that act was to implement the treaty of 1788 with France. The first section provided that the judge of the federal district where an incident occurred should provide the assistance to the French consul required by that agreement in cases of shipwreck and desertion, as well as any other situation contemplated by the treaty.[110] The act went on to define the functions of United States consuls abroad. The specifically maritime functions were not nearly as broad in scope as envisaged in the treaty. The consul was authorized to receive protests and declarations which any member of a United States ship's company might choose to make.[111] They were also authorized to undertkae the administration of any wrecked vessel of the United States, provided that, and during the time that, the master or other representative of the owner was not available for that purpose.[112] Section 7 authorized consuls to relieve distressed seamen at a rate not exceeding 12 cents per day per man, at the expense of the United States, and to order the master of any American vessel on a homeward voyage to transport them there without remuneration.[113] Finally, in case of sale of a United States ship abroad, unless the crew had consented to discharge there either by their contract of employment or at the time of the sale, the consul was charged with the duty of assuring that the master provided the seamen with transportation back to the place of signing on. On his refusal, the consul was authorized to take local action, presumably with assistance of local authorities, to arrest the ship, goods belonging to the master, or the master himself, and to hold the same until he complied.[114]

As noted in the preceding paragraph, the consular functions specifically defined in the act of 1792 were not nearly sufficient to fully implement the treaty of 1788 with France. However, performance of general treaty powers by American consuls was permitted by the last

[109] Carr, "The American Consular Service," 1 *A.J.I.L.* 891, 894 (1907).

[110] 1 Stat. 254.

[111] Sec. 2, 1 Stat. 255.

[112] Sec. 3, *id.*

[113] 1 Stat. 256. There was a limitation of not more than two repatriates per 100 gross tons of the ship involved. This section was substantially re-enacted on February 28, 1803, without the 12 cent limitation. Sec. 4, 2 Stat. 203, 204.

[114] Sec. 8, *id.* at 256–257. This section was re-enacted by the Act of February 28, 1803, but without consular authority to take local enforcement action. Sec. 4, 2 Stat. 203–204.

section of the Act, in addition to any duties implied by the nature of their position.[115] This last provision was a necessary part of the statute, since without it, an American consul abroad might, and probably would, have felt obliged not to act even in a situation in which he was entitled to under an applicable treaty or where the local authorities tacitly or expressly admitted his competence to act.

As it became apparent that the existing statutory duties of consuls were inadequate for the desired control and promotion of shipping, Congress enlarged those powers by the Act of February 28, 1803.[116] This act imposed a duty on masters of vessels of the United States at the first port of re-entry to produce all members of the crew as it consisted when the ship left for her foreign voyage or excuse his failure to do so by showing a consular discharge of the missing persons. It was made discretionary with the consul whether he would consent to such discharge.[117] The master was also obligated to deposit the ship's papers with the consul on the vessel's arrival. He was required to return them when satisfied that the ship had been duly cleared by local authorities for departure and that the master had complied with all duties imposed by statutes of the United States. For failure to comply, the master was subject to a 500 dollar fine recoverable at the suit of the consul involved.[118] The treaty with Sweden of 1783,[119] which contained a general provision concerning the right to consular representation was supplemented in 1816 [120] by a more complete agreement which contained some specific definition of consular authority. Article 5, second paragraph, stated:

> The consuls and their deputies shall have the right, as such, to act as judges and arbitrators in the differences which may arise between the captains and crews of the vessels of the nation whose affairs are entrusted to their care. The respective governments shall have no right to interfere in matters of this kind, except the conduct of the captain and crew shall disturb the peace and tranquillity of the country in which the vessel may be, or that the consul of the place shall feel himself obliged to resort to the interposition and support of the executive authority to cause his decision to be respected and maintained. It being, nevertheless, understood, that this kind of judgment, or award, shall not deprive the contending parties of the right which they shall have, on their return, to recur to the judicial authorities of their own country.[121]

115 Sec. 9, *id.* at 257.
116 2 Stat. 203–205.
117 Sec. 1, *id.* at 203.
118 Sec. 2., *id.;* see *Harrison v. Vose,* 50 U.S. (9 Howard) 372 (1850).
119 8 Stat. 60.
120 8 Stat. 232.
121 *Id.* at 236.

This clause raises several points of interest. Generally, it follows the pattern of the French treaty of 1788, in that it makes the consul the final arbiter of differences internal to the ship's company while it is in the country to which he is appointed. The fact that the parties to the dispute may, according to the article, seek any available judicial relief on returning to home port presents no particularly significant problem as regards the relationship of the parties to the treaty. What United States seamen do in their homeland which happens to impair the commerce of the United States cannot be of any legal interest to Sweden, nor can the United States attribute the detriment to any but a deficiency in her own domestic law, the price in terms of commercial cost being avoidable by unilateral change in that law. A similar provision was contained in the French treaty of 1788,[122] but there was no such provision implicitly obligating the local executive to enforce the consul's judgment within the jurisdiction. Another innovation was the provision extending consular authority to vessels of other countries whose affairs are "entrusted to their care." This provision might be significant in a situation in which a third country which does not maintain consular representation in one of the states requests the other to represent it there.[123]

In 1824, The United States concluded a rather comprehensive treaty with the Republic of Colombia, it being the first with another state of the Americas.[124] Although it contained a provision contemplating a consular convention which would "declare specially the powers and immunities of the consuls," [125] it nevertheless contained various provisions which pertain to consular authority. The parties agreed that the commerce and navigation of each would benefit by advantages conferred on any third nation by the other. This was coupled with a provision that, if an advantage granted to a third state was conditional upon some compensation, the other party too would be subject to that condition.[126] Article 4th of the same treaty specifically places merchants and navigators of each on a most-favored-nation basis regarding their activities within the territory of the other.[127] Presumably, both

[122] Art. XII, 8 Stat. 106, 114.

[123] This extension of consular authority would probably accrue to the benefit of a state with an applicable "most-favored-nation" treaty clause.

[124] Convention of Peace, Amity, Navigation, and Commerce, October 3, 1824, 8 Stat. 306.

[125] Art. 30th, *id.* at 320.

[126] Art. 2d, *id.* at 306. It is possible that that type of provision may make all most-favored-nation benefits mutual, particularly if, as is usually the case, the agreement with the third state confers reciprocal benefits.

[127] *Id.* at 308.

provisions would include expediting their commercial activities, including exemption of seamen from local jurisdiction to the extent that that has been granted to any third state.[128] At any rate, the 26th article expressly placed consular "rights, prerogatives and immunities" on a most-favored-nation basis.[129] It would seem that either "rights" or "prerogatives" would include the exercise of jurisdiction over maritime affairs to the same extent as consuls of any third state. Finally, it contained a clause pertaining to consular handling of desertions from national vessels, similar to the clause in the French Treaty of 1788.[130] Soon after the conclusion of the treaty with Colombia, one was concluded with the Federation of the Centre of America which contained provisions similar in all respects.[131]

United States activity in the international consular law legislation field after this time greatly accelerated. The treaties, insofar as they pertain to consular authority over maritime affairs, may be conveniently classified by the method adopted to define that authority. Some treaties contained only specific provisions expressly defining the authority and contained no general provisions under which a consul might claim to act in absence of specific authority. There were only five of this type concluded by the United States, and all of them prior to 1900, namely those with Sweden and Norway, Greece, the Hanseatic Republics, Denmark and the United Kingdom.[132] Each of the first four contained a clause authorizing consuls to sit as "judges and arbitrators" of disputes between the "captains and crews of the vessels belonging to the nation whose interests are committed to their charge, without interference of the local authorities" unless the dispute disturbs the "order or tranquillity" of the place where the ship is or the consular officer require "their assistance to cause their decisions to be carried into effect or supported." There was no express obligation upon the local authorities to grant such assistance, but the obligation is readily inferable from the language used. The clause reserved to the disputants a right to resort to the judiciary of their own state to contest the decision of the consul.[133] That provision probably would not have been essential, since it is hard to conceive what interest one state could

[128] This point is not settled. See *post* at pp. 136 *et seq.*

[129] *Id.* at 172

[130] Art. 29th, *id.* at 318.

[131] 1825, Art. 2d, 28th, 31st and 32nd, General Convention of Peace, Amity, Commerce, and Navigation, 8 Stat. 322, 334, 336.

[132] Appendix A, #'s 22, 36, 55, 71 and 104.

[133] 8 Stat. 352, 504; 10 Stat. 96; 13 Stat. 606.

have in the ultimate resolution in another of a dispute confined to persons in whom it has no interest. It is possible that this provision was purely for the guidance of municipal judiciary when asked to take cognizance of a dispute which had already been determined by a consular officer. If it were not in the clause, and there were no provision of local legislation covering the problem, he might have felt that *res judicata* was a bar to any further proceedings.

The treaties with Greece and Denmark also contained a provision defining the consular authority in cases of seamen deserting from national vessels in the receiving state, as did the agreement with the United Kingdom.[134] The article common to these three treaties provided that the consul was empowered to apply to the local authorities, documenting his application with such official papers as the crew list, for arrest and disposition of a deserter. He could either be placed in the custody of the master of the vessel or held in prison, at the option of the consul, for a period not in excess of two months pending a decision by the consul as to what to do with him. If once released, he could not be molested again for the same complaint.

In addition to those treaties conferring only limited and expressly defined consular authority over maritime affairs, there was a second type which contained, in addition to certain specially defined authority, general provisions from which the authority to act in a case not covered by an express provision might be inferred. In this category, one finds the treaties with Prussia, Russia, Hanover, Portugal, Hanover, Austria, the Two Sicilies and Venezuela.[135]

Each of the treaties in this group contained a provision similar to the one in the preceding group authorizing consuls to reclaim deserters with the assistance of the local authorities.[136] In fact, this is a provision that is common to almost every commercial treaty of the United States up to 1915 when the Seamen's Act made it statutorily beyond an American consul's authority to molest deserters from American ships in any way, and also deprived foreign consuls of any local assistance in the United States in reclaiming deserters.[137] Each also

[134] 8 Stat. 498, 504; 13 Stat. 605, 606–607; 27 Stat. 961.

[135] Appendix A, #'s 24, 30, 40, 41, 44, 46, 61 and 70. In the second treaty with Hanover, there was a clause permitting the accession of other Germanic States, two of which, Oldenburg and Mecklenburg-Schwerin, did in fact accede. 9 Stat. 66, 67.

[136] 8 Stat. 382, 448, 556, 566; 9 Stat. 60–61, 154–155; 11 Stat. 100–101; 12 Stat. 1157–1158.

[137] *Post* at p. 50. The provision is so common that I have ignored it for classification purposes; *i.e.* even though it is a specific authority, I have classified treaties which contain it and no other specific authority as general.

contains a provision similar to the one previously described permitting consuls to sit as judges and arbitrators in disputes involving members of the ship's company.[138]

The provisions in treaties of this group which I have referred to as conferring general or indeterminate authority may be further subdivided. First, there is the provision which says that consuls shall enjoy the same "privileges and powers" as the consuls of any third state or of the most favored nation.[139] Assuming that some third state's consuls had been granted the "power" to determine intra-ship's company disputes, this type of clause would apparently confer that same power on the consuls of the other party to the treaty. Second, there is the clause which provides that, if any third nation is granted any particular "favor" [140] or "favor, privilege or immunity" [141] in either "navigation or commerce" [142] or "navigation and duties of customs," [143] it shall immediately become common to the other party to the treaty. This is subject to the caveat that if the favor granted to the third state was conditional or in return for some consideration, it becomes common to the other party to the treaty, subject to the same condition.

The problem of construction implicit in this type of clause is whether a grant of consular authority over shipboard problems to a third state is a "favor in navigation or commerce" and therefore would inure to the benefit of the other party. A collateral problem is whether the language subjecting the other party to the same conditions upon which the favor to the third state was predicated includes the implied condition that the power be mutual, as it usually would be if derived from a treaty with the third state. In other words, suppose states A and B are parties to a treaty containing a provision of this type, neither having conferred any specific consular authority on any third state; A then concludes a treaty with Z under which the consuls of each have certain authority over a particular maritime problem; does B get this privilege without conferring the reciprocal privilege upon A, or does the clause importing conditions to the granting of the right to any third party make it subject to B's granting the same right to A?

138 8 Stat. 382, 448, 556, 564; 9 Stat. 60–61, 154–155; 11 Stat. 101; 12 Stat. 1157–1158. In the convention with the Two Sicilies, the language was "to judge in the quality of arbitrators," but the rest of the clause was the same.

139 8 Stat. 382, 556, 564; 9 Stat. 154; 12 Stat. 1157–1158.

140 8 Stat. 450, 12 Stat. 1148–1149.

141 11 Stat. 98.

142 8 Stat. 450, 11 Stat. 98, 12 Stat. 1148–1149.

143 9 Stat. 59.

Since the placing of maritime matters as fully as possible in the hands of the consul tends to expedite the maritime commerce of his state, or at least places the responsibility for any interference with it upon his state, the grant of this authority would seem to be the grant of a "favor," "privilege," or an "immunity" to the "commerce," or more specifically, the "navigation" of a third state within the purview of this clause. It would follow that the other party to such a treaty would immediately become entitled to the same right.[144]

Whether the other party to a most-favored-nation clause should, in any case, be entitled to a right granted conditionally to a third state without also satisfying the same condition is doubtful. The right granted to the third state is defined in part by the condition to it, but is a right nevertheless. It seems rational to assume that such a conditional right would become available to the other party to such a clause in its conditional form; otherwise, a greater right is conferred by the clause than the original grantee received. This is more than the treaty provides. At any rate, most of the clauses giving the parties the benefit of any right granted to a third state expressly made the entitlement subject to the same condition, so at least in regard to those treaties, the problem did not exist.

The introduction of an express provision concerning conditional most-favored-nation rights raises the question whether, when the grant to the third state is by way of an agreement wherein the third state reciprocally grants the same right, the reciprocal grant was a "condition" to the giving of the right to the third state. If so, then the other party to a most-favored-nation clause would not get the same right without its being subject to the same condition, namely, reciprocity. If not, the other party would get the right without being required to grant it in return. Since the normal situation in treaty negotiation is that legal rights are granted reciprocally, and any right would not be granted unless it were to be reciprocal, there is an implied condition to every treaty grant (in absence of clear intent to the contrary) that it be reciprocal. Following this line of reasoning, then, a treaty grant of a right to a third state is only available to the other party to the most-favored-nation agreement subject to the same condition of reciprocity. In fact, of course, the right which is granted subject to reciprocity is defined by that condition like any other, and therefore should be available to the other party only in that same

[144] The U.S. State Department took an opposing view of that construction of such a clause. IV Hackworth, *Digest of International Law* 702.

form; otherwise, it would be getting better than the most-favored-nation treatment to which it is entitled.

It should be pointed out that the clauses granting consular powers on the basis of most-favored-nation treatment were not made expressly subject to any condition, whether of reciprocity or otherwise. This introduces another problem of construction, namely, whether the failure to include such a provision in the one clause and its inclusion in another in the same treaty might not require that a grant of consular powers to a third state, even on a condition, should not be available to the other party unconditionally. The best answer to this is that the right itself is defined by the condition, and it is that right to which the other party is entitled.

As a conclusion it would seem that the best position is that all most-favored-nation clauses, whether directly concerning consular powers or only indirectly related to them through their reference to rights in navigation or commerce, and whether or not expressly subject to conditions to the grant to third states, including reciprocity, confer upon the parties all rights granted to third states subject to the same conditions as were imposed upon the third state.[145]

The next type of commercial treaty used by the United States during this period, and this was by far the most extensively used form, was one relying solely upon the most-favored-nation clause, either expressly with regard to consular authority, or implicitly by reference to favors or rights in navigation or commerce. In this group, one finds almost uniformly, however, as previously noted, express authority to reclaim deserters with the aid of the local authorities. Treaties in this category are referred to in the footnote.[146] Although not all of the treaties in this group contain identical provisions, they do all contain clauses either expressly or implicitly conferring upon the parties a right to most-favored-nation treatment insofar as consular authority over maritime affairs is concerned. Since these clauses have been analyzed in detail in the discussion of the preceding category of treaties, I shall move on to the next group.

145 But see Schwarzenberger, Georg, "The Most Favoured-Nation Standard in British State Practice." XXII *Brit. Y.B.Int. L.* 96, where the auther concludes that in the case of unconditional clauses the parties take the benefit without the price. There is a difference between "price" and "condition". The consideration for a concession does not qualify the concession, whereas the condition does.

146 Appendix A, #'s 21, 23, 25, 26, 28, 29, 33, 35, 37, 39, 43, 45, 47, 48, 49, 52, 53, 54, 57, 58, 65, 67, 69, 73, 74, 75, 76, 78, 83, 85, 87, 88, 95, 102, 113, 135, 136, 137, 142 and 143. Some of the more recent treaties listed herien will be discussed at a later point. They are listed at this point only because they show that the most-favored-nation approach to commercial treaty negotiation has continued right up to modern times.

The classification for the purposes of this discussion is consular conventions generally. These are classified separately because the provisions contained in them were not part of an agreement primarily concerned with some other problem. These treaties were negotiated by men who were directing their minds to the specific problem of how much and what type of authority should be conferred upon a consular official of one state within the territory of another. The earliest of these conventions, except for the one with France of 1788,[147] was not concluded until 1850 with New Granada.[148] It provided that the consul was entitled to accompany any member of the ship's company at any time when he was dealing with local authorities; [149] was authorized to take depositions from members of the ship's company, either on board the ship or ashore and to certify them; [150] had authority to adjudicate the rights of interested parties when goods had been damaged at sea, provided there was not a contract providing otherwise or one of the interested parties was not a national of the receiving state; [151] could arbitrate disputes between two of his own nationals upon their agreement to submit the dispute to him for disposition; [152] was authorized to maintain order on board ships of his state and to decide disputes between members of the ship's company, provided that any act complained of did not interfere with the peace of the port or affect local residents or nationals of a third state; [153] could administer the problems involved in national vessels wrecked in the territorial waters of the receiving state, provided and until the master or other owner's agent was available to assume those duties; [154] and finally he was accorded the right to demand the assistance of the local authorities in arresting and detaining at his pleasure, for a period not in excess of two months, any deserter who was not a citizen of the local state.[155]

Other consular conventions are indicated below.[156] There have been other consular conventions concluded since the one with Sweden in 1910,[157] starting with the one with Germany of December 8, 1923, but that one marked the beginning of a different approach by the United

147 *Supra* note 87.
148 10 Stat. 80.
149 Art. III (4), *id.* at 82.
150 Art. III (5), *id.* at 82–83.
151 Art. III (6), *id.* at 83.
152 Art. III (7), *id.*
153 Art. III (8), *id.*
154 Art. III (9), *id.* at 83–84.
155 Art. III (11), *id.* at 84.
156 Appendix A, #'s 56, 79, 81, 82, 84, 86, 89, 91, 92, 93, 95, 96, 107, 108 and 112.
157 Appendix A, #112.

States to questions of consular authority in treaties, which attitude has continued up to the present day. Therefore, the treaties subsequent to those listed in the preceding footnote will be discussed in a later chapter.

Each convention in this group contained a provision similar to that in the treaty with New Granada [158] concerning the consul's authority in cases of desertion from a national vessel, with the exception of the treaty with Serbia.[159] Also, with the exception of that treaty and the one with Spain, [160] each contained a provision authorizing the consul to take charge of salvage operations in a manner similar to the provision in the treaty with New Granada.[161] Each also included a provision giving the consul exclusive authority over everything internal to the ship and the ship's company, and most required the local authorities to assist him upon his request, including arrest and incarceration of any member of the ship's company.[162] All but five of them [163] contained provisions permitting the taking of depositions of members of the ship's company by the consul. Only three [164] did not contain provisions similar to the one in the treaty with New Granada permitting the consul to adjust the rights of the parties interested in damages to goods at sea.[165] Only one other contained a provision permitting the consul to accompany members of the ship's company in their dealings with local authorities; [166] and none other contained a provision authorizing the consul to serve as arbitrator on submission of a dispute between nationals of his state.[167] In addition to the provisions in common with the treaty with New Granada, seven contained provisions conferring most-favored-nation treatment regarding consular authority.[168] Three of them contained provisions permitting the consul to assume complete control of the internal administration of the ship, including all documentary control, and guaranteed that he

[158] *Supra* note 148.

[159] 22 Stat. 963.

[160] 33 Stat. 2105.

[161] *Supra* note 154.

[162] The treaty with Serbia, being essentially a release by the United States of its extraterritorial rights under its treaties with the Ottoman Empire, implicitly left the consul with this authority over internal problems of his state's vessels by reserving such jurisdiction as existed under the old capitulations over ships and citizens. Thus, in this one troaty only, the consular authority over this type of problem was not mutual. 22 Stat. 963.

[163] Appendix A, #'s 79, 81, 82, 86 and 92.

[164] Appendix A, #'s 56, 95 and 112.

[165] *Supra* note 151.

[166] Salvador, 1870, Art. 33rd (4th), 18 Stat. 725, 741.

[167] *Supra* note 152.

[168] Appendix A, #'s 82, 84, 89, 91, 96, 107, and 112. The clause in the treaty with Salvador made "all privileges and concessions" in "commerce and navigation" conferred upon any third state available to the other party. Art. 3rd, 18 Stat. 725, 726.

be notified before a ship of his state was to be searched, or as soon thereafter as possible, if this was impossible, and also before any member of the ship's company was examined or questioned pursuant to any legal proceeding.[169] One other treaty [170] contained a provision similar to that in the New Granada convention authorizing the consul to serve as arbitrator of disputes submitted to him by his fellow countrymen.[171] Finally, only the treaty with Germany contained a provision permitting the consul to take charge of the effects of deceased seamen and passengers and to dispose of them pursuant to the laws of his state.[172]

All of the treaties of the United States thus far considered provided the consular officer with some extraterritorial jurisdiction, but carefully limited that authority to matters pertaining to maritime commerce. None of them recognized any official capacity to resolve disputes involving United States citizens other than seamen; [173] and all of them were concluded with states which adhered to a jurisprudential system not fundamentally different from that of the United States; *i.e.* they were all states of the European tradition. In the next succeeding section, a group of treaties known as capitulations will be discussed. These treaties were all concluded with states having, in the view of the United States (which was a view common to the countries of the European tradition), a fundamentally different social and legal system, a system which gave no reasonable assurance of a fair and just resolution of controversies in which an American national might be involved. Most of them were Arabic or Oriental countries which had no common social heritage with the United States. The treaties concluded with these states were, as might be expected, fundamentally different from those concluded with states which did share a common sociological background with the United States. Different from those treaties which assumed unfettered local jurisdiction over everyone within the territory except those defined by the agreement itself (primarily mariners), treaties with these alien states uniformly placed all nationals of the United States beyond the reach of local law and authority, and only exceptionally subjected them to it for limited purposes. These treaties,

[169] Austria-Hungary, 1870, Art. X, 17 Stat. 821, 826–827; Germany, 1871, Art. XII, 17 Stat. 921, 927–928; Greece, 1902, Art. XVI, 33 Stat. 2133.

[170] Salvador, 1870, Art. 33rd (7th), 18 Stat. 725, 742.

[171] *Supra* note 152.

[172] 1871, Art. XI, 17 Stat. 921, 927.

[173] The treaty with Serbia, *supra* note 159, is the only exception, and it will be considered in the next section.

conferring much broader jurisdiction on consular officers than the others, necessarily conferred jurisdiction over maritime affairs too.

Although it may be true that all extraterritorial jurisdiction, including that over maritime commerce, is rooted in the medieval belief in personal law, it seems clear that there must have been some other motive inducing the United States (and other states of common ancestrage) to conclude treaties of one type with the one group of states, and of another type with the other. One reason why the Arabic and Oriental states were prepared to concede the greater extraterritorial jurisdiction to the European states, and later to the United States, may have been that they were already conditioned to expect it by their own inheritance of a belief in personal law.[174] The motive of the United States appears to have been different. Apparently the primary factor inducing the insistence upon unilateral extraterritoriality was fear of the consequences to American nationals should they become embroiled in what was considered a barbaric legal system.

> ... at first, from the total difference of religious habits and feelings, it was necessary to withdraw as far as practicable British subjects from native courts, then in the progress of time commerce increasing, and various nations having the same interest in abstaining from resort to the tribunals of Mussulmans, etc., recourse was had to consular courts; and by degrees the system became general....[175]
>
> The President is impressed with the importance of continued concert between the treaty powers in Japan, at least until after the revision of the treaties, and until the government of Japan shall have exhibited a degree of power and capacity to adopt and to enforce a system of jurisprudence, and of judicial administration, in harmony with that of the Christian powers, equal to their evident desire to be relieved from the enforced duties of extraterritoriality.[176]

Evidence of this underlying fear as the force motivating the United States in seeking extraterritorial jurisdiction is found in some of the treaties concluded with these states. In article IV of the Treaty of Peace, Amity, Commerce, and Navigation with Corea,[177] the United States agreed to surrender its extraterritorial rights there when convinced that the laws and procedures of justice were consistent with standards in the United States.[178] Further evidence is to be found in

[174] Since it was not a reciprocal right, even this is doubtful. Perhaps nationalism with its concomitant territoriality psychosis had not yet become the force in those countries that it had in the European and American states.

[175] II Moore, *Digest of International Law* 667. For similar rationale on the policy underlying the institution, see *The Indian Chief*, 165 E.R. 367, 374–375.

[176] Mr. Fish, Sec. of State, to Mr. Nicholas Fish, chargé at Berlin, No. 703, Sept. 2, 1874, For. Rel. 1874, 460; V Moore, *Digest of International Law* 752.

[177] 1882, 23 Stat. 720, 721–722.

[178] See also Art. XV, Treaty with China, Oct. 8, 1903, 33 Stat. 2208, 2215.

treaties between the United States and the powers holding mandates from the League of Nations over the various fragments of the Turkish Empire after World War I. In the convention with France, as Mandatory over Syria and Lebanon, the United States renounced its extraterritorial rights in return for France's undertaking the obligation to establish an adequate judicial system there.[179] In fact, whenever a European power became responsible for the functioning of the judicial system in one of these countries, the United States surrendered her special treaty rights there.[180]

Additional evidence of this attitude is to be found in legislation of the United States. For example, in 1874, an Act was passed authorizing the President to suspend the operation of the extraterritorial regime in Egypt if and when he became satisfied that nationals of the United States would receive treatment in Egyptian courts comparable to that accorded in United States courts.[181] On March 27, 1876, President U.S. Grant did in fact suspend the operation of that regime in Egypt to the extent that Egyptian courts had been established with procedures designed to dispose of controversies and problems previously handled by the consular courts.[182]

The most obvious distinction between the treaties concluded with European and related states and those with the Oriental and Arabic states was the lack of mutuality in the latter. The procedure generally followed in negotiating a treaty with a European state was to accord rights on a strict mutuality basis, whether by use of most-favored-nation clauses which, because of the treaty pattern of the parties with other states, served the end of mutuality, or by wording each clause so that the rights and obligations thereunder were mutual. It is true that some capitulations in fact used most-favored-nation language; *e.g.* the treaty of 1868 with China provided that a citizen of either residing in the

[179] 1924, Art. 5, 6, 43 Stat. 1821, 1823. The treaties of September 7, 8, 1944, with Syria and Lebanon terminated this agreement. 58 Stat. 1491, 1493. These treaties served as a recognition by the United States of the independent sovereignty of Syria and Lebanon. See also the Convention with Great Britain of 1924 concerning the Mandate of Palestine. Art. 8, 9, 44 Stat. 2184, 2186.

[180] Treaty of 1905 with Great Britain re East Africa and Zanzibar, Art. I, 34 Stat. 2870; 1925, Great Britain re Togoland, 44 Stat. 2433; 1930, Great Britain re Iraq, Art. 7, Sched. I, 47 Stat. 1817, 1819, 1821; 1904, France re Tunis, Art. I, 33 Stat. 2263–2266. A similar attitude of Great Britain and Germany was evinced by the treaty of 1899 wherein the three powers relinquished all extraterritorial rights in the Samoan Islands to the United States and Germany respectively, which powers thereby became responsible for judicial administration in their respective territorial allotments. 31 Stat. 1878.

[181] 18 Stat. 23–24. The constitutional effect of such a directive to the executive is not material to this problem.

[182] 19 Stat. 662–663.

other was entitled to the same privileges, immunities and exemptions as the citizens of the most-favored-nation.[183] However, the United States had granted no extraterritorial rights to any third state over its citizens while in the United States, whereas China had granted such rights to various European states. Therefore, the effect of the clause, although mutual in form, was in fact to confer greater jurisdictional rights on the United States than upon China. Actually, since various European states had concluded capitulatory treaties, with these countries, all the United States need have done in order to acquire the same rights was to conclude most-favored-nation treaties which would automatically have conferred the same rights upon the United States. Turkey, for example, from a very early time had granted privileges of self government to communities of Christians living there, and later entered into a treaty with France conferring these rights on French nationals residing there.[184] In 1675, similar rights were granted by treaty with England.[185] Any treaty concluded thereafter by the United States with Turkey pertaining to this subject and containing a most-favored-nation clause would incorporate thereby the most generous provisions of all of these arrangements for the benefit of the United States. Such a clause would also serve to assure that the United States also got the benefit of any future concession conferred upon any third state.[186]

Under some of the capitulatory treaties, the United States acquired its extraterritorial jurisdiction solely by most-favored-nation clauses incorporated in them.[187] Others contained both most-favored-nation clauses and clauses providing express consular authority over certain types of problems.[188] In these treaties, as in those containing no most-favored-nation clause, the most common provision was one conferring upon the United States consul exclusive jurisdiction over any incident

[183] Art. VI, 16 Stat. 739–740. See also Art. V, Treaty of 1857 with Persia, 11 Stat. 115, 116.

[184] Schuyler, *American Diplomacy* 59 (1886).

[185] Piggot, *Exterritoriality, The Law Relating to Consular Jurisdiction and to Residence in Oriental Countries* 273 (1907).

[186] That was the evident purpose of Art. 9 of the Treaty of 1854 with Japan, 11 Stat. 11, 12.

[187] China, treaties of 1868, Art. VI, and 1903, Art. II, 16 Stat. 739–740 and 33 Stat. 2208, 2209. These were superimposed upon other more detailed conventions on the same subject. Ottoman Empire, Treaty of 1862, Art. I, 12 Stat. 1213, 1217; Egypt, Treaty of 1884, 24 Stat. 1004; Zanzibar, Treaty of 1886, Art. II, 25 Stat. 1438, 1439; Congo, Treaty of 1891, Art. I, V, XII, 27 Stat. 926, 927, 928–929–930, 932. This last treaty also contained a provision pertaining to the reclaiming of deserters similar to such provisions in treaties with European countries.

[188] Appendix A, #'s 34, 62, 63, 66, 77, 94, 97 and 101.

which involved only United States nationals.[198] Coupled with the exclusive jurisdiction over disputes involving only Americans, it was not uncommon to find a provision giving the consul jurisdiction of any dispute which involved an American as defendant, but providing that the local authorities should have jurisdiction of actions in which a local subject was defendant,[190] or giving him a joint jurisdiction with local authorities of any dispute involving Americans and locals.[191] Generally, in cases where joint jurisdiction was provided, the defendant was to be punished by the laws and authorities of his own country.[192] In the treaty of 1830 with Turkey, the consul was entitled to be present at civil trials between United States and Turkish subjects,[193] as was also the case in the treaty of 1856 with Persia.[194] In the treaty with Morocco of 1836, there was a provision permitting the consul to be present and to assist at a trial of a citizen of either party charged with wounding or killing a citizen of the other, the trial to be in a Moroccan court applying Moroccan law.[195] There were a few treaties which simply removed United States nationals from the jurisdiction of local officials for all purposes.[196]

In those situations which involved nationals of the United States and a third state, the jurisdictional problem was implicitly provided for in those treaties which provided consular jurisdiction over Americans for all purposes. Of course, if the third state had a similar treaty, there would have been a direct conflict of jurisdiction between it and the United States. However, that would not involve the local authorities in the matter. The same problem would not have arisen in situations where a third state's national was involved with an American and each had treaties with the territorial sovereign providing for exclusive consular jurisdiction of cases involving their nationals as defendants.

[189] Appendix A, #'s 32, 34, 42, 62, 63, 66, 68, 77, 90, 94, 97, 101. The treaties with Japan and Corea (68 and 97) inferentially provide that jurisdiction by providing that the consul has authority over any suit in which an American is a defendant.

[190] Japan, 1858, Art. VI, 12 Stat. 1051, 1056; Corea, 1882, Art. IV, 23 Stat. 720, 721–722; Tonga, 1886, Art. XII (criminal acts only) 25 Stat. 1440, 1443. In the last one, an American could be defendant in Tongan courts if no United States law covered the act complained of.

[191] China, 1844, Art. XXIV, 8 Stat. 592, 594; Siam, 1856, Art. II, 11 Stat. 149, 150; China, 1858, Art. XVIII, XXVIII, 12 Stat. 1023, 1029; Madagascar, 1881, Art. VI (7), 22 Stat. 952, 958.

[192] Siam, Japan, Madagascar, Samoa and Tonga. *Id.*

[193] Art. IV, 8 Stat. 408, 409. He had exclusive jurisdiction of all criminal charges against an American.

[194] Art. V, 11 Stat. 115, 116.

[195] Art. 21, 8 Stat. 484, 486.

[196] Borneo, 1850, Art. 9, 10 Stat. 89, 90; Lew Chew, 1854, 10 Stat. 211. The latter pertained only to seamen, who had to be returned to the ship's master for punishment. Apparently, there was no consular officer there.

The local authorities would not become involved because no local subject was a party to the dispute as a defendant, but the consul of the defendant would have jurisdiction. If the two treaties were different, it would depend upon their substance whether there was a conflict of jurisdiction. In a few treaties of the United States, this type of problem was anticipated. In the treaties with China of 1844 and 1858,[197] and in the treaty of 1856 with Persia, [198] it was provided that in a controversy between a citizen of the United States and one of a third state, the jurisdictional problem would be regulated by agreement between the two states whose nationals were involved, without interference of the local authorities.

In addition to provisions granting the United States extraordinary consular jurisdiction over American nationals – *i.e.* provisions not found in treaties with European states – there were also some provisions concerning jurisdiction over maritime affairs common in treaties with both classes of states. The most common of these was a clause concerning the arrest and return of mutineers and deserters from United States ships.[199] Additionally, in the treaties with China and Siam, it was provided that ships of the United States should enter and clear through the consul, who would make necessary reports to the local authorities.[200]

Although the problem of local assistance to United States consuls in the exercise of their jurisdiction over their countrymen must have been a real one, in only two of these treaties did the other party assume a general obligation to provide assistance.[201] It may be that no express provision concerning local assistance was deemed necessary in most cases, either because the United States had sufficient force available to control the relatively small number of Americans in the country, or because the local authorities and the consular officer had a community of interest in the maintenance of order which would cause aid to be granted even though there was no contractual obligation.

Although there would appear to have been a definite economic

197 Art. XXV and XXVII, 8 Stat. 592, 597; 12 Stat. 1023, 1029.

198 Art. V, 11 Stat. 115, 116.

199 China, 1844, Art. XXIX, 8 Stat. 592, 598. This treaty also expressly stated that merchant vessels of the United States were to be under the exclusive jurisdiction of the United States while in China. China, 1858, Art. XVIII, 12 Stat. 1023, 1027. In this article, it was also provided that seamen, among others, were to be under the "superintendence" of the consular officer. Madagascar, 1881, Art. XI (2), 22 Stat. 952, 960; Tonga, 1886, Art. X, 25 Stat. 1440–1442.

200 China, 1844, Art. VI, 8 Stat. 592, 593, 1858, Art. XIX, XXII, 12 Stat. 1023, 1027, 1028; Siam 1856, Reg. III, V, 11 Stat. 149, 152, 153. This type of provision is not to be found in any other United States treaty.

201 Siam, 1856, Art. VI, 11 Stat. 149, 151; Japan, 1858, Art. IX, 12 Stat. 1051, 1058.

advantage to be derived from capitulatory concessions, in that the trade and commerce of the United States with the granting state could be expedited to the extent that the United States deemed advisable, and could at least be placed on a competitive basis with that of any third state; as pointed out previously,[202] concern with treatment of United States nationals rather than the economic benefits seems to have been the primary factor motivating the seeking of such concessions. This is not to say that economic considerations did not also play their part. In the treaty of 1858 with China, even import duties chargeable on United States products were subjected partially to the control of the United States consul. Article XX provided that disputes between importers and local customs officials concerning weights and valuations for customs purposes should be adjusted by agreement between the consul and the superintendent of customs.[203] The purpose of such a provision must have been to assure United States merchants of non-discriminatory treatment. However, this was the only provision in any one of the capitulatory treaties which was obviously and primarily concerned with economic considerations. The extraordinary jurisdictional regimes established by these treaties were primarily assurances of civilized treatment for United States citizens while in a territory where the legal system was deemed to be below standards of a civilized state, as understood by the United States, and they were liquidated as rapidly as was consistent with that view. As soon as a judicial system came into existence which gave some assurance of just treatment to aliens, the applicable capitulatory regime was voluntarily terminated by the United States. It is true that the rising tide of nationalism, with its accompanying pressure for complete administrative control of all incidents of national life, must have had its effect, but it appears that the United States did not cling unnecessarily to these privileges when the professed purpose of their existence had passed.

As noted previously, whenever a European state became responsible for the administration of the legal system within one of the burdened territories, the United States relinquished its extraterritorial privileges;[204] and even where no state upon which the United States was prepared to rely in establishing a just legal administration had become responsible, these privileges were relinquished as and when the United

[202] *Supra* pp. 39 *et seq.*
[203] 12 Stat. 1023, 1028.
[204] *Supra* note 180.

States felt assured of civilized procedures.[205] In 1894, a treaty was concluded with Japan whereby all extraterritorial rights except those pertaining to maritime affairs – which were to be found in most commercial treaties with states of Europe as well as elsewhere – were relinquished.[206] In 1920, the same type of treaty was concluded with Siam; [207] in 1931, with Turkey; [208] in 1937, with Egypt; [209] and in 1943, with China.[210] In 1956, Congress passed a joint resolution which clearly stated the policy of the United States against the continuance of any capitulatory regime and authorizing the President to terminate the last one in existence, namely that with Morocco.[211] The multilateral treaty of October, 1956, in which the United States joined in recognizing the unlimited sovereignty of Morocco over the international zone in Tangier marked the termination of the last remnant of the capitulatory network built up by the United States in the preceding century.[212]

Although the history of consular jurisdiction as it developed in the United States is most comprehensively to be found in the treaty making activity of the United States, this activity was necessarily, to some extent, paralleled and complemented by legislative activity. The treaty of 1788 with France produced the Implementing Act of May 4, 1826.[213] The act of March 2, 1829,[214] implemented similar treaties with other states. The only difference in substance between it and the earlier act was that it was made generally applicable to this class of treaties rather than, as the earlier one was, being limited to implementation of only one treaty (with France), and the time during which a deserter could be held in prison awaiting the pleasure of his country's consul was limited to two months instead of three as in the prior act. This latter difference was apparently unrelated to any existing international treaty obligation, since provisions in some of the treaties subsequent to the one with France but before this act obligated the receiving state

205 As regards Egypt, see *supra* note 182. When Serbia had detached itself from the Turkish Empire, the United States gave up most of its extraterritorial jurisdiction by treaty with Serbia. 1881, Art. XII, 22 Stat. 963, 971.

206 29 Stat. 848.

207 42 Stat. 1928.

208 47 Stat. 2432.

209 53 Stat. 1645. This was a multilateral convention involving all the treaty powers which had extraterritorial privileges there.

210 57 Stat. 767.

211 70 Stat. 773.

212 TIAS 3680, 7 USTIAS 3035.

213 *Supra* notes 109, 110.

214 4 Stat. 359–360.

to hold the deserter longer than two months.[215] Perhaps this was Congress' way of forcing the executive into concluding treaties which were consistent with their ideas as to fair play.

Although some of the treaties in existence at the time of the Act of 1829 contained other obligations on the part of the receiving state to provide the consul with official assistance in carrying out his functions of controlling internal order on board ship,[216] that Act only provided for assistance to him in performing the function of reclaiming deserters.[217] It was not until 1846 that Congress acted to authorize the United States courts, Commissioners and marshals to provide assistance required by the various treaties to consuls in maintaining the internal order on vessels of their states.[218] Apparently, until the passage of that Act, the United States officials would not have had authority to give requested assistance notwithstanding the treaty obligations.

In 1864, a further act, entitled "An Act to provide for the Execution of Treaties between the United States and foreign Nations respecting Consular Jurisdiction over the Crews of Vessels of said Foreign Nations in the Waters and Ports of the United States," was passed.[219] One distinction from its predecessor was that its operation was expressly conditioned upon the President's being satisfied that reciprocal authority for local assistance existed in the other country the consul of which sought assistance. The other was that authority under the Act did not extend to imprisonment of an American citizen who happened to be employed on a foreign vessel. If it transpired upon arraignment that the seaman who had been arrested at the instance of a foreign consul was an American citizen, he was to be released forthwith. This was a departure from the provision common to the treaties with which the statute dealt. Those provisions did not distinguish by citizenship between members of a ship's company. Therefore, it would appear plausible that an American citizen who deserted form a Prussian vessel,

[215] See, *e.g.*, Art. XI, Treaty of Commerce and Navigation with Prussia of 1828, which specified three months (8 Stat. 378, 382), and Art. X of the Treaty with Russia of 1832 (8 Stat. 444, 448–449), which specified four.

[216] See Art. X, Treaty with Prussia, 8 Stat. 378, 382 – "The consuls ... to sit as judges and arbitrators ... between the captains and crews of the vessels ... without the interference of the local authorities, unless ... Consuls ... should *require their assistance to cause their decision to be carried to into effect or supported* ...." [emphasis supplied].

[217] This was also true of the Act of 1826. *Supra* note 213. For the operation of the 1829 Act, in conjuction with the Treaty of 1832 with Russia (8 Stat. 444.), see *Tucker v. Alexandroff*, 183 U.S. 424 (1901).

[218] 9 Stat. 78–79. This Act expressly mentioned the provision in the treaty with Prussia, the quotation of which appears in footnote 216, *supra*, and referred to similar provisions in other treaties.

[219] June 11, 1864, 13 Stat. 121–122.

or was guilty of an infraction on board which induced the consul to demand his arrest and incarceration pending the vessel's sailing from the United States, would be subject to the treaty's operation. However, it was not uncommon to find in those treaty clauses pertaining to jurisdiction over the internal order of national vessels a provision that the consul's judgment should not operate to deprive the parties to such a dispute of recourse "to the judicial authority of their own country." [220] One might infer from this language the intent to limit consular authority to situations involving only crew members nationals of his own state. On the other hand, it would have been possible to construe it as meaning that the courts of the flag state would have ultimate jurisdiction of such disputes regardless of the nationality of the disputants.

It was also common to find in those clauses pertaining deserters provision that the arrested man should be held "until the time when they shall be ... sent back to their own country by a vessel of the same nation." [221] This might give rise to the same inference as that discussed in conjunction with internal disputes on board ship. The Act also provided that the arrested man should be committed to prison or returned to his vessel if the court examining into the matter was satisfied that the act complained of concerned only the internal order and discipline of the vessel and "does not effect [affect] directly the execution of the laws of the United States, or the rights and duties of any citizen of the United States." This would seem to have constituted a further attempt by Congress to exclude American citizens from the operation of the treaty. The maximum period of dentention in prison was two months. However, by this time, the Congressional will had made itself felt, and the more recently concluded treaties of the United States on the subject contained only a two month obligation.[222]

The last legislation on judicial assistance to foreign consuls was passed in 1911.[223] That act provided that United States district courts and Commissioners should

> have the power to carry into effect according to the true intent and meaning thereof, the award or arbitration or decree of any ... [consular officer] of any foreign nation ... [made pursuant to] authority conferred on him ... [by treaty] to sit as judge or arbitrator in such differences as may arise between the captains

[220] *E.g.* Art. VIII, Treaty with Russia of 1832, 8 Stat. 444, 448.
[221] *E.g.* Art. IX, *id.*
[222] *E.g.* Art. III (II) of the Consular Convention with New Granada of 1850, 10 Stat. 80, 84.
[223] The Judiciary, Ch. 11, Sec. 271, 36 Stat. 1163–1164.

and crews of the vessels belonging to the nation whose interests are committed to his charge, application for the exercise of such power being first made to such court or commissioner, by ... such consul .... And said courts or commissioner may ... carry into full effect such award ... and to enforce obedience thereto by imprisonment ... until such award ... is complied with, or the parties are otherwise discharged thereupon, by the consent in writing of such consul ....

This act did not refer to the problem of deserters from foreign ships in the United States, so presumably the old act pertaining to arrest and imprisonment on application of consuls would have continued in force.[224] The act also made no reference to release of an American citizen if he were arrested on application of a foreign consul.[225] This may have been inadvertence or a recognition by Congress that such a provision was arguably inconsistent with treaty obligations of the United States.

The problem pertaining to desertions was, it was apparently thought by Congress, finally put to rest by the Seamen's Act of 1915. It will be recalled that commercial treaties had uniformly up to that time contained provisions authorizing consular officers to effect, with the aid of local authorities, the arrest, incarceration and return of deserters to their ships or home countries. Largely as a result of the lobbying of the International Seamen's Union of America, Congress finally became convinced that some of the economic ills of American seamen and of the merchant shipping of the United States resulted from competition from foreign merchant ships which were paying substandard wages to their seamen and providing them with substandard conditions on board. It was thought that the United States might indirectly, through legislation, effect an equalization of wages and conditions between American ships and their foreign competitors. It was thought that a change in the legal climate eliminating or mitigating punishment for desertion might encourage seamen on foreign vessels with poor wages and working conditions to desert in United States ports. The foreign ship master would then be forced to replace the deserters with seamen at a wage determined by the United States labor market. The threat of easy desertions in American ports would also tend to compel general improvement of conditions on board foreign vessels. The long range effect of such legislation, then, would be to raise wages and improve conditions on foreign ships competing with the American merchant marine,

[224] *Supra* notes 217, 218.
[225] See 13 Stat. 122, *supra* note 219.

making competition with them more profitable. An anticipated collateral benefit was that American shipowners would not oppose so violently or with such persuasiveness all social legislation tending to improve the lot of American seamen at the price of higher operating costs.[226]

Briefly, the legislative history on the desertion problem was as follows: In 1790, Congress passed an act which provided that a deserting American seaman should be imprisoned until the ship was ready to sail, at which time he would be returned to the ship. The cost of detention would be deducted from his wages.[227] In 1829, an act was passed providing for arrest and delivery of a seaman deserting from a foreign vessel, upon application by a consul of the flag state, provided that country had a treaty with the United States so providing.[228] In 1872, desertion from an American ship was made punishable by three months' imprisonment and forfeiture of all or part of wages due and effects left on board.[229] In 1895, imprisonment for desertion from American coastwise vessels was abolished.[230] In 1898, the penalty of imprisonment for desertion from American ships was abolished completely except when occurring in a foreign port.[231] Statutes providing imprisonment for desertion were held constitutional by the Supreme Court in 1897 over the claim that they were invalid under the thirteenth amendment because subjecting seamen to involuntary servitude.[232] Those statutes, it is clear, tended to deprive American seamen of the strike as an effective weapon in bergaining with the shipowner. For a strike to be effective, workmen must must be free to leave the job. Mitigation of the rigors of the American seaman's economic position as compared with his fellow laborers ashore could well begin by providing him with the strike weapon. One provision of the Seamen's Act of 1915 had that effect:

[226] Albrecht, *International Seamen's Union of America, A Study of its History and Problems* (U.S. Bureau of labor Statistics, Bulletin No. 342, June, 1923). For reference to a similar argument, see *Lauritzen v. Larsen*, 345 U.S. 571, 593 (1953).

[227] Ch. XXIX, Sec. 7, 1 Stat. 134.

[228] Ch. XLI, 4 Stat. 359–360.

[229] Ch. CCCXXII, Sec. 51, 17 Stat. 273. For failure or neglect without reasonable cause to join the ship when she was about to put to sea, or being absent without leave not amounting to desertion, the penalty was imprisonment for not more than one month and forfeiture of two days' pay for each day's absence.

[230] Ch. 97, 28 Stat. 667.

[231] Ch. 28, Sec. 19, 30 Stat. 760. The penalty for desertion in a foreign port was reduced to one month's imprisonment.

[232] *Robertson v. Baldwin*, 165 U.S. 275 (1897).

That in the judgment of Congress articles in treaties and conventions of the United States, insofar as they provide for the arrest and imprisonment of officers and seamen deserting or charged with desertion from merchant vessels of the United States in foreign countries, and for the arrest and imprisonment of officers and seamen deserting or charged with desertion from merchant vessels of foreign nations in the United States and the Territories and possessions thereof, and for the co-operation, aid, and protection of competent legal authorities in effecting such arrest or imprisonment and any other treaty provision in conflict with the provisions of this Act ought to be terminated, and to this end the President be, and he is hereby, requested and directed, within ninety days after the passage of this Act, to give notice to the several Governments, respectively, that so much as hereinbefore described of all such treaties and conventions between the United States and foreign Governments will terminate on the expiration of such periods after notices have been given as may be required in such treaties and conventions.[233]

In the same Act, the punishment for desertion from an American ship was reduced by eliminating the imprisonment provision.[234] This act, it is apparent, served the dual purpose of providing American seamen with the strike weapon in their battle for improved economic status while at the same time making it more difficult for competing foreign shipowners to operate at lower cost, since their seamen, if dissatisfied, could now desert without fear of criminal consequences or of being returned to their ships. Also, if he deserted, he might get employment on a vessel of the United States where wages and conditions could be more favorable.

Apparently, Congress was not satisfied with merely making it more attractive to foreign seamen to desert in American ports by relieving them of the fear of arrest and imprisonment at the application of their consul. As part of the same act, it was provided that:

Every seaman on a vessel of the United States shall be entitled to receive on demand from the master ... one-half part of the wages which he shall have then earned at every port where such vessel ... shall load or deliver cargo ... and all stipulations in the contract to the contrary shall be void: ... Any failure ... to comply ... [shall] release the seaman from his contract and he ... [is] entitled to full payment .... [N]otwithstanding any release signed by any seaman, any court having jurisdiction may upon good cause shown set aside such release and take such action as justice shall require: *And provided further.* That this section shall apply to seamen of foreign vessels while in harbors of the United States, and the courts of the United States shall be open to such seamen for its enforcement.[235]

[233] Ch. 153, Sec. 16, 38 Stat. 1184. On termination of those treaty provisions, statutes pertaining to judicial assistance to foreign consuls in reclaiming deserters was to become ineffective.

[234] Ch. 153, Sec. 7, 38 Stat. 1166. The penalty, as amended, was foreiture of all or any part of wages due and effects left on board.

[235] Ch. 153, Sec. 4, 38 Stat. 1165.

The obvious effect of this statute, when coupled with the sections previously discussed, was to help the American seaman finance a strike out of his wages, and the foreign seaman his desertion. Once he had decided to sever his employment with the ship, he could first demand half his wages due when his ship reached an American port. If they were refused, he could collect the wages then due, in full, in an American court, upon the ground that the statute had relieved him of his contract. If the master complied with the statute and gave him fifty percent, he would have at least that much to live on ashore while seeking other employment, possibly on an American ship.

To be sure that the foreign seaman contemplating desertion in an American port would be likely to have a substantial sum due him in earned wages when he made his bid for freedom, it was provided that it was "unlawful ... to pay ... in advance ... or to pay ... [or] make any order, or note, or other evidence of indebtedness ... to ... any person, for the shipment of seamen when payment is deducted or to be deducted from a seaman's wages." [236] This was expressly made applicable to foreign vessels when in the United States. By making advance payment of wages for any purpose unlawful, it was assured that the seaman would have available for his demand at least the wages which he had earned on the current voyage. Otherwise, it might have been possible for the foreign shipowner to obligate substantially his entire income for the voyage before it began thus making his right to fifty percent of wages due in an American port of very little value.

Congress also attempted to assure that the foreign shipowner would be forced to replace deserters by paying the higher price in the American market, by providing that foreign ships leaving ports of the United States should comply with manning scale rules.[237] Presumably, the desertions which occurred in United States ports which were induced by the other legislation discussed would bring the vessel below the manning requirements of United States law and force the master to hire seamen at the higher wages prevailing in American ports.

It might appear that the attempt by Congress in 1915 to approach a solution to the economic ills of the American merchant marine by the legislative program of encouraging desertions from foreign ships in American ports would conflict with any rational immigration policy. It would seem that to encourage desertion might be also to encourage illegal immigration. This problem was recognized by Congress, and to

[236] Ch. 163, Sec. 10 (a), 38 Stat. 1168.
[237] Ch. 153, Sec. 13, 38 Stat. 1169–1170.

some extent there was a reconciling of the two interests. In 1917, Congress passed an act to regulate the immigration of aliens to, and their residence in the United States.[238] Ir was made an offence punishable by a five thousand dollar fine, for which the ship could be held liable *in rem*, to knowingly sign on articles or bring to the United States as one of the crew any alien with intent to permit him to land in violation of the laws and treaties of the United States, or falsely and knowingly to represent that such person was a bona fide member of the crew.[239] It also provided for a $ 1000 fine, for which the ship could also be held responsible *in rem*, for negligent failure to detain on board any alien excluded from the United States by any law or treaty after notice in writing by an immigration officer or the Secretary of Labor to do so.[240] Finally, there was an escape clause, the evident intent of which was to offer encouragement to desert. It provided that the only action which could be taken against an alien who had landed in violation of the act was, for the ensuing three year period only, he would be subject to being taken into custody upon a warrant of the Secretary of Labor, but that even then he would merely be subjected to examination as to his qualifications for permanent admission to the United States. If he were found to be inadmissible, he would simply be deported to the country from which he came.[241] Under this statute, even if he landed illegally, the alien seaman deserter would be safe if he could keep out of custody for three years. If unsuccessful in this, he might still be found admissible for continued residence.[242]

The other side of the legislative picture concerning consular authority consisted of those enactments which authorized or required an American consular officer to do some act or perform some duty with regard to American seamen who came to the country in which he was serving. The legislative implementation of the capitulatory treaties will be taken up immediately after this section.

[238] 39 Stat. 874.
[239] Sec. 31, *id.* at 895.
[240] Sec. 32, *id.*
[241] Sec. 34, *id.* at 896.
[242] This was supplemented by the Act of May 26, 1924, which provided that no alien seaman excluded from admission to the United States should be permitted to land except for medical treatment or pursuant to such regulations as the Secretary of Labor might prescribe for his ultimate deportation. It was further provided that proof that such alien seaman was reported by the master as a deserter would be prima facie evidence of a failure to detain on board or deport after being required to do so by the immigration officer or Secretary of Labor. The Secretary of Labor was authorized, if he found that undue hardship would be caused the seaman if he were deported on the vessel from which he deserted, to deport him on another vessel but at the expense of his own ship. Ch. 190, Sec. 19 (c), 43 Stat. 153, 164–165.

The first legislation on the subject of consular authority over seamen came into effect in 1792.[243] This was followed by the statute of 1803 which has been previously discussed.[244] These were followed by a more detailed act in 1840.[245] Congress clearly designated the American consul as the officer with ultimate control of the relationship between seamen and their ships while in foreign ports. In order that his intervention should not be avoided by preventing complaints from reaching him, it was expressly provided that crew members should be free to see the consul for that purpose, or if he could not go ashore for any reason, the master was to inform the consul of the situation and ask him to go on board to receive the complaint.[246] That provision remained in force until 1872, when it was changed to require the master to send a seaman ashore in custody if necessary, and provided a one-hundred dollar fine for the master's failure to arrange a consultation with the consul upon request of a seaman.[247]

Prior to the passage of the Act of 1840, there was no lawful way that a seaman or any number of them could protect themselves against the dangers or discomforts of a ship which was unseaworthy or improperly manned or equipped. That statute provided that if any officer and a majority of the crew should complain in writing to the consul about an alleged deficiency, the consul must appoint two men of experience in maritime affairs to investigate and report to him as to what need be done, if anything, to put the vessel in proper condition.[248] Their report was required by the act to state whether in their opinion the ship was sent to sea in an unsuitable condition. The cost of investigation was required to be borne by the master, but he was authorized to deduct it from the wages of the complainers if the complaint proved unjustified. The consul was required to examine the report and either approve it or dissent, giving his reasons. If the consul approved a report that the ship was sent to sea unsuitably provided in any important or essential particular through neglect or design, he was required to discharge any seamen who demanded it, exacting three months' extra pay. If the condition arose through mistake or accident not reasonably forseeable, no discharge was to be granted if the condition were corrected within a reasonable time. Otherwise, seamen requesting it

[243] 1 Stat. 255–256. See text at note *supra* 109.
[244] 2 Stat. 203. Text at note *supra* 116.
[245] 5 Stat. 394–397.
[246] § Sixteenth, *id.* at 396.
[247] Ch. 322, Sec. 38, 17 Stat. 262, 269–270.
[248] Ch. 48, § Twelfth, 5 Stat. 396.

were to be discharged and granted one month's extra pay.[249] It is probable that this would have been considered a continuing of the voyage contrary to the agreement, entitling the seamen to their discharge under the ninth section of the same act.[250] That section provided the consul with general authority to discharge seamen if satisfied that their complaint that the voyage was being continued contrary to the agreement was justified, or that they had fulfilled their contract. It further provided that, upon such discharge, the consul should exact three months' extra pay unless convinced that the situation was beyond the control of the master.[251] The fifth section provided that the consul could, on the joint application of the master and mariner, grant the discharge without requiring payment of extra wages, but on terms which he determined would relieve the United States of any expense of maintenance and repatriation.[252]

Although the statute under consideration did not expressly require that a seamen be signed on before the consul in a foreign port, it did require the consul to enter newly shipped seamen on the crew list.[253]

The statute of 1840 obligated consuls to discountenance insubordination and to reclaim deserters "by every means within their power," including requests for assistance from local authorities.[254] Once a deserter was apprehended, the consul was to investigate into the

[249] § Fourteenth, *id.*

[250] *Id.* at 395.

[251] This provision was substantially re-enacted in 1855. Ch. 133, Sec. 19, 10 Stat. 619, 625, and 1856, Ch. 127, Sec. 26, 11 Stat. 62. In 1873, it was provided that the consul should conduct a hearing into the cause of a mariner's discharge, and if satisfied that it was caused by his own fault, could remit the 3 months' extra wages. Ch. 242, 17 Stat. 580. In 1884, the provision was modified by permitting the consul to discharge provided he was satisfied that the employment contract was completed or that the seaman was entitled to his discharge under any act of Congress or general principles or usage of maritime law. The extra wages, which were reduced to one month's, could be remitted by the consul unless he found that the voyage was designedly and unnecessarily continued contrary to the agreement or that the man's discharge was required because of an injuriy received in the employ of the ship. Ch. 121, Sec. 2, 23 Stat. 53, 54.

[252] 5 Stat. 395. In 1855, this provision was modified by requiring the consul to question the seaman privately to determine whether it was in his interest to be discharged. His finding was required to be entered on the crew list and articles along with the decision to remit the three months' extra wages. Ch. 133, Sec. 15, 17, 10 Stat. 624. Even prior to this change, all discharges were required to be entered on the crew list and articles. 1840, Ch. 48, Sec. 7, 5 Stat. 395.

[253] Sec. 8, *id.* The deficiency was corrected in 1872. Ch. 322, Sec. 15, 17 Stat. 265. The master was required to replace lost crew members with the consent and through the agency of a consular officer where one was available, the change being endorsed on the articles and crew list. If no consul was available, he was required to report the addition at the next port of call where there was one stationed. In 1915, this area was codified, the only change of substance being that the master was obligated to replace lost seamen with persons of equal or higher grade. Ch. 163, Sec. 1, 38 Stat. 1164.

[254] § Eleventh, 5 Stat. 395–396.

underlying facts and, if satisfied that the desertion was caused by cruel or unusual treatment by the master or officers, discharge the seaman, exacting three month's extra wages.[255]

The statute establishing consular jurisdiction regarding complaints of unseaworthiness was broadened in 1872 to require investigation into complaints by three or more crew members that water and/or provisions for the crew were deficient. The consul was authorized to order rectification of substandard conditions, the master being subject to a penalty of 100 dollars on failure to comply.[256]

In 1884, provision was made for discharge by the consul of seamen on vessels sold abroad. He was required to collect one month's extra wages unless the master and seaman agreed to substitute employment.[257] In 1888, the consul was statutorily required to retain all monies collected on behalf of the seaman upon his discharge for any reason and to pay out of them expenses incident to his maintenance and repatriation.[258]

The United States legislation concerning consular authority over seamen's affairs will be seen to have been incomplete as to coverage of problems likely to arise, but by the middle of the 19th century, Congress had made it manifest that the consul was to have ultimate control of all United States maritime problems in foreign countries to the extent that this was permitted by treaty and consistent with Congressional policy. On the other hand, as will be seen in the ensuing section, Congress built a rather complex statutory edifice in its attempts to provide for the exercise of American consular jurisdiction in the countries with which the United States had capitulatory conventions.

Although the United States had a capitulary arrangement with Turkey as early as 1830,[259] and before 1848 had similar treaties with

[255] § Seventeenth, *id.* at 396–397. His reasons for discharge were to be entered on the crew list and articles. This provision was re-enacted in 1884. Ch. 121, Sec. 6, 23 Stat. 55. In 1915, the provision was modified by deleting that portion which authorized the arrest of deserters. Ch. 153, Sec. 8, 16, 17, 38 Stat. 1167, 1184.

[256] Ch. 322, Sec. 36, 17 Stat. 269. If the complaint was found to be unjustified, each person who complained was liable to forfeiture of not more than one week's pay to the master. In 1915, the whole area of unseaworthiness was codified. Upon a complaint in writing signed by the first and second officer or a majority of the crew that the vessel was in an unsuitable condition to go to sea because unseaworthy or insufficiently or unsatisfactorily supplied with provisions or equipment, the consul was to appoint three inspectors to investigate and report to him. He was to use the report as under prior law. Ch. 153, Sec. 5, 38 Stat. 1165.

[257] Ch. 121, Sec. 5, 23 Stat. 54–55.

[258] Ch. 61, Sec. 3, 25 Stat. 80. The 1915 act provided that sick or injured seamen should be returned at the expense of the government if, by emergency, they were not actually discharged before the consul. The master was merely required to send them to the consul. Ch. 153, Sec. 19, 38 Stat. 1185.

[259] 8 Stat. 408.

Muscat, [260] Morocco [261] and and China,[262] it was not until that year that legislative action was taken to implement those treaties; [263] and when taken, it pertained only to Chian and Turkey. Prior to the passage of that act, presumably, United States consuls must have acted under executive authority without legislative sanction, and subsequently must have continued to do so in Muscat and Morocco.

The Act of 1848 conferred upon the consul original jurisdiction, both procedurely and substantively, in all criminal matters. If the amount in controversy in a civil action was not more than five hundred dollars, and if the penalty in a criminal prosecution was not more than one-hundred dollar fine or sixty day's imprisonment, the determination by the consul was final. If the possible penalty in a criminal matter exceeded that limit, the consul had the power to decide the case alone if the penalty did not exceed a five-hundred dollar fine or ninety days' imprisonment. However, under these circumstances, the defendant had the right of appeal to the United States Commissioner to China (Ambassador to Turkey). If the possible penalty or amount in controversy exceeded these latter limits, the consul was required to summon American citizens – up to four in a criminal matter, but not less than four in a capital case, and two or three in a civil case – to sit with him on the trial. Even in these cases, the consul made the final decision, but if one of the citizen-judges disagreed, there was an absolute right of appeal to the Commissioner. If the vote was unanimous, there was no right of appeal except in capital cases (Murder, insurrection or rebellion against the Chinese government). Criminal cases in which the possible penalty was between a fine of one-hundred dollars or imprisonment for sixty days and five-hundred dollars or ninety days could be processed in the same way if the consul chose. There was no right of appeal from the decision of the Commissioner, but in a capital matter he was authorized at his discretion to submit the decision to the President of the United States for possible pardon or commutation.

Controlling law, for the resolution of all matters, was designated as the statutory law of the United States. If that law did not cover the problem, the common law was to be applied; and if still deficient the United States Commissioner was authorized to promulgate decrees and regulations to satisfy the need. He was also authorized to establish,

[260] 1833, 8 Stat. 458.
[261] 1836, 8 Stat. 484.
[262] 1844, 8 Stat. 592.
[263] 9 Stat. 276–280.

with the advice of the United States consuls in that country a complete judicial procedure for the resolution of controversies which were by treaty subject to United States jurisdiction.

As an incident of the statutory scheme, Congress authorized civil settlement of criminal matters by agreement of the parties with concurrence of the consul. Additionally, the consul was specially authorized to seek aid from local authorities in carrying out the duties prescribed.

In 1860, Congress enacted a general plan [264] expressly operative in China, Turkey, Persia, Tripoli, Tunis, Morocco and Muscat to the extent permitted by the relevant treaty in each country. In the case of Turkey, there was authorization of the exercise of civil jurisdiction as permitted by the laws and usage of Turkey in her dealings with "the Franks" or "other foreign Christian nations." [265] Additionally, consuls in "uncivilized places" were invested with jurisdiction in civil cases up to one-thousand dollars, and in criminal matters where the penalty did not exceed a one-hundred dollar fine or sixty days' imprisonment.[266] Perhaps this statute was intended to control in Borneo, Lew Chew and Siam. Substantively, the act was the same as its predecessor except that the decrees and regulations of the ministers, both as regards procedure and substance were to be submitted by him from time to time to the Secretary of State for presentation to Congress for approval or modification.[267]

In 1866, the powers conferred upon United States consular officers in 1860 were extended to those in Egypt,[268] and in 1870 to Madagascar.[269]

The Act of 1870 vested the superior judicial authority of the consular system in the Secretary of State for the time being.[270] It also provided a right of appeal to the Minister to China or Japan in civil cases involving five-hundred to twenty-five-hundred dollars. If the amount in controversy exceeded that limit, and in all criminal matters,

[264] Ch. 179, 12 Stat. 72–79.
[265] Sec. 21, *id.* at 76. At that time, the United States also had capitularies with Borneo (1850, 10 Stat. 89.), Lew Chew (1854, 10 Stat. 211.) and Siam (1856, 11 Stat. 149.). They were not covered by the statute. As a result, it would have been necessary for consuls there to act under executive authority.
[266] Sec. 30, *id.* at 78–79.
[267] Sec. 6, *id.* at 73–74.
[268] Ch. 296, Sec. 11, 14 Stat. 322.
[269] Ch. 189, Sec. 7, 16 Stat. 184.
[270] Sec. 2, *id.* at 183–184.

there was a right of appeal to the United States circuit court for the district of California.[271]

Congress finally passed an act in 1878 which extended the statutory judicial authority of consuls to those in any country with which the United States had a treaty granting extraterritorial rights, its scope being limited by the terms of the particular treaty involved.[272]

The criminal jurisdiction of United States consuls in China was extended in 1887 to the trials of offences against the opium trafficing laws of that country.[273] Such an act was necessary to any consular authority over that type of offense, since all jurisdiction of consular officers prior to that time was defined by United States law, and would not therefore extend to crimes under Chinese law.[274]

The volume of litigation involving Americans in China finally reached a point where Congress found it necessary to establish a special court to handle the problem.[275] This court exercised all extraterritorial jurisdiction of the United States in China except that the consular courts retained original jurisdiction over civil cases involving not more than five-hundred dollars and criminal cases where the penalty did not exceed one-hundred dollars' fine or sixty days' imprisonment. Apeals from consular decisions were to the United States court for China in all cases, as were all appeals from the consular courts of Korea.[276] Appeals from the United States Court for China were permitted to the ninth circuit court of appeals and thence to the Supreme Court of the United States.[277] Governing law remained the same as previously prescribed,[278] and the procedure as nearly as possible identical with that which prevailed in the consular courts.[279]

The consular regime defined by treaty and implemented by statute continued in force in each country until terminated by treaty. By 1956 the only country in which the United States continued to exercise extraterritorial authority under a capitulatory treaty was Morocco. Apparently, Congress did not favor its continuance for any extended

271 Sec. 3 and Sec. 5, *id.* at 184.
272 Ch. 193, 20 Stat. 131.
273 24 Stat. 409.
274 The only comparable provision was that making it a capital offense to engage in a rebellion or insurrection against the Chinese government. Of course, that act became a crime by United States law under the statute which prescribed the penalty. Ch. 179, sec. 15, 12 Stat. 75.
275 1906, Ch. 3934, 34 Stat. 814.
276 Sec. 1, 2, *id.* at 814–815.
277 Sec. 3, *id.* at 815.
278 *Supra* p. 56; Sec. 4, *id.*
279 Sec. 5, *id.* at 816.

period. On August 1, 1956, the following joint resolution was passed:

> Whereas the laws of the United States invest the ministers and consuls of the United States in certain countries, including Morocco, with judicial authority so far as the exercise of the same is allowed by treaty with such countries and in accordance with usage in such countries; and
>
> Whereas the consuls of the United States in Morocco are permitted to exercise jurisdiction over American nationals under the treaty between the United States and Morocco signed September 16, 1836, [8 Stat. 484.] and the Act of Algeciras signed April 7, 1906; [34 Stat. 2905.] and the exercise by custom and usage the same jurisdiction over subjects of Morocco or others who may be designated as "protoges" under the Convention of Madrid signed July 3, 1880; and
>
> Whereas Morocco is now the only foreign country where the consuls of the United States exercise such jurisdiction; and
>
> Whereas it is the policy of the United States to discontinue the exercise of extraterritorial jurisdiction in Morocco at such time as it becomes appropriate: Therefore be it
>
> *Resolved* ... That the relinquishment by the President, at such time as he considers this appropriate, of the consular jurisdiction of the United States in Morocco is hereby approved and section ... of the Revised Statutes ... pertaining to the exercise of such jurisdiction are repealed effective upon the date which the President determines to be appropriate ....[280]

CONCLUSION

The history of United States consular jurisdiction reflects two major purposes being served by governmental policy which was implemented by executive and legislative action. First, it was necessary to accommodate two conflicting interests, namely the interest in unimpeded international commerce which is of benefit to all countries, and the interest in maintaining peace and good order within the national territory. In order to encourage a free flow of commerce among the various nations, it was necessary to arrange international relations in such a manner that there would be a minimum of interference with the functioning of ships in foreign ports. This approach to stimulation of commerce has been traced back into the earliest beginnings of international trade. Local legislation supplemented international agreement to accomplish the desired result. The exercise of jurisdiction over either the ship or members of her crew while in port could of course only serve to detain her. On the other hand, it was not considered practicable to attempt to remove such ships entirely from the power of local authorities. There were possible extreme situations in which, in order to

[280] Ch. 807, 70 Stat. 773–774.

prevent serious social disturbance, it would be essential that local authorities intervene in the affairs of the vessel. These two interests could be seen in conflict at the outset of United States international relations. The consular treaty concluded by Benjamin Franklin with France was rejected by Congress because it granted too great an exemption from local jurisdiction to ships of one state within the territory of the other. However, the treaty which was finally concluded between them conferred substantial jurisdiction to consuls over ships of their respective states. Thereafter, in all treaties with states which dealt as equals, there were attempts at reconciliation of these competing interests.

The legislation on the subject generally only implemented the executive policy as expressed in treaties, and usually lagged far behind the treaty development, never more than partially implementing the rather extensive powers which United States consuls were conventionally granted over shipping. There were two instances in which this was not the case – in which Congress seized the initiative in affecting the legal position of the consul in shipping. Both of these instances involved his authority in case of desertion. First, Congress limited the time during which a United States court could hold a deserter in jail, pending disposition by his consul, to two months. This was inconsistent with provisions in most of the then existing treaties. The effect was to cause the executive to negotiate later treaties which embodied the two month term rather than the three or four month provision previously commonly found.

The other instance referred to occurred in the enactment of the Seamen's Act of 1915 in which Congress effectively called for the termination of treaty obligations to give assistance to foreign consuls in the arrest of deserters, and eliminated the authority of United States consuls to effect such arrests abroad. This, it is clear, is a departure from the policy of leaving maritime commerce as fully as possible in the power of a representative of the flag state. It was the feeling of Congress that this departure, although probably having a detrimental effect on the shipping of foreign states, would benefit that of the United States by tending to equalize the wage and accommodation costs of United States operators and their foreign competitors. The idea was to encourage, rather than discourage, dissatisfied foreign seamen to desert in American ports, thereby forcing the employer to rehire at the rate current in America and to improve wages and conditions generally in order to eliminate the source of dissatisfaction. This process would involve him in greater expense and would tend to equalize his costs with those of American operators.

The other main stream of United States activity during the period involved the removal not only of maritime commercial matters from the cognizance of local authorities in certain countries, but also of all American nationals to the extent that such agreements could be concluded. These treaties differed from those previously discussed in that they were not reciprocal. Some appeared to be reciprocal, but were in form only. They granted to both states most-favored-nation treatment insofar as consular authority was concerned. However, in view of the fact that, different from the other state, the United States had conferred no non-maritime extraterritorial privilege on any third state, the result was that the United States acquired rights which the other party did not.

Although it is incidentally true that these treaties which conferred extraterritorial jurisdiction over United States nationals abroad would tend to confer a benefit on the foreign commerce of the United States, the main purpose, apparently, of the United States in seeking such treaties was to protect Americans from the operation of what were deemed to be uncivilized jurisprudential systems in states with fundamentally different social systems. Generally, these states were to be found in the Arabic world and the Orient, in addition to a few in parts of Africa.

The general tenor of the "capitulations" was that American nationals were placed to a large extent under the authority of the United States consul in the state involved. The terms of agreement were largely inherited from the early French treaties which had been concluded with the Ottoman Porte prior to United States independence. These had in turn been reflected in the treaties of England with the Porte and with other countries of alien social and legal systems. Evidence of the fact that the primary reason for the conclusion of capitularies by the United States lay in the fear of the effect of an alien legal system upon American nationals may be found in recitations of treaties themselves. In some, the process of their own liquidation was related to a prior establishment of a "civilized" court system. Evidence is also to be found in legislation of the United States. However, the best evidence is the fact that they were abrogated by the United States as fast as the judicial system in the various subservient states were found to be of a standard acceptable to the United States, and when any European power became responsible for the operation of the system. In the case of China, the United States even aided in the development of an adequate judicial system, which led to the termination of extraterritorial rights there.

The system of capitularies has now been completely liquidated by the United States, leaving as a residual of extraterritorial jurisdiction the reciprocal authority of consuls over their national shipping in foreign parts, which is limited by the legitimate interest of the local authorities in maintaining law and order. It is the bounds of this authority that will be examined in the succeeding chapters.

CHAPTER III

SEAMEN OVER WHOM CONSULAR OFFICERS HAVE AUTHORITY

The problem dealt with in this chapter is primarily the definition of the class of persons over whom a consular officer may exercise authority because they are seamen of his state.

Since the consul is an official of the sending state, his authority to act in the first instance is derived from the municipal law of the sending state. Lacking authorization under the law of the sending state, either by statute or executive rule, he would not have official capacity to take any action which could raise questions of conflict with the law of the receiving state. On the other hand, the receiving state could not question the validity of his act on the ground that it was unauthorized by the municipal law of his state, but only upon the ground that such authorization would constitute a violation of international law.[1]

There were several dissents from the proposition that one state cannot question the domestic validity of another state's act, but the majority opinion seems sound. If Turkey was not precluded from asserting jurisdiction over the French officer by any rule of international law, then it is incompteent for France to claim that the jurisdiction was applied inconsistently with Turkish law or that the Turkish statute actually implemented violated well established international legal principles. Presumably the Turkish officials could have chosen a statute which was not inconsistent with international law, or the Turkish legislature could have passed a legitimate one.[2] The same type of problem could arise as the result of a consul's exercise of authority over a seaman. If the sending state could legitimately authorize the action taken, the fact that it did not in fact do so can be of no concern to

[1] *The S. S. Lotus, P.C.I.J.*, ser. A., No. 10, Hudson, *II World Court Reports* 20, 39.

[2] It should be noted that there was no claim for denial of justice, which could raise a question of the validity of the municipal law which was implemented. The only question was the right to exercise jurisdiction, not how it was done.

the receiving state. As between the two states, the only question can be whether the action by the sending state through its official, the consul, was or was not consistent with the international law controlling between the parties. If so, the sending state could rightly respond to a claim that the act had not been municipally authorized or had been authorized inconsistently with the domestic law of the sending state, that that question is one for it alone to decide. The relationship between a state and its officials depends upon municipal law, and only that state can construe its law and regulate the terms of the relationship, including the authority of the agent.

Although it is not competent for another state to question a United States consul's action on the ground that it was unauthorized by United States law, he would not in fact act in a particular matter unless he at least thought there was municipal legal authority for his action, regardless of the international legal position. Therefore, in the usual case, an international legal attack upon particular consular action will collaterally bring into question the legitimacy of the act under United States law. Additionally, there is a direct bond between United States municipal law and international law on any subject cognizable in international law. The Constitution imports treaty provisions into the municipal law system,[3] and the Supreme Court has incorporated the general international law.[4]

The United States Constitution [5] makes treaties to which the United States is a party the supreme law of the land. That provision would seem to simplify the problem of the relationship between United States municipal law and treaty provisions by merely making the treaty provisions supreme over any inconsistent provision of local law. However, as the area has developed, the Constitution has not in fact eliminated all conflict between what may be the treaty rule on any subject and municipal law on the same subject. It is true that is has effectively dealt with the problem of inconsistency between a treaty provision and the content of the law of any particular political subdivision of the United States. Provided that the treaty provision has become incorporated into the municipal law of the United States, it takes precedence over any inconsistent state or local law,[6] whether the local law

[3] Article VI, 1 Stat. 19.

[4] *The Paquete Habana*, 175 U.S. 677 (1900). *In Hilton v. Guyot*, 159 U.S. 113, 163 (1895) the Court said that international law as well as private international law is "part of our law, and must be ascertained and administered by the courts of justice, as often as such questions are presented in litigation."

[5] Article VI, 1 Stat. 19.

[6] *Ware v. Hylton*, 3 Dall. 199 (1796); *cf. United States v. Belmont*, 301 U.S. 324, 331 (1937).

was promulgated before or after the treaty came into force. The question of when it becomes incorporated into United States municipal law will be discussed at a subsequent point.

With regard to inconsistencies between self-executing treaty provisions and statutory law of the United States, the position is somewhat different.[7] If there is a clear and direct conflict, the one which is later in time will be held controlling in any litigation in a United States Court,[8] and presumably an administrative official would be bound by the one which later came into force.[9] As a matter of construction, if the later statute can be construed consistently with the earlier treaty provision, that will be done on the theory that Congress will not be presumed to have intended to act inconsistently with treaty obligations of the United States.[10] The unsatisfactory alternative would be that the United States has incurred by the subsequent Congressional action an international legal liability to another country. It is logical that if this result can be avoided by the process of construction, a court should avoid it, whether the treaty provision has become incorporated into the municipal law of the United States or not. It is true that if the treaty has not as yet become incorporated into municipal law, the court technically need not consider it. However, that fact does not mean that it constitutes no international obligation of the United States. Thus, even though not obligatory municipally, a court should construe legislation, if such construction is possible, as not inconsistent with a treaty obligation.

The question of whether a particular treaty provision has become part of the municipal law of the United States is one which is not always easily answered. Treaties have been classified by the courts into two categories, those which automatically became part of municipal law upon their ratification, and those which require some implementing legislation or executive action to become effective as part of domestic law. The former are referred to as "self-executing," and the latter "non-self-executing."

Self-executing provisions are those which are intended to and are so phrased as to provide a rule which the courts [11] or administrative

[7] If the treaty is non-self-executing, the problem does not arise, since it would have no domestic effect without legislation. See, *e.g.* Art. 12, Convention for the Protection of Submarine Cables, 1884, 24 Stat. 989, 996.

[8] *Whitney v. Robertson*, 124 U.S. 190, 195 (1887).

[9] See Reiff, "The Enforcement of Multipartite Administrative Treaties in the United States," 34 *A.J.I.L.* 661, 670n (1940); Cook v. United States, 288 U.S. 102 (1933).

[10] See *The Chinese Exclusion Case*, 130 U.S. 581, 600 (1888).

[11] See *Foster v. Neilson*, 2 Peters 253, 314 (1829).

officials[12] can apply in an appropriate case without the aid of implementing legislation. Non-self-executing provisions are those which amount to a contractual obligation of the United States to take particular legislative action, or executive action where the executive is competent to act.[13] A second type of non-self-executing treaty is that which amounts to a general statement of attitude on the part of the signatories which by its nature requires no particular action to be taken.[14]

Although there is no constitutional provision making customary international law operative in United States courts the Supreme Court has incorporated it into municipal law, at least where not in conflict with any Congressional act. In *The Paquete Habana,* while the United States was at war with Spain, and Cuba was blockaded by the United States Navy, two fishing vessels owned and operated by Spanish nationals were seized by the blockading warships and brought into Florida as prizes of war. The United States District Court, after a trial, condemned the vessels and ordered them sold as prize, "the court not being satisfied that as a matter of law, without any ordinance, treaty or proclamation, fishing vessels of this class are exempt from seizure." [15] There was no treaty to which the United States was party which required the exemption of such vessels from capture during time of war. The Constitutional provision incorporating threaty obligations into United States domestic law therefore could have no effect upon the problem, and there was no domestic legislation or executive act which regulated the subject. Thus, the question was squarely raised in the Supreme Court whether the courts of the United States are required to apply substantive rules of customary international law in deciding cases to which they apply. If there was no such obligation, the decision of the District Court could not be disturbed. The Court first traced the origins and growth of the usage among civilized nations in exempting fishing vessels from capture as prize.[16] It then considered the opinions of

[12] See *Cook v. United States,* 288 U.S. 102 (1933). Administrative officials frequently have to determine whether a treaty provision is self-executing. For example, the report of the Commissioner of Navigation of 1913 on page eight, refers to the Radiotelegraphic Convention of 1912 (38 Stat. 1672) and says that the Commerce Department, along with the Navy Department, War Department and Treasury Department, began enforcing the self-executing provisions of that treaty at the earliest time that the requisite arrangements could be completed.

[13] See *Cotzhausen v. Nazro,* 107 U.S. 215 (1822).

[14] *E.g.,* Art. I, General Pact for the Renunciation of War, Aug. 27, 1928, 46 Stat. 2343, 2345–2346 – "The . . . Parties solemnly declare . . . that they condemn recourse to war . . . ."

[15] *Supra* note 4, at 679.

[16] *Id.* at 686–700.

leading text writers on international law as to whether this usage had grown into a rule of international law.[17] The Court finally determined that there was such a rule and that it was binding upon them in this situation.[18] The decision of the District Court was reversed, the Court holding that "International law is part of our law, and must be administered by the courts of justice of appropriate jurisdiction, as often as questions of right depending upon it are duly presented for their determination. For this purpose, where there is no treaty, and no controlling executive or legislative act or judicial decision, resort must be had to the customs and usages of civilized nations ...." [19]

A statement similar to that of the Court in *The Paquete Habana* had been previously made in *Hilton v. Guyot*,[20] which case, however, involved not a question of a rule restricting the power of the United States to act in a particular way *vis-à-vis* a foreign national, but of an international rule regulating rights as between individuals, nationals of different states. The question was whether the courts of the United States were required to give effect to a money judgment in favor of a French national by a French court against an American national. It was held that it was not necessary to give effect to that judgment, but the Court had found that there was an international rule to the effect that such a judgment was not entitled to enforcement unless the country the courts of which granted it recognized and gave effect to the judgments of the courts of the forum state. Since the courts of France did not give effect to judgments of United States courts without relitigating the controversy out of which it arose, similar treatment was accorded the French judgment. Thus, although the plaintiff was not entitled to enforement of his French judgment in the courts of the United States, this was because of the effect of an international law rule, not in derogation of one.

The New York Court of Appeals subsequently refused to apply the rule espoused by the Supreme Court in *Hilton v. Guyot* in a case which was, however, distinguishable on its facts.[21] In that case, the plaintiff was an American national who had sued a French national in a French court and lost, and then sought to re-litigate the issue in the courts of the State of New York. He was held to be barred by the previous

[17] *Id.* at 700–708.

[18] *Id.* at 708. The ensuing pages deal with the question of whether the Court could take judicial notice of the particular rule involved or whether it must be proved as a fact. 708–712.

[19] *Id.* at 700.

[20] 159 U.S. 113, 163 (1894).

[21] *Johnston v. Compagnie Générale Transatlantique*, 242 N.Y. 381, 152 N.E. 121 (1926).

judgment of the French court. The case was clearly distinguishable from *Hilton v. Guyot* and, it is submitted, was correctly decided;[22] but the dicta of the Court of Appeals to the effect that it was not bound by the Supreme Court's prior decision is subject to the most serious question. The Constitution confers upon the federal government exclusive control of international relations. Therefore, if the Supreme Court of the United States declares a particular rule of international law and that it is the supreme law of the land – *e.g.* reciprocity in the enforcement of foreign judgments – it would appear that every state of the United States is bound to apply that rule thereafter.

In *The Paquete Habana*, the court considered the international legal bounds of governmental action against a national of another state, and decided that customary international law defining the limits of such action was part of the law of the United States. In *Hilton v. Guyot*, the customary international law rule of reciprocity in the enforcement of foreign judgments was held to apply as between two individuals whose controversy came within its ambit. Closely related to this problem is the question of whether there is any international law rule pertaining to the choice of law governing the resolution of a controversy between two individuals where there are contacts with the laws of more than one sovereign. In *Hilton v. Guyot*, the Court said "International law, ... including ... questions arising under what is usually called ... conflict of laws, and concerning the rights of persons within the territory and dominion of one nation, by reason of acts, private or public, done within the dominions of another nation – is part of our law, and must be ascertained and administered by the courts of justice, as often as such questions are presented in litigation between man and man ...."[23]

Hilton v. Guyot involved a conflict between the law of France and that of the United States. More accurately stated, the controversy would have been decided differently if the law of France had been applied rather than that of the United States. Under the law of France the re-litigation of the controversy was barred, whereas the plaintiff was required by the Court's decision to relitigate on the merits. This depended upon a finding by the Court that there was a positive rule of international law permitting a state to refuse enforcement of a foreign judgment if the state whose courts gave the judgment refused effect to judgments of the forum state.

[22] It involved a plaintiff attacking the judgment of a court the jurisdiction of which he himself invoked. *Res judicata* is clearly applicable.

[23] 159 U.S. 113, 163 (1894).

In the usual conflict of laws situation, there has been no prior litigation of the controversy, and the court of the forum is forced to choose between the laws of two or more states each of which has some contact with the transaction. That was the problem with which the Court was faced in *Lauritzen v. Larsen.*[24] An action was brought in the United States District Court for the Southern District of New York for personal injuries sustained by a seaman of Danish nationality on board a ship of Denmark while in Cuban waters. The employment contract had been concluded in the United States, and under it he was to be returned to the United States at the end of the voyage. However, it also provided that Danish law and the collective bargaining contract with the Danish seamen's union should be controlling in any controversy arising out of the employment. The action was against his employer, a Danish national, the owner of the vessel on which he was employed. The plaintiff contended for the application of United States law,[25] while the defendant insisted upon the application of Danish law, which did not provide an injured seaman with a cause of action for damages for personal injuries, but gave him an exclusive remedy similar to wormen's compensation.[26] The Court held that there was an international maritime law rule for determining controlling law in such a situation, which required the identification ans weighing of the various contacts between the transaction and the national interest served by the assertion of authority.[27] It then carefully analyzed all the various connecting factors, finally concluding that maritime law required the application of Danish law to the controversy. Since Danish law provided an exclusive remedy, the seaman was deprived of the benefit of any American law, including the Jones Act. As the Danish statute was not pleaded, the question of an exclusive Danish forum was not raised, and the action was dismissed.[28] This case in conjunction with *Hilton v. Guyot* and *The Paquete Habana* appear to go a long way towards complete incorporation of customary international law into the domestic law of the United States; and in the area of control of international commerce and maintenance of international relations – both of which are involved in problems of a state's authority over its seamen and

[24] 345 U.S. 571 (1953).
[25] More specifically, The Jones Act, 46 U.S.C. 688.
[26] Although the tort occurred in Havana harbor, neither claimed that Cuban law was applicable to the controversy.
[27] 345 U.S. 571, 582 (1953).
[28] The Court said that United States municipal law conflict of laws rules would have produced the same effect. *Id.* at 592.

both of which have been constitutionally subjected to the control of the federal government – these decisions are binding in both state and federal courts.

Since international law is largely incorporated into United States municipal law, it is likely that any statutory or administrative rule pertaining to an area with international implications will reflect the view of the promulgating authority as to the internationally acceptable standard. It is unlikely that either Congress or an administrative department of government would intentionally act in a manner which it felt would involve the United States in international legal liability.

UNITED STATES STATUTES

In the nature of things, it is to be expected that any statutory treatment of the question of who are seamen over whom a state's consular officers may exercise authority will deal with the problem only incidentally, and not for the purpose of definition. In other words, the question of what people are seamen of the United States will arise in the context of a statute dealing, for example, with criminal acts on board ship, and it is not to be expected that any express comprehensive definition which will be of value for all purposes will be found. It is likely that a particular person may be an American seaman for one purpose and not for another.

UNITED STATES CRIMINAL STATUTES

Congress has passed certain criminal statutes which were expressly designed to apply only to acts of seamen. Tha introductory clause to section 701 of Title 46 of the United States Code states: "Whenever any seaman who has been lawfully engaged or any apprentice to the sea service commits any of the following offences, he shall be punished as follows": [29] Section 713 then provides the only definition of the persons who are within the scope of the term "seamen":

> ... every person having the command of any vessel belonging to any citizen of the United States [30] shall be deemed to be "master" thereof; and every person

[29] 38 Stat. 1166.

[30] The term "citizen of the United States" includes corporations and other business entities the controlling interest in which is owned by citizens of the United States, and, in the case of corporations, the president and managing directors are citizens of the United States, and the corporation itself is organized under the laws of the United States or of a State, Territory, District or Possession thereof. 46 U.S.C. 802, 39 Stat. 729.

(apprentices excepted) who shall be employed or engaged to serve in any capacity on board the same shall be deemed and taken to be a "seaman"; and the term "vessel" shall be understood to comprehend every description of vessel navigating on any sea or channel, lake or river ... and the term "owner" shall be taken and understood to comprehend all the several persons, if more than one, to whom the vessel shall belong.[31]

It is apparent that Congress intended by this Act to prescribe rules of conduct for all seamen on vessels owned in whole or in part by citizens of the United States. Since the definition of "vessel" is expressly framed to encompass such a vessel wherever it may be navigating, it must have been within the contemplation of the legislature that the offence described might be committed in the waters of a foreign state or otherwise under circumstances requiring consular officer involvement.

The United States Code, *Crimes and Criminal Procedure*,[32] preliminarily defines the "special maritime and territorial jurisdiction of the United States" as including

(1) The high seas, any other waters within the admiralty and maritime jurisdiction of the United States ...[33] and any vessel belonging in whole or in part to the United States or any citizen thereof, or to any corporation created, by or under the laws of the United States, or any State, Territory, District, or possession thereof, when such vessel is within the admiralty and maritime jurisdiction of the United States ....[34]

(2) Any vessel registered, licensed, or enrolled under the laws of the United States, and being on a voyage upon the waters of any of the Great Lakes, or any of the waters connecting them, or upon the Saint Lawrence River where the same constitutes the International Boundary Line.[35]

The term "vessel of the United States" is defined as one "belonging in whole or in part to the United States, or any citizen thereof, or any

[31] R.S. § 4612, 1898. Section 1703 (b) of Title 19 of the United States Code (49 Stat. 519), which pertains to violations of the customs laws of the United States by illegal importations reads: "Every vessel which is documented, owned, or controlled in the United States, and every vessel of foreign registry which is, directly or indirectly, substantially owned or controlled by any citizen of, or corporation incorporated, owned, or controlled in the United States, shall, for the purposes of this section, be deemed a vessel of the United States." 19 U.S.C. 1708 imposes criminal penalties upon the master or crew member of such a vessel, under five hundred net tons, which is used for the illegal importation of alcoholic beverages into the United States.

[32] Title 18 U.S.C.

[33] The provision "and out of the jurisdiction of any particular state" which is omitted here is not significant in the international legal sphere, since it refers to the relationship between the federal government of the United States and the various state governments thereof. *United States v. Bevans*, 3 U.S. (Wheat.) 326, 386–387 (1818).

[34] *Id.*

[35] Subd. (5) prepeats the provision concerning ownership of vessels for aircraft flying over admiralty waters. 18 U.S.C. 7; 62 Stat. 685, 66 Stat. 589.

corporation created by or under the laws of the United States, or of any State, Territory, District, or Possession thereof.[36]

These statutes are consistent *inter se* in that, in each, the waters upon which jurisdiction is asserted are any which are navigable, and the vessels any belonging in whole or in part to Americans and navigating those waters.[37] The purpose was to provide a general jurisdictional definition to avoid the necessity of repeating in each pertinent criminal statute a full definition of the statutory prescription.[38]

An examination of the specific prescriptive rules contained in the United States Code goes no further towards clarifying what persons are considered "American seamen" for the purpose of exercise of criminal jurisdiction over them. The general pattern is to define an act by the place of its commission, *e.g.* on "a vessel of the United States," [39] "on board of any American vessel," [40] "within the special maritime and territorial jurisdiction of the United States," [41] "within the admiralty and maritime jurisdiction of the United States," [42] and by the persons whose activity is subject to control.[43]

It is apparent that the United States asserts a right to prescribe the conduct of all persons on board any vessel owned in whole or in part by a citizen or company of the United States wherever that vessel may be within navigable waters anywhere in the world. Whether another state would be required to recognize this asserted jurisdiction by permitting the United States consul to take control of a person who had committed a proscribed act on board is a question which will be considered in a subsequent chapter.

[36] 18 U.S.C. 9, 62 Stat. 685.

[37] The Supreme Court of the United States has defined the waters subject to the admiralty jurisdiction of the United States as any waters where commercial navigation is carried on. *Genesee Chief v. Fitzhugh*, 53 U.S. (12 How.) 443 (1851); *ex Parte Boyer*, 109 U.S. 629 (1884), re canals; *In re Ross*, 140 U.S. 453 (1891), re foreign territorial waters.

[38] See reviser's note immediately following section 7 in the U.S. Code.

[39] 18 U.S.C. 2191, 2192, 2193, 2194, 2273, 62 Stat. 800, 804.

[40] 18 U.S.C. 2198, 62 Stat. 802.

[41] 18 U.S.C. 81, 1111, 1112, 1113, 1363, 2031, 2111, 62 Stat. 688, 756, 764, 795, 796.

[42] 18 U.S.C. 1656, 1658, 1659, 2191, 2192, 2193, 2273, 2276, 62 Stat. 774, 775, 800, 804.

[43] "master, officer, seaman, or other person employed on board of any American vessel," 18 U.S.C. 2198, 62 Stat. 802; "Whoever," § 2031, *id.* at 795. There are many which apply generally to whoever is within the place where the action is proscribed. "Whoever, being of the crew of a vessel of the United States," §§ 2192, 2193, *id.* at 800; "master or officer of a vessel of the United States" § 2191, *id.* at 800; "citizen of the United States," § 1652, *id.* at 774; "captain or other officer or mariner of a vessel, § 1656, *id.* at 774; "crew", § 166, *id.* at 775; "master," § 1582, *id.* at 772; "citizen or resident of the United States," §§ 1585, 1586, *id.* at 773; "captain, master, or commander of any vessel," § 1587, *id.* at 773; "master . . . of any vessel," § 1588, *id* at 773; "master or person in charge or command of any private vessel, foreign or domestic, or a member of the crew," § 2274, *id.* at 804; "master of any . . . vessel," § 2278, *id.* at 805; "seaman," § 1655, *id.* at 774.

STATUTES OTHER THAN CRIMINAL

The statutes considered in this section were not primarily designed to confer or assert jurisdiction over persons who may be described as seamen. However, they may have an effect upon the application of a particular statute to the persons described. They are considered in this section only on the narrow question of what persons may be for some limited purpose subject to the authority of an American consular officer in a foreign port.

Congress has provided for the compulsory execution of statutory contracts of employment between the "master of every vessel bound from a port in the United States to any foreign port ... with every seamen whom he carries to sea as one of the crew.[44] The terms of this Act are broad enough to affect the shipping of seamen on foreign vessels sailing from United States ports. However, in the cases in which that question was posed, the courts have uniformly held that it was not applicable.[45] In *Ktistakis v. The Star*, the court decided the issue purely on the basis of the registry of the vessel and apparently was not presented with the problem of whether ownership by United States nationals would dictate a different conclusion.[46] The same is true of the other two cases cited. In *The Elswick Tower*, the Court decided as a matter of statutory construction that, since Congress had in other parts of the same act made them expressly applicable to foreign vessels [47] and had not done so in this part, they must not have intended it to be applicable. In The *Montapedia*, the Court cited another part of the same act which required seamen to be signed on American vessels in a foreign port before a United States consul as evidence of a similar Congressional intent.[48] The argument is that if the United States asserts the applicability of its statutory law to seamen signing on its vessels in a British port, it implicitly recognizes the same right in Britain. In that case, however, the Court seemed prepared to apply the section to a foreign flag vessel owned by a citizen of the United States because of another part of the same act

[44] 46 U.S.C. 564, R.S. § 4511, 1878.

[45] Liberian flag ship, *Ktistakis v. The Star*, 192 F. Supp. 895 (E.D. Va. 1961); British vessel, *The Elswick Tower*, 241 Fed. 706 (S.D. Ga. 1917); British vessel, *The Montapedia*, 14 Fed. 427 (E.D. La. 1882).

[46] It will be remembered that for the purposes of the criminal statutes, ownership by United States nationals was expressly made a criterion subjecting the vessel and persons on board to various criminal sanctions. *Supra* p. 71.

[47] Advances of wages invalid. 46 U.S.C. 599, 38 Stat. 1168.

[48] 46 U.S.C. 569, R.S. § 4517, 1878.

so defining "vessel." [49] Using this argument, it would appear that the plaintiff in *Ktistakis v. The Star* would have prevailed if the vessel involved was owned in whole or in part by an American national.

Two other questions raised by the section under discussion are which persons on board "vessels" covered by the statute are within the category of "seaman whom he carries to sea as one of the crew," and the legal significance of a person's not having signed such articles. The first question seems to be adequately answered by 46 U.S.C. 713.[50] That section defines "seaman" as "every person ... who shall be employed or engaged to serve in any capacity on board ...." It is unnecessary to canvass all the cases on the question, but it seems clear that the United States Supreme Court is prepared to give the term the broad scope which it appears to have. In *Uravic v. Jarka Co.*[51] an American longshoreman casually on board a German ship for the handling of cargo was held to be a "seaman." [52]

The question of the effect of signing, or failure to sign, articles upon the status of a particular individual is a matter which seems on principle to be clear. The statute assumes that a person may serve on board a ship without having signed articles and yet be a "seaman" and "one of the crew." It also provides for certain types of voyages which may be made without the benefit of a signed contract. It would be irrational to conclude that seamen sailing without the statutory agreement, whether consistently or inconsistently with the act, should for that reason be deprived of benefits to which all seamen are entitled by general maritime law or some other statute. The act is remedial in nature, and for the benefit of seamen. An evasion of it by the shipowner, or an inadvertent failure to comply, should have no adverse effect on the rights of its beneficiaries. In common sense, the only effect of a failure to sign articles should be that the seaman is not bound by their terms where they depart from general maritime law or from the standard set by statute or custom of the port where he was engaged. This seems to have been the assumption of Judge Learned Hand in *The Falco* [53] when he said "The fact that he had not signed articles ... might affect the duration of his service and his right to

[49] 14 Fed. 427, 428; 46 U.S.C. 713, R.S. § 4612, 1878.

[50] R.S. § 4612, 1878.

[51] 282 U.S. 234, 239 (1930).

[52] It is true that Congress subsequently took longshoremen out of the scope of the statute for the purpose of actions for personal injuries (Longshoremen's and Harbor Workers' Compensation Act, 1927, 33 U.S.C. 901 *et seq.*, 44 Stat. 1424 *et seq.*) but that does not affect the broad construction which has been given to the statute under consideration.

[53] 20 F. 2d 362 (2d Cir. 1927).

throw up his job, but did not qualify its incidents, or define its character, while he remained at work ...." [54]

The various seamen's wage statutes have been either construed to apply to foreign vessels in United States ports or, by their terms, have been made applicable.[55] The act which governs the rights of "any seaman" in case of loss of the vessel,[56] has been applied to determine the rights of foreign seamen suing in a United States Court.[57] The same is true of the succeeding section [58], which regulates the rights of seamen improperly discharged after signing articles.[59] The section which penalizes the "master or owner of any vessel" for failing to pay wages to a seaman within a certain period of time [60] has also been held applicable a foreign seaman in an action against a foreign vessel.[61] If the foreign vessel was not in a port of the United States, however, the action could not be maintained.[62] The section which makes it illegal to pay any seaman any part of his wages prior to their actually being earned [63] has also been applied to foreign vessels in United States ports.[64] The terms of the act itself made it applicable to foreign vessels,[65] the real question in *The Neck* [66] being whether an extant treaty changed its effect. In *Patterson v. The Eudora*,[67] as well as *The Neck*, the seamen were signed on in a United States port.[68] Of course, the section requiring payment on demand of half-wages due to seamen in each port of loading or discharge [69] is applicable to foreign vessels in United States ports since the Seamen's Act of 1915.[70] The only case on the applicability of the section which invalidates contracts under which seamen give up their lien upon the ship or any other remedy for the

[54] *Id.* at 363. See also *Jameson v. The Regulus*, 13 Fed. Cas. 336 (No. 7198) (D. Pa. 1800).
[55] 46 U.S.C. 591–611, R.S. §§ 4524–4548.
[56] 46 U.S.C. 593, R.S. § 4526, 1898, 30 Stat. 755.
[57] *Avgoustis v. Erini Shipping Co.*, 177 F. 2d 461 (2d Cir. 1949).
[58] 46 U.S.C. 594, R.S. § 4527, 1878.
[59] *Id.*
[60] 46 U.S.C. 596, R.S. § 4529, 30 Stat. 756.
[61] *The Fletero v. Arias*, 206 F. 2d 267 (4th Cir. 1953), *cert.* denied, 346 U.S. 897 (1953); *The Sunderborg*, 47 F 2d 723 (4th Cir. 1931), *cert.* denied, 284 U.S. 618 (1913).
[62] *Transportes Maritimos v. Almeido*, 5 F. 2d 151 (2d Cir. 1925), transferred, 265 U.S. 104 (1924).
[63] 46 U.S.C. 599, 30 Stat. 763.
[64] *The Neck*, 138 Fed. 144 (W.D. Wash. 1905); *Patterson v. The Eudora*, 190 U.S. 169 (1903).
[65] Subd. (f), *supra* note 63.
[66] *Supra* note 64.
[67] *Supra* note 64.
[68] The effect of these statutes will be considered at greater length in Chapter V.
[69] 46U.S.C. 597, R.S. § 4530, 1898, 30 Stat. 756.
[70] Ch. 153, § 4, 38 Stat. 1165.

enforcement of wage claims,[71] has held that it is inapplicable to shipping articles made in a foreign port relating to a foreign vessel.[72] For the purpose of determining applicability of these statutes, no distinction has been drawn between foreign ships beneficially owned by Americans and those which are not.

Although the wage statutes have been rather uniformly applied to seamen on foreign vessels while in the United States, it should not be inferred that this is any indication of Congress' or the courts' attitude towards the general question of which seamen a state is entitled to treat as subject to its authority while in foreign ports. There is no doubt that these same persons would be subject exclusively to the jurisdiction of the foreign consul for some other purposes. These are remedial statutes which constitute an area of special local competence. Of course, to the extent that they deprive the officials of the registration state (consular officers) of authority to deal with these problems, they validate a like deprivation of United States authority abroad over vessels registered in the United States and thus narrow the total scope of consular authority over maritime matters.

There are certain legislative acts which assume the necessity of intervention by United States consular officers in foreign ports. It is important to determine which seamen come within their scope, since they constitute an implied assertion by Congress that their objects are proper subject matter for the exercise of United States authority abroad. These acts refer to "seamen" without any clarifying terminology,[73] "seamen of the United States," [74] or couple the term "seaman" with "merchant vessel," [75] "merchant vessel of the United States," [76] "vessel of the United States," [77] or simply "vessel." [78] There seems to be no significance in the varying terminology used. Since another section [79] of the same act defines "seaman" as a person employed on a "vessel belonging to any citizen of the United States," all these sections may be interpreted to affect the rights of persons employed on any vessel belonging to a citizen of the United States,

[71] 46 U.S.C. 600, R.S. 4535, 1878.

[72] *The Countess of Dufferin*, 6 Fed. Cas. 643 (No. 3280) (E.D. N.Y. 1878).

[73] *E.g.*, 46 U.S.C. 569, 38 Stat. 1164.

[74] *E.g.*, 46 U.S.C. 678, R.S. § 4577, 1878.

[75] *E.g.*, 46 U.S.C. 570, R.S. § 4517, 1878.

[76] *E.g.*, 46 U.S.C. 662, R.S. § 4565, 1878.

[77] *E.g.*, 46 U.S.C. 679, R.S. § 4578, 1878.

[78] *E.g.*, 46 U.S.C. 624, R.S. § 4541, 1878; 46 U.S.C. 656, R.S. § 4559, 1878; 46 U.S.C. 658, R.S. § 4561, 1878; 46 U.S.C. 682, R.S. § 4580, 1878; 46 U.S.C. 685, R.S. § 4583, 1878.

[79] 46 U.S.C. 713, R.S. § 4612, 1878.

regardless of the distinctions among the terms actually employed. Each of these sections constitutes an implicit assumption by Congress that United States consular representatives abroad may, consistently with international law, treat as seamen subject to their authority, as defined, anyone employed aboard a vessel beneficially owned wholly or in part by an American citizen.[80] For this purpose, the place of registration does not seem to have been considered as a possibly relevant factor by the legislature, nor have the courts of the United States considered the problem.

In *The Montapedia* [81] the court held that the Act of 1872 requiring the shipment of seamen in United States ports before a shipping commissioner [82] was not applicable to a British vessel. No issue was raised as to whether the vessel was American owned. The theory was that Congress had, by making it mandatory in the same act that seamen be shipped on American vessels abroad before a United States consul, implicitly assumed the same competence in a British consul in the United States. The courts have also held that aliens serving on American vessels were entitled to relief by United States consuls abroad if destitute within the meaning of the appropriate statutes.[83] Here, too, no question was raised regarding definition of vessels subject to the statute.

The significance of statutes which require or permit consular action *vis-à-vis* seamen on American ships abroad is that, in those and similar areas, a foreign state would be within its rights to similarly instruct its consuls serving in the United States. Having claimed a right in foreign states, the United States could not deny its legality if asserted by foreign consuls within its territory.

TREATY PROVISIONS

It appears from an examination of the treaties and conventions in the formation of which the United States has been involved, that the executive branch of the government has always been committed to the position that beneficial ownership of the vessel is not significant on the question of which country has ultimate jurisdiction over and on it. The state of the vessel's registration has uniformly been desig-

[80] "citizen" is defined *supra* note 30. 46 U.S.C. 802, 41 Stat. 1008.

[81] 14 Fed. 427 (E.D. La. 1882).

[82] 46 U.S.C. 565, R.S. § 4512, 1878.

[83] 46 U.S.C. 593, 678, 683, R.S. § 4526, 30 Stat. 755, R.S. § 4577, 1878, R.S. § 4581, 30 Stat. 752. *Matthews v. Offley*, 16 Fed. Cas. 1128 (No. 9290) (C.C.D. Mass. 1837); see *The Santa Elena*, 271 Fed. 347 (S.D. N.Y. 1920).

nated as the country with ultimate control over it. It is true that, by the statutory law of the United States, ownership by American nationals has always been a prerequisite to the right to register.[84] Therefore, if a vessel is registered in the United States, it is necessarily wholly owned by American citizens or corporations "organized and chartered under the laws of the United States, or of any state thereof, the President and managing directors of which shall be citizens of the United States ...." [85] However, the converse is not true – a vessel owned by an American citizen is not statutorily required to be registered in the United States. If registered elsewhere, the different attitude of the executive from that of Congress becomes significant.

The United States became a member of the International Labor Organization on June 28, 1919.[86] The various conventions of the I.L.O. pertaining to seamen designate the country of registration as the state responsible for treaty enforcement on board, and uniformly make the national law of that state controlling on questions not directly covered by treaty provisions.[87] It is true that not all of these conventions are in force and binding on the United States,[87a] but they do reflect the attitude of the Department of State to the extent that they are in force, and apparently the United States representative at the I.L.O. conferences out of which these conventions grew raised no objection to the final wording insofar as it pertained to this problem.

Since the beginning of international intercourse by the United States as a sovereign state treaties concluded with other powers have always expressly or implicitly asserted that a party's ascription of its nationality to a vessel by registration was conclusive upon the other. The treaty of Amity and Commerce with France of February 6, 1778, provided for identification of vessels by presentation of documents

[84] The first statute on the subject was the Act of Dec. 31, 1792, ch. 1, § 2, 1 Stat. 288. The current law is found in 46 U.S.C. 11, R.S. § 4132, 37 Stat. 562, 38 Stat. 698.

[85] *Supra* note 30.

[86] 49 Stat. 2712.

[87] 1926 Conventions: Simplification of the Inspection of Emigrants on Board Ships, Art. 3 (refers to "the country whose flag the vessel flies"), III Hudson, *International Legislation* 1898, 1899, 1931; Repatriation of Seamen, Art. 1, 6, *id.* at 1981–82, 1984; Seamen's Articles of Agreement, Art. 1, 3, 4, *id.* at 1986, 1987, 1988. 1936 Conventions: Minimum Requirement of Professional Capacity for Masters and Officers on Board Merchant Ships, Art. 1, 4, VII Hudson 440, 441, 442; Annual Holidays with Pay for Seamen, Art. 1, 2, *id.* at 446, 447–8, 449; Liability of the Shipowner in Case of Sickness, Injury, or Death of Seamen, Art. 1, 2, 4, *id.* at 453, 454–455, 456, 456–457; Sickness Insurance for Seamen, Art. 1, 3, 4, *id.* at 462, 463–464, 465, 465–466; Hours of Work on Board Ship and Manning, Art. 1, *id.* at 470, 471–472.

[87a] Only the 1936 Convention on minimum professional capacity of officers and on liability of shipowners in case of sickness, injury and death are in force and ratified by the United States. 54 Stat. 1683, 1693.

issued by either party, the documents constituting the sole basis for determining whether the vessel was entitled to the benefits guaranteed by the agreement.[88] Thereafter, no less than fourty-three treaties of the United States clearly made registration of a vessel by one party binding on the other.[89] In many of them, there were also provisions conferring power upon consular officers to perform some function related to the seamen on board a vessel so registered.[90]

A provision usually found in more recent treaties of the United States covers the question of nationality of merchant vessels substantially as follows:

> Vessels under the flag of either Party, and carrying the papers required by its law in proof of nationality, shall be deemed to be vessels of that Party ....[91]

This clause makes no reference to the conditions under which either party to the treaty is entitled to enter a ship in its national registry. In view of the absence of any limitation upon the right of either party to register vessels, it would appear to follow that the parties did not intend to restrict that action. Implicit, therefore, in the format of these treaties is the sasumption that either party could register a vessel owned wholly or in part by aliens. In fact, they implicitly leave the question solely to the arbitrary discretion of the registering state.

The proper construction of these treaty clauses might differ from that dictated by the plain meaning of their language if it could be shown that the municipal law of both states made national ownership a condition to the right to register. The argument would run that, since the parties both restricted the registration right to vessels beneficially owned by their own nationals, the registration test of nationality contained in the treaties included by inference the test of national ownership.

The law of the United States has always been that a ship not wholly owned by United States nationals may not be registered as a vessel of the United States.[92] However, an examination of the municipal law of

[88] Art. XXV, 8 Stat. 12, 26–28.

[89] Appendix A, #'s 2, 3, 4, 8, 9, 10, 11, 12, 13, 19, 20, 29, 39, 43, 49, 54, 57, 61, 65, 67, 69, 70, 72, 75, 76, 83, 84, 85, 88, 102, 105, 107, 113, 116, 119, 122, 123, 124, 126, 130, 131, 136, 142a.

[90] These provisions will be considered in Chapter V.

[91] Treaty of Friendship, Commerce and Navigation with Greece, 1951, Art. XXI, TIAS 3057, 5 TIAS 1829, 1889–1891 (1954). Similar provisions are found in the treaties, Appendix A, #'s 149, 150, 152, 155, 157, 158, 159, 161, 162, 163, 164, 168a, 170 and 171. The treaty of 1963 with Japan contains a substantially similar provision. # 174.

[92] *Supra* note 84.

the other signatory states discloses that they could not have been contracting under the assumption that the right to register a vessel depends upon the nationality of its owners. Denmark requires only a two-thirds beneficial ownership by nationals or residents of five years' standing.[93] The Federal Republic of Germany permits registration if the majority of the partners-owners personally liable for the debts of the partnership and of those entitled to represent the firm are German nationals, provided they have a voting majority under the partnership contract.[94] In the case of corporations, it is sufficient if German nationals constitute a majority of the board of directors.[95] In the case of Greece, alien ownership of one-half interest or less in a vessel will not prevent its registration.[96] Irish law prohibits any alien ownership of vessels there registered unless the alien is a citizen of a state with which Ireland has a treaty by which such alien is entitled to such ownership. The Irish act also designates as Irish any ship owned by Irish nationals and not registered elsewhere, even though not registered in Ireland.[97] The law of Japan prohibits alien ownership of interests in Japanese ships, but will permit ownership by a foreign corporation provided that all the directors are Japanese subjects and the head office is located in Japan.[98] Korean law is similar.[99] Under the law of The Netherlands, aliens only who are residents may own up to one-third interest in a "Netherlands ship," and corporate ownership is limited to those incorporated under local law, have their head offices there, of which two thirds of the shares are registered in the name of citizens, and the majority of directors are resident citizens; or lacking such stock registration, all directors are citizens, three-quarters of them residents, and three-quarters of the supervisors citizens, two-thirds of whom are residents.[100] Nicaraguan law expressly recognizes the right of an alien to register his ship upon compliance with the dictates of local law.[101] The law of Israel merely states that a ship registered there has Israeli nationality.[102]

It appears from the foregoing survey of the law of states with which

[93] "Laws Concerning the Nationality of Ships," *U.N.L.S.*, ST/LEG/SER. B/5, p. 39.
[94] *Id.* at 64.
[95] *Id.*
[96] *Id.* at 69.
[97] *Id.* at 85. This makes explicit what is implicit in the treaty, namely that an Irish owned vessel may be registered in the United States if United States law permitted.
[98] *Id.* at 90.
[99] *Id.* at 93.
[100] *Id.* at 111.
[101] *Id.* at 123.
[102] *Id.* at 86.

the United States has treaties that there is no common denominator requirement for the right to register a vessel under local law. Thus, there would appear to be no justification for construing the treaty provisions concerning vessel nationality other than consistently with their plain meaning. It appears, therefore, that the attitude of the executive branch of the United States government, as derived from these treaties and those concluded throughout the earlier history of the United States, is that registration is conclusive evidence of nationality, and that the validity of a registration may not be questioned upon the ground that the vessel was owned wholly or in part by aliens.

It is possible, of course, to construe the treaty designation of vessel nationality as restricted to nationality for treaty purposes. That construction would confer a different meaning upon identical provisions according to the content of the rest of the particular treaty under consideration. In the treaty of 1954 with Germany,[103] the only other provisions concerning vessels are Article XX,[104] which accords vessels of one party within the territory of the other national and most-favored-nation treatment, and Article XXII,[105] which authorizes re-crewing in the territories of the other party. Pursuant to Article XXVIII,[106] the maritime jurisdictional provisions of the 1923 treaty[107] were continued in force until a consular convention replaces it. The vessel nationality provision in the 1954 treaty would presumably affect the scope of those provisions of the 1923 treaty. Thus, in the case of the treaty with Germany, the clause under consideration would be definitive in quite a broad problem area.[108] On the other hand, in the Treaty of 1955 with Iran,[109] the only provision concerning national vessels, other than the definition clause, is Article X (3),[110] which grants national and most-favored-nation treatment to vessels of one party in the territory of the other.[111] To confine the effect of the clause in the treaty with Iran to the one narrow problem of whether a particular

[103] TIAS 3593, 7 USTIAS 1839.
[104] *Id.* at 1860.
[105] *Id.* at 1862.
[106] *Id.* at 1868.
[107] Art. XXII, XXIII, XXVIII, 44 Stat. 2132, 2147–2148, 2151–2152, 2152–2153, 2156.
[108] The 1923 treaty gave the consul competence to take depositions from members of the ship's company, to adjudicate on disputes intra-ship's company and to take control of salvage operations under certain circumstances.
[109] TIAS 3853, 8 TIAS 899.
[110] *Id.* at 907–8.
[111] Article X (6) (*Id.* at 908.) merely continues the definition, making it clear that it includes all vessels, whether publicly or privately owned. Article XIII (*Id.* at 909–10.) may considerably broaden the consul's maritime competence. That will be discussed at a subsequent point.

vessel is to be granted access and treatment on a national and most-favored-nation basis, and not to other problems not expressly mentioned in the treaty, such as which of the consuls of two competing states is to take action in the resolution of disputes on board, would seem to produce illogical results. A vessel might be admitted to an Iranian port only because it was a United States vessel as defined by the treaty, but held to be a Greek vessel while there because, say, the vessel was owned by a corporation, all of the shares of which were beneficially owned by a Greek national.

Any such restrictive construction of the clause under consideration would be inconsistent with its clear meaning and therefore not likely to prevail in any particular controversy. If there is no good reason to depart from the clear meaning of a treaty clause, it should prevail.[112] Additionally, any such construction would be inconsistent with the rule of liberal construction enunciated by the United States Supreme Court in *Jordan v. Tashiro*.[113]

> The principles which should control the diplomatic relations of nations, and the good faith of treaties as well, require that their obligations should be liberally construed so as to effect the apparent intention of the parties to secure equality and reciprocity between them .... Upon like ground, where a treaty fairly admits of two constructions, one restricting the rights that may be claimed under it and the other enlarging them, the more liberal construction is to be preferred.[114]

It would appear that the better interpretation of this clause, then, would be that it defines the nationality of merchant vessels for all purposes between the parties, and not only for the expressly stated treaty purposes.

The attitude of the executive appears always to have been that registration is conclusive on the question of vessel nationality. Since these treaties also grant certain consular authority over seamen on board the designated vessels, they also evince conviction that those seamen at least are subject to the authority of the United States to that extent while in foreign waters.

Brief mention should be made at this point of the Convention on the

[112] Maximov v. U.S., 373 U.S. 49 (1963). See Fachiri, "Interpretation of Treaties," 23 *AJIL* 745–752 (1929). For an analysis of the decisions of the Permanent Court of International Justice on this question, see Hyde, "The Interpretation of Treaties by the Permanent Court of International Justice," 24 *AJIL* 1–19 (1930). Particular attention should be given to the unequivocal articulation of that principle in *P.C.I.J.*, Ser. A, No. 1 (The Wimbledon).

[113] 278 U.S. 123 (1928).

[114] *Id.* at 127.

High Seas [115] and its effect on the question of the conclusiveness of registration on the nationality of a vessel. Preliminarily, it should be noted that at least until such time as it is binding upon both the United States and the other party to one of the bilateral treaties previously discussed in this section, it will have no effect upon the obligation of each to give full effect to the registration of a vessel by the other.[116] The question is the effect it will have, if any, upon this question under those circumstances. It should be pointed out that Article 30 provides that "The provisions of this Convention shall not affect conventions or other international agreements already in force, as between States Parties to them." However, the convention may reflect a changing attitude on jurisdictional questions, and therefore must be considered.

Article 5 of the Convention states:

1. Each State shall fix the conditions for the grant of its nationality to ships, for the registration of ships in its territory, and for the right to fly its flag. Ships have the nationality of the State whose flag they are entitled to fly. There must exist a genuine link between the State and the ship; in particular, the State must effectively exercise its jurisdiction and control in administrative, technical and social matters over ships flying its flag.

2. Each State shall issue to ships to which it has granted the right to fly its flag documents to that effect.

Article 6 provides for exclusive jurisdiction in the flag state over a ship on the high seas. Article 10 obligates that state to ensure that such ships are governed in matters of navigation, construction, labor conditions, and seaworthiness in accordance with international standards. Article 11 expressly reserves to the flag state jurisdiction to take penal or disciplinary action against a member of the ship's company for an act in the navigation or management of the ship on the high seas.[117] That article also provides that a vessel may only be detained as a result of an incident occurring on the high seas by the officials of the flag state. Articles 12, 13 and 27 recognize implicitly that only the flag state has authority to control a vessel and those on board while on the high seas. The plan of the convention insofar as it deals with vessels and their personnel is to first define the jurisdictional link between state and vessel which justifies or obligates the state to take action

[115] TIAS 5200, 13 USTIAS 2312.

[116] The Convention was ratified by the United States on April 12, 1961.

[117] The state of which the actor is a national is given concurrent jurisdiction. Only the issuing state is authorized to take action against a marine competency document, regardless of the nationality of the holder or of the ship on which the holder served.

concerning it, and then to define specific international obligations and the circumstances out of which they arise.

The United Nations Convention on the Territorial Sea and the Contiguous Zone,[118] which was concluded at the same time as the Convention on the High Seas, defines the rights and duties of a littoral state *vis-à-vis* vessels of other states while in its territorial waters. It does not define the relationship with a ship which gives another state standing to complain of violation by the littoral state of the duties defined.[119] The same is true of the Convention on the Continental Shelf.[120] Since these conventions were concluded at the same time as the Convention on the High Seas, and were ratified by the United States at the same time, it seems safe to assume that the lack of a definition of vessel nationality in them was intended to be supplied by reference to the Convention on the High Seas.

The question resolves itself to this: whether the wording of Article 5 of the Convention on the High Seas, taken in conjunction with its other provisions and those of the Territorial Sea and Continental Shelf conventions, establish a different test of merchant ship nationality from that otherwise adhered to by the Department of State. If so, it necessarily follows that a different rule may also apply as to which seamen are subject to the consular authority of which country.

The specific language which raises the question is: "There must exist a genuine link between the State and the ship; in particular, the State must effectively exercise its jurisdiction and control in administrative, technical and social matters over ships flying its flag.[121] In its most basic form, does this language mean that registration is not a conclusive test of the nationality of a merchant vessel but merely raises an inference of nationality which may be rebutted by the showing of no genuine link between the vessel and the state of registration? [122]

[118] U.N. Doc. A/CONF. 13/L. 52.

[119] *E.g.*, articles 14–20 pertaining to innocent passage.

[120] TIAS 5578, 15 USTIAS 471.

[121] The rest of the article merely codifies what has otherwise been the United States position.

[122] The language of the Article discloses an equivalence between "nationality," "registration" and "the right to fly its flag." Therefore, any of these terms may be used to describe the legal connection between a vessel and a state which confers upon the state the rights in and around a vessel which are defined by the Conventions under examination. It is not intended to canvass all the literature evoked by the adoption of this article by the International Law Commission in its draft convention, and its subsequent inclusion in the Convention finally concluded. See, *e.g.*, Jessup, The United Nation Conference on the Law of the Sea, 59 *Calumbia L. Rev.* 234, 255 *et seq.* (1959); Watts, "The Protection of Merchant Ships", 33 *Brit. Yb. Int'l L.* 52, 68 *et seq.* (1957); McDougal, Burke and Vlasic, "The Maintenance of Public Order at Sea and the Nationality of Ships," 54 *A.J.I.L.* 25 (1960); McDougal and Burke, *The Public Order of the Oceans* 1013–1076 (1962).

If so, who may rebut that inference and under what circumstances?

If there is a question as to whether the consul of Panama may exercise authority over seamen on board a vessel owned by a Greek national but registered in Panama and carrying a crew of diverse nationalities, may a court of the United States question his right to do so on the ground that there is no "genuine link" between the ship and Panama? [123]

If the question arose, as suggested, in the context of a court proceeding, it would be open to the court, even in the face of the article, to give conclusive effect to the fact of registration as an act of state. That construction is permissible, in view of the format of the article. It starts with a statement of the right of a state to fix the conditions for the attribution of its nationality to a ship, and then goes on to mention the requirement of "genuine link." A court might well decide that it has no competence to decide whether a foreign sovereign had complied with the mandate of the article, but only whether there had in fact been an attribution of nationality. The question of compliance with "genuine link" then would be a question which could only be raised on an intergovernmental basis.

There is no question that courts of the United States cannot question the validity of an act of an instrumentality of a foreign government on the ground that the act was inconsistent with the municipal laws of that state.[124] Thus, no question could be raised in a United States court as to the validity under local law of an attribution of nationality to a vessel.

One question raised by the "genuine link" provision of the Convention on the High Seas is whether such an attribution of nationality can be questioned in a United States court on the ground of its inconsistency with international law, defined by that clause, between parties signatory to the Convention. In *Banco Nacional de Cuba v. Sabbatino*,[125]

[123] In the case of a vessel registered in the United States, there will necessarily be a "genuine link" between the ship and the United States because of the registration prerequisites in the controlling statutes. See text *supra* at note 84.

[124] *Hudson v. Guestier*, 8 U.S. 293 (1808); *Bernstein v. Van Heyghen Frères Société Anonyme*, 163 F. 2d 246, 249 (2d Cir. 1947), *cert.* denied, 332 U.S. 772 (1947). *In Canada Southern R. Co. v. Gebhard*, 109 U.S. 527 (1883), the Supreme Court of the United States did in fact discuss the validity of a Canadian statute under Canadian constitutional law, but decided in favor of its validity. The Court also examined into conformity with the laws of Mexico of an official act of land confiscation. *Sabaviego v. Maverick*, 124 U.S. 261 (1888). Apparently, the Supreme Court is today convinced that such an inquiry is not permissible – that the validity under local law is conclusively presumed. *Banco Nacional de Cuba v. Sabbatino*, 376 U.S. 398, 415, n. 17 (1964).

[125] *Id.*

the Supreme Court decided that an act of the government of a foreign state in taking property within its own territory could not be questioned in a court of the United States upon the ground that the act was inconsistent with customary international law.[126] The court, it is true, was careful to restrict the effect of its decision to the particular problem involved, and specifically recognized the possibility that conflict of the sovereign act with a treaty provision might warrant the possibility of a different result.[127] The court also discusses the fact that there is a division of opinion as to the rule of customary international law controlling in the particular controversy, which would not be the case when the rule is defined in a treaty. However, the policy which underlies the refusal of courts to review the validity of acts of a foreign government for consistency with its own municipal law and customary international law would seem to dictate the same result in cases where the attack is based upon conflict with conventional international law.[128]

The court in *Sabbatino* based its refusal to adjudicate on the international legality of the Cuban expropriation on the ground that any determination could interfere with the maintenance of international relations, including the negotiation of agreements looking to reparation for the taking, which function has been entrusted by the Constitution to the executive branch of government.[129] It is no less true of the international intercourse involved in treaty interpretation that judicial action attacking the validity of a sovereign act because allegedly inconsistent with the provision of a treaty could adversely affect the position of the executive in its negotiations with the government involved. More specifically, if the consul from Honduras claims standing in court because the vessel involved is registered in Honduras, the court certainly should not refuse his claim on the ground that there was no "genuine link" between the vessel and Honduras which justified the registration. That is a question which should only be raised by the executive in negotiating with Honduras or with some other state claiming interest in the vessel.

The fact that the courts of the United States probably will not question vessel nationality on the ground that no "genuine link" existed between the registering state and the vessel is not a complete answer to the problem. There is a serious question as to whether the

[126] *Id.* at 940.
[127] *Id.*
[128] *Contra,* Verzijl, "The United Nations Conference on the Law of the Sea," Geneva, 1958, 6 *Nederlands Tijdschrift voor Internationaal Recht* 115, 118 (1959).
[129] *Supra* note 127 at 941–943.

United States executive is not in a different position from that which it has historically held, as a result of United States participation in and ratification of the Convention. It is true that the representative of the United States at the United Nations Conference on the Law of the Sea argued against the retention of the requirement of "genuine link" in the Convention on the ground that it implicitly authorized non-recognition by one state of another's registration if no such link existed, and failed to define the term in a way that would aid in determining the circumstances in which that power could be exercised.[130] Nevertheless, the United States did in fact ratify the Convention with that provision intact, and therefore must be taken to be bound by it in dealing with other states which are also parties, at least where it does not conflict with existing treaty arrangements between them.[131]

In the case of the United States, there is such a network of bilateral treaties containing provisions on the subject of vessel nationality that the clause in question will have very little scope, but there is still some possibility of conflict arising out of its existence. There can be no doubt that a "genuine link" exists between the United States and vessels registered under its laws. United States legislation concerning requisites for vessel registration [132] are sufficient assurance of that. However, vessels registered abroad coming into contact with the United States will not necessarily have a sufficient relationship with the country of registration to justify its attribution of nationality. It would depend upon the pertinent provisions of municipal law of the registering state and whether they had been complied with in the particular case. It appears then, that in one rather limited type of situation, the executive has authority to deny legal effect to a foreign registration, namely, where no genuine link actually exists between the ship and state and there is no convention between the United States and the registering state making registration alone conclusive on the question. Whether the executive may arm the courts with a like power by letter of appropriate import [133] is an open question in the Supreme Court.[134]

The question of what contacts between ship and state constitute genuine links will have to await the event of that question arising in an

[130] "United Nations Conference on the Law of the Sea," *Official Records*, Vol. IV Second Committee, p. 64–65, A/Conf. 13/40.

[131] Convention on the High Seas, Article 30, 13 USTIAS 2320.

[132] *Supra* at 84.

[133] See *Bernstein v. N.V. Nederlandsche-Amerikaansche*, 210 F 2d 375 (2d Cir. 1954).

[134] *Banco Nacional de Cuba v. Sabbatino*, 376 U.S. 398, 420 (1963).

international conflict. It seems clear that no satisfactory formula can be devised in advance of the fact.[135] Perhaps the requirement is so ambiguous that only in the extreme situation where there is no contact other than registration between the ship and registering state would the United States be justified in denying effect to a foreign registration. Indeed, there is a strong suggestion by the International Court of Justice that a State's attribution of nationality to a vessel is not subject to review by another State. In its advisory opinion construing the effect of Article 28(a) of the Convention for the Establishment of the Intergovernmental Maritime Consultative Organization as affected by Article 5 of the "unratified Geneva Convention on the High Seas," it had this to say:

> That Article itself provides: "Each State shall fix the conditions for the grant of nationality to ships, for the registration of ships in the territory, and for the right to fly its flag ..." The Court having reached the conclusion that the determination of the largest ship-owning nations depends solely upon the tonnage registered in the countries in question, any further examination of the contention based on a genuine link is irrevelant ....

The clear inference is that any claim that the validity of a grant of nationality is dependent upon the existence of a genuine link cannot be sustained.[135a] The court assumed without discussion that a state has legal control over all vessels registered under its laws.

> In order effectively to carry out these recommendations and to promote maritime safety in its numerous and varied aspects, the co-operation of those States who exercise jurisdiction over a large portion of the world's existing tonnage is essential.[135b]

EFFECT OF INDIVIDUAL NATIONALITY

For some purposes, the question of who are seamen of a particular state turns on the question of nationality of the individual involved. There is more likelihood of conflict between the United States and another country if the consul of one attempts to exercise authority over a national of the other who happens to be at the time serving on a ship of the sending state. Therefore, it would be well at this point to dis-

[135] See McDougal and Burke, *The Public Order of the Oceans* 1013 *et seq.* (1962); remarks of Mr. Demeur of the Holy See, Mr. Franchi of Italy and ensuing discussion on question in United Nations Conference on the Law of the Sea, Vol. IV 59, 61–68, A/CONF. 13/40.

[135a] 1960 I.C.J. 150, 171.

[135b] *Id.* at 170–171.

cuss nationality of individuals generally, with no reference to their incidental status as seamen. Thereafter, I shall discuss the effect of the fact that a person of one nationality is for the time being serving on a ship of another.

There seems to be little question that, generally, the attribution of nationality by a state to an individual is not open to question by another state. Lauterpacht, in *Oppenheim's International Law*, makes this explicit.[136] The Permanent Court of International Justice, in 1923, said:

> The question of whether a certain matter is or is not within the jurisdiction of a State is an essentially relative question; it depends upon the development of international relations. Thus, in the present state of international law, questions of nationality are, in the opinion of the Court, in principle within this reserved domain.[137]

It is also true, however, that the question of nationality attribution is not exclusively in the domain of domestic law. The exclusiveness may be affected by the term of a treaty,[138] and possibly by certain other considerations of international legal significance. In the *Nottebohm Case*,[139] the International Court of Justice reaffirmed the general principle in the following words:

> It is for Liechtenstein, as it is for every sovereign State, to settle by its own legislation the rules relating to the acquisition of its nationality .... It is not necessary to determine whether international law imposes any limitation on its freedom of decision in this domain. Furthermore, nationality has its most immediate, its most far-reaching and, for most people, its only effects within the legal system of the State conferring it. Nationality serves above all to determine that the person upon whom it is conferred enjoys the rights and is bound by the obligations which the law of the State in question grants to or imposes on its nationals. This is implied in the wider concept that nationality is within the domestic jurisdiction of the State.[140]

In *Nottebohm*, however, it was held that, when a problem on the international plane arises, the solution to which turns upon the effect-

136 Vol I, Sixth ed., 1940, p. 586.

137 *P.C.I.J.* Ser. B., No. 4, p. 24. In that case, the Court decided that the dispute between Great Britain and France concerning certain French nationality decrees having effect in Tunis and Morocco were not within the exclusive jurisdiction of France because of certain treaty obligations assumed by France. However, this did not affect the validity of the general rule espoused. In *P.C.I.J.* Ser. B., No. 10, concerning the exchange of Greek and Turkish populations, the court implicitly reaffirmed this principle conditioned by the same caveat, that a state may, by treaty, give up its arbitrary discretion in matters of nationality. The same is true of *P.C.I.J.*, Ser. B, No. 7, Acquisition of Polish nationality.

138 *Id.*

139 1955 I.C.J. 4.

140 *Id.* at 20.

iveness of a State's attribution of nationality, the question must of necessity be resolved by application of international legal principles, which may conflict with the domestic law of the attributing state. Guatemala was held not required to recognize as effective the conferral by Liechtenstein of its nationality upon Nottebohm. This result was predicated upon the fact that the individual involved did not have a relationship with Liechtenstein which corresponded with the minimum contact recognized in international law as a basis for conferring nationality. The actual relationship was one purely formal in nature, and there was in fact a more substantial connection with Guatemala, the very state which, it was claimed, was required to give credit to his designation as a Liechtenstein national.[141]

It appears clear then, and upon principle unquestionable, that where a State's rights and duties under international law are concerned, an attribution of nationality will only be effective if some minimum substantial contact exists between the individual and the acting state, and if the state against whom the demand of recognition is made has not an equally substantial contact.

In the situation where the question involved is the exercise of jurisdiction or the right to extend protection to a seaman on a merchant vessel, if he happens also to be a national of the vessel state by the laws of that state there could be little doubt that there is sufficient contact to justify its claiming him as a national for all international legal purposes. Service aboard a national vessel is a rather substantial contact which, it is submitted, should be recognized as a sufficient basis for conferral of nationality. However, if he happens to be a national of one state serving on the vessel of another, the problem is not so simple. If the question arises in a third state, that state would have to decide whether, under a treaty or customary international law, he was a seaman of the state of the vessel and thus subject to the exercise of that state's consular authority. The flag state might well claim that service aboard a national merchant ship is sufficient contact with it to justify its claim that the man has a derivative nationality from the ship and therefore is subject to the jurisdiction of that state.

This was a problem implicit in the Hilson claim decided by the United States-German Mixed Claims Commission in 1925.[142]

[141] This case has been cited as the justification of the "genuine link" provision in the Geneva Convention on the High Seas. *Supra* p. 84. See McDougal, Burke and Vlasic, "Maintenance of Public Order at Sea and the Nationality of Ships." 54 *A.J.I.L.* 25 (1960). Watts, A.D., "The Protection of Merchant Ships," 1957 *Brit. Yb. Int'l* L. 52.

[142] Decisions and Opinions 231, III Hackworth, *Digest of International Law* 418–420.

The Commission was charged by international agreement with fixing the liability of Germany for injury to "the United States or its nationals." Hilson was an alien sailing on an American ship which was sunk by a German submarine. The United States claimed that he was a "national" of the United States under the agreement, and therefore that the Commission should fix the liability of Germany for his injuries. The umpire decided that he was not a "national" of the United States, and therefore that the Commission was without authority to decide the matter. The United States representative maintained alternatively that it could extend its protection to the injured seaman pursuant to customary international law, the contact with an American vessel being sufficient bond in international law to justify its claim. This question was not decided by the umpire since it was outside its jurisdiction. In a similar situation where the umpire was not similarly bound by the terms of a treaty reference, but could decide on the basis of customary international law, the umpire held that service on an American vessel was sufficient contact with the United States to justify its espousal of his claim for damages from Mexico for wrongful seizure of his vessel and his subsequent imprisonment.[143] Perhaps the most clear expression of the principle that a seaman takes, for some purposes, the nationality of his ship will be found in the correspondence between the United States and Mexico concerning a mutiny on board an American vessel in a Mexican port involving Mexican subjects. The Mexican government refused to permit the ship to depart unless it was given jurisdiction over the Mexican nationals. The United States Department of State sent the following instruction to the Embassy in Mexico:

> By signing on American steamship *Harvester* the Mexican citizens became subject to laws of the United States and should be treated as other members of crew of vessel without regard to their citizenship .... Inform authorities of this view and informally urge that vessel be permitted to discharge and load cargo without further delay.[144]

On being assured of reciprocity in conversely similar cases, the Mexican government permitted the vessel to depart with the mutineers on board. It is apparent, then, that Mexico and the United States both

[143] 3 Moore, *Digest of International Law* 795.
[144] IV Hackworth, *Digest of International Law* 880.

adhered to the view that these seamen, although Mexican nationals, were subject to the law of the United States.[145]

It is true that the United States' position on the question of derivative nationality [146] of seamen has not always been the same. In the case of the wrongful wounding of an alien seaman, returning to an American vessel on which he was serving, by the authorities of the Dominican Republic, the Department of State said, "If Smith were an American citizen, I should say that he is entitled to the intervention of this Department to secure an indemnity for his injuries. He is not, however, an American citizen ...." [147] This case and others of a similar nature [148] were affected by the then extant consular regulations which set forth that aliens shipping on American vessels were "American seamen" only if they "regularly shipped in an American vessel in a port of the United States" or "regularly shipped in an American vessel, whether in a port of the United States or a foreign port, who have declared their intention to become citizens of the United States and have served three years thereafter on an American merchant vessel." [149] The provision in the current Foreign Affairs Manual on the subject designates a foreign national as an "American seaman" if he once ships on an American ship in a port of the United States and thereafter until he deserts from an American vessel, ships on a foreign vessel or abandons his calling as a seaman.[150] This provision, too, leaves scope for not treating some aliens serving on board American vessels as "American seamen." For instance, if an alien signed on in a foreign port, he would not be within that definition of "American seaman." The ensuing section describes as "Advantages of status (as American seamen)" that it "entitles a seamen to certain privileges of protection and relief *under the laws of the United States.*" [151] The wording of that section makes it clear that the definition in the preceding section does not reflect the attitude of the State Department as to what persons are "American seamen" in international law, but

[145] The question of concurrent jurisdiction over a particular person for a particular act will be considered in a later chapter. The point for which this case is considered here is that service on a national vessel may for some purposes be considered an even stronger contact than nationality itself.

[146] Mr. Bayard, Sec. of State, in communication with Mr. Hubbard, min. to Japan, on November 10, 1888, said "the flag imparts nationality." III Moore, *Digest of International Law* 800.

[147] Mr. Uhl, Act. Sec. of State, to Messrs. Goodrich *et al.*, Apr. 10, 1894, *id.* at 788–799.

[148] See *id.* at 799–800.

[149] *Id.* at 799.

[150] *Foreign Affairs Manual,* 12–20–61, section 513. 1–2.

[151] Emphasis supplied. *Id.* at section 513. 1–3.

who are such under the domestic law of the United States. Thus, the department should not permit this particular section to influence its opinion when the question arises in an international context.

CONCLUSION

The question of what persons are subject to the authority of consuls because they are seamen of his state depends upon the problem context in which the question is posed. If the question is whether a particular individual is entitled to the benefit, or subject to the dictates, of a particular statute of the United States, that is a purely domestic question and must be determined by construction of the statute involved and any other expressions of Congressional intent. On the other hand, a statute which authorizes or requires a particular action to be taken abroad, either expressly or implicitly raises problems of international law. Additionally, statutes which require or permit action by local authorities affecting the rights of seamen while in the United States raise international legal problems. To the extent that a statute authorizes or requires consular action abroad, it limits the ability of the United States to object to a similar exercise of authority within the United States; to the extent that it authorizes or requires action by local authorities within the United States, it restricts the scope of foreign consular authority and renders it difficult to object to a similar restriction on American consular authority abroad. It may also be that the statute requires or admits an act in contravention of international law, but at the least it has the effect of widening or diminishing the scope of consular authority relative to seamen in the relations of the United States with other states. There are some statutes which have been made applicable to seamen on any ship which happens to be in a United States port, such as the seamen's wage statutes. Those acts amount to an assertion of competence, in the particular area involved, over seamen on foreign vessels. To that extent, they constitute a practical surrender of of like competence to foreign states over American vessels abroad.

As a broad generalization, Congress has acted in a manner intended to affect persons serving on vessels owned in whole or in part by citizens of the United States. This, of necessity, includes vessels registered in the United States, because of the statutory registration requirements. It does not, however, follow that these statutes do not apply to certain vessels registered abroad. It depends upon the registration laws of the particular foreign state whether it is possible for an American citizen to own an interest in a vessel registered there. If so, then the statutes referred to would be applicable to seamen on such a ship.

In those areas affected by United States statutory law, the executive branch is necessarily affected in its dealings with foreign governments by the expressed intent of Congress. As concluded in the preceding paragraphs, the Department of State could not very persuasively argue that a foreign state has no power to do an act affecting American vessels similar to that authorized by United States statutes relative to foreign vessels. However, in problem areas unaffected by United States legislation, the executive has unfettered latitude in letting what it views as the international legal rules governing a problem to have effect.

The executive, on the whole, has rigidly adhered to the position that a state is free to treat as its seamen those persons serving on vessels registered pursuant to its laws. This has been demonstrated by an unbroken chain of international commitments from the earliest history of the United States as an independent state down to the present time. This attitude has been carried to the extent of insisting upon treating as an American seaman a national of another state serving on an American vessel, even in dealings with the very state of which he is a national. The only deviation from this attitude has been in the adherence to the Geneva Convention on the High Seas, which provides that a "genuine link" must exist between a state and a vessel to which it attributes its nationality. Even this deviation, however, is slight. Another clause of the same convention preserves the *status quo* between the United States and the many states with whom it has treaty commitments on the subject – all of which provide that registration is conclusive on the question of vessel nationality, and make no reference to any pre-requisite to such registration. Additionally, all vessels registered in the United States must have a "genuine link" with the United States before they could be admitted to registry. Thus, insofar as the international relations of the United States are concerned, the provision of the Geneva Convention can have little effect, at least for the forseeable future.

In the succeeding chapters, where dictated by the subject matter under discussion, questions dealing with the persons subject to authority will be considered in more detail than they have been herein.

CHAPTER IV

GENERAL JURISDICTIONAL PROBLEMS

CONSUL AS AN OFFICIAL OF THE SENDING STATE

This chapter is intended as a resume of general problems of jurisdiction, without detailed consideration of specific fact situations, related to the maritime context. The purpose is to consider generally the circumstances under which states do exercise jurisdiction over persons who also have contacts with other states and those in which they do not. Putting it differently, there are certain bases, or contacts between a person and a state, which are more or less uniformly recognized internationally as sufficient to justify an exercise by that state of jurisdiction over the person. Some of these bases are considered sufficient by some states and not by others. Also, there are some situations in which, by international law more than one state may have a right to exercise its authority. In this latter type situation, one of the two may defer to the other either because of comity or because a positive rule of international law gives to one state the primary right to act.

Particularly in the maritime context, there will be situations in which a state enjoying power over a person because of his location within its territory desires for one reason or another, or is required by law, to defer to another state which also has some contact with the person. In such case, the practical problem arises as to what official of the second state may effectuate the authority thus conferred. If a vessel of the United States is within waters of the United Kingdom, and some official action is indicated with regard to someone on board; provided British authorities concede the right of the United States to take action (either because of a rule of law or otherwise), that action can only be taken through the agency of some person exercising the official authority of the United States. It is also necessary, on occasion, to have an official available to define and interpret the law. That official has historically been a consular officer.

In order to form a clearer idea of the areas in which the consul is likely to function, this chapter will deal with those general rules of international law and comity which have the effect of conferring upon one state the power to prescribe and enforce rules of conduct in another. In the areas thus defined, then, it will presumably be the consul of the foreign state who will determine what action to take, if any. The next chapter will be devoted to a consideration of specific problem areas.

To the extent that international law or voluntary local official action authorizes one state to exercise control within another, the absence of an official of the foreign state makes it necessary to dispose of the problem through a designated representative of a third state or leave the problem unresolved. The history of the evolution of the consul as an official of one state in the territory of another for the purpose of effectuating the laws of his state pertaining to maritime matters is considered in Chapter II. This material is intended to supplement and make current that treatment of the topic.

In absence of treaty provision, there is no general legal right of a state to maintain consular representation within the territory of another.[1]

Apparently, the United States has never taken the position that she is entitled to establish a consulate in any state without governmental consent of that state or consent of the group in *de facto* control of the territory involved.[2] Even during the era of the capitulations it will be remembered, although the right of establishing consulates was not always reciprocal,[3] it was always based on consent of the state where the consulate was to be established.[4] For the purpose of defining the United States position, then, it is necessary to consider the various treaties to which the United States is party.

The Pan American Consular Convention of 1928 provides that

[1] See I *Oppenheim's International Law* 747 (6th ed. 1947); Puente, "The Nature of the Consular Establishment," 78 *U. of Pa. L. Rev.* 329 (1930) Project No. VIII of the *International Commission of Jurists*, 1927, "Consuls," Art. 3, 22 *A.J.I.L.* Spec. Supp. 255 (1928). The Harvard Draft Convention on Legal Position and Functions of Consuls, Sec. II, Art. 2, would create such a duty on the part of signatories, on a most-favored-nation basis, to any state with which diplomatic relations are maintained. However, the commentary to that article makes it clear that no such duty exists under general international law, the article itself being a generalization from various bilateral treaty provisions. 26 *A.J.I.L.* Supp. 193, 229–231 (1932).

[2] See IV Hackworth, *Digest of International Law* 666–699.

[3] See treaty with Siam of 1833, 8 Stat. 454.

[4] The United States has, on occasion, established consulates in geographic areas under the control of groups not recognized as the government of the area. IV Hackworth, *Digest of International Law* 684–699. This has always been done with the consent, tacit or express, of the *de facto* authorities, however.

"States may appoint in the territory of others, with the express or tacit consent of the latter, consuls who shall there represent and defend their commercial and industrial interests and render to their nationals such assistance and protection as they may need."[5] Consent, either tacit or express, was required of the territorial state before another state was entitled to establish consular posts there.

The most recent international instrument on the subject, namely the Vienna Convention on Consular relations,[6] provides that "The establishment of consular relations between states takes place by mutual consent." [7] This provision differs from the Pan American Convention in two significant ways: 1.) It provides for mutual consent, thereby excluding a non-reciprocal granting of the right. The Pan American Convention would admit the possibility of a state's acquring the right to establish a consulate in another without granting a similar right in return. 2.) It does not expressly provide that the consent may be tacit. It seems clear on principle that such consent need not be express in order to be effective. However, the next subdivision of the article provides that "The consent given to the establishment of diplomatic relations between two states implies, unless otheriwse stated, consent to the establishment of consular relations.[8] It might be argued that, the convention having mentioned a specific type of implied consent, all others are thereby excluded.[9] At any rate, it is clear that both conventions require the consent of the receiving state to the establishment and continuance of a consular establishment.

All the current bilateral treaties of the United States which deal with questions of consular relations represent at least tacit mutual consent to the establishment of consulates.

The legal position of the consular officer with regard to the maritime interests of the sending state may also be discovered by an examination of the treaties to which the United States is a party. The Pan American Convention,[10] does not deal extensively with the problem. Article 1 [11] says that consuls "shall there [in the receiving state] represent and

[5] Art. I, 47 Stat. 1976, 1977.

[6] U.N. Doc. A/CONF. 25/12, Apr. 23, 1963, 57 *A.J.I.L.* 995 (1963).

[7] Art. 2 (1).

[8] Art. 2 (2).

[9] The third subdivision of the same article then adds another specific class of tacit consent to the continued existence of consular relations by stating that the severance of diplomatic relations does not *ipso facto* involve the severance of consular relations. Art. 2 (3). Article 4 subjects such incidents as location of consular posts and changes in them to the consent of the receiving state.

[10] *Supra* note 5.

[11] *Id.* at 1977.

defend their [sending states] commercial and industrial interests and render to their nationals such assistance and protection as they need." Article 10 [12] says that "Consuls shall exercise the functions that the law of their state confers upon them, without prejudice to the legislation of the country where they are serving." The representation of commercial interests and protection of nationals would encompass the resolution of various maritime problems, at least insofar as such was permitted by the laws of the receiving state and the actions of local officials there. Article 10, by permitting the exercise of functions defined by the laws of the sending state clearly makes him an official of the sending state empowered, in absence of local legislation to the contrary, to enforce the provisions of the shipping laws of his state. The extent of this authority would have to be determined by examination of the legislation and treaties of the United States, on the one hand to determine the authority conferred upon United States consuls abroad, and on the other, the restrictions upon the authority of foreign consuls here.[13] At any rate, it is clear that this convention designates the consul as the official of the sending state who may occupy the jurisdictional void caused by a failure of local officials to take cognizance of any maritime problem, either because local law does not permit them to act or because they choose in their discretion not to.

The Vienna Convention on Consular Relations [14] deals with the question of consular functions in somewhat greater detail than does the Pan American Convention. Here, too, the consular officer is authorized to protect "the interests of the sending state and of its nationals," but this authority is expressly circumscribed by "the limits permitted by international law."[15] No doubt, that limitation would be implicit in the Pan American Convention, so there is no real difference of substance. Additionally, he is expressly authorized to perform "certain functions of an administrative nature, provided that there is nothing contrary thereto in the laws and regulations of the receiving state."[16] Specifically with regard to maritime matters, he is authorized to exercise "rights of supervision and inspection provided for in the laws and regulations of the sending state ... and in respect of their crews."[17] The following subdivision of the same article provides for

[12] *Id.* at 1978.
[13] Detailed examination is reserved for chapter V.
[14] *Supra* note 6.
[15] Article 5 (a), 57 *A.J.I.L.* 995, 997 (1963).
[16] Art. 5 (f), *id.* at 998.
[17] Art. 5 (k), *id.* This subdivision also applies to national aircraft, where similar problems are involved.

"extending assistance to [those same] vessels and aircraft ... and to their crews, taking statements regarding the voyage of a vessel, examining and stamping the ship's papers, and, without prejudice to the powers of the authorities of the receiving state, conducting investigations into any incidents which occurred during the voyage, and settling disputes of any kind between the master, the officers and the seamen insofar as this may be authorized by the laws and regulations of the sending state."[18] These latter two subdivisions, similarly to the Pan American Convention, establish the consular officer as an official of the sending state sent for the purpose, *inter alia*, of applying the law of the sending state as it applies to national vessels and their crews. The final subdivision [19] is a general provision having the same effect and expressly providing for the performance by the consul of any acts "not prohibited the laws and regulations of the receiving state or to which no objection is taken by the receiving state or which are referred to in the international agreements in force between the sending state and the receiving state." This constitutes the clearest definition of the consul as an official of the sending state with authority to deal with any problem arising out of the operation of his nation's ships, at least where there is no conflict with local law, or where local authorities deign to act even though authorized to do so by local law.

The bilateral treaties to which the United States is a party do not expressly deal with the official capacity of the consul. However, in the convention of June 6, 1951, with the United Kingdom,[20] he is authorized to "take measures for the enforcement of the shipping law of the sending state." [21] A similar provision is to be found in the treaty of 1950–1952 with Ireland.[22] To the extent that he enforces the shipping laws of the sending state, he is an official of that state. These conventions also deal in some detail with powers of consuls over general maritime problems.[23] These powers are so broadly phrased as to place the consular official in fact in the position of being the official of the sending state administering its shipping within the receiving state. Similar provisions are contained in many other treaties of the United States, in addition to which, provision is sometime found conferring upon consuls the "rights, privileges, exemptions and immunities ... in con-

[18] *Id.*
[19] Art. 5 (m), *id.*
[20] TIAS 2494, 3 USTIAS 3426.
[21] Art. 21 (4), *id.* at 3443.
[22] Art. 22 (4), TIAS 2984, 5 USTIAS 949, 992.
[23] *E.g.*, Art. 21 (3), 22 of Treaty with U.K., 3 USTIAS 3426, 3442.

formity with modern international usage,"[24] or language of similar import.[25] To the extent, then, that international usage provides consular officers with official capacity to deal with maritime problems, these treaties would protect him in the exercise of that authority.

There is substantial evidence of international usage conferring upon consular officers official capacity to take action in any matter involving the merchant shipping of his state, at least where this action does not come into conflict with the wishes of the local officials.[26]

In addition to the treaty provisions already mentioned, many of the treaties to which the United States is a party provide that the consul shall have the "rights, privileges, exemptions and immunities" of the most favored third state.[27] This type of clause, of course, incorporates the provisions of many other treaties concerning the official capacity of consular officers. It may be that there is such a network of common provisions on the subject as to constitute a rule of customary international law.[28] In the *Lotus Case,* the majority opinion, discussing the French argument that there was a customary rule of international law conferring upon the flag state exclusive jurisdiction over acts occurring on a ship on the high seas, assumed that a sufficiently broad network of treaties containing common provisions on the subject could establish a customary rule of law.[29] In the case of *The Wimbledon,* the same court used the treaties defining the regime of the Suez and Panama canals as "illustrations of the general opinion according to which when an artificial waterway connecting two open seas has been permanently dedicated to the use of the whole world, such waterway is assimilated to natural straits ...." [30] There are innumerable treaties to which the United States is a party which contain clear language defining explicitly or implicitly the maritime administrative capacity of consular officers. There are many similar treaties to which the United States is not a party which contain similar provisions. It is submitted that the

[24] Consular Convention of 1947 with the Philippines, Art. I 2, 62 Stat. 1593, 1594.

[25] Treaty with Yemen (1946), Art. II, 60 Stat. 1782–1783; Nepal (1947), Art. 2, 61 Stat. 2566, 2567; Ethiopia (1951), Art. III (1), 4 USTIAS 2134, 2137–2138; Iran (1955), Art. XIII (1), TIAS 3853, 8 USTIAS 899, 909–910.

[26] See Colombos, *The International Law of the Sea* 277, 279, 295, 298 (5th rev. ed. 1962.); I *Oppenheim's International Law* 750 (6th ed., 1947). The United States' position concerning this usage is clearly set forth in IV Hackworth, *Digest of International Law* 876–883.

[27] See *e.g.*, Treaty of Friendship, Commerce and Consular Rights With Germany (1923), Art. XVII, 44 Stat. 2132, 2147–2148.

[28] See *Oppenheim's International Law* § 18, p. 27 for a discussion of treaties containing "general" international law. (6th ed. 1947).

[29] *P.C.I.J.* Ser. A, No. 10, 25–27.

[30] *P.C.I.J.* Ser. A, No. 1, 28.

common provisions of these treaties constitute in fact a rule of customary international law on the subject.

The statutory law of the United States does not deal generally with the official status of United States consuls *vis-à-vis* American maritime commerce. However, insofar as the subject is dealt with statutorily, no other official is authorized to assume any official function in the area, and consular officers are expressly granted substantial special authority. For example, they are authorized to receive protests and declarations from members of a ship's company,[31] to maintain records of United States vessels arriving and departing and changes in the crew,[32] and to retain ship's papers until payment of all demands and wages on account of such ships.[33] This latter provision implicitly gives him the power to determine the legitimacy of the demand and its extent before releasing the papers. Other sections obligate the masters of American vessels to deposit the papers with the consul.[34] Additionally, consuls are authorized under certain circumstances to issue provisional certificates of registry to vessels abroad,[35] and to officiate as shipping commissioner at the signing on of a seamen in a foreign port [36] or receive the report of one shipped at a prior port where no consular officer was stationed.[37] In case of the death of a seaman, the consul is authorized under certain circumstances to take custody of his wages and effects.[38] If certain conditions are fulfilled, he is empowered to survey a vessel for seaworthiness and to discharge crew members from one found to be unseaworthy.[39] He is also authorized to take action upon complaint of improper provisioning or supplying of a ship.[40] Under statutorily defined conditions, the consular officer is authorized to discharge seamen and collect wages due, and sometimes to assess and effect penalty wages.[41] There is also statutory authority for United States consuls to take charge of salvage operations involving vessels of United States nationality.[42] When disciplinary or criminal problems

[31] 22 U.S.C. 1173, R.S. § 1707, 1878.
[32] 22 U.S.C. 1174, R.S. § 1708, 1878.
[33] 22 U.S.C. 1185, R.S. § 1718, 1878.
[34] 46 U.S.C. 354, 355, R.S. §§ 4309, 4310, 1878.
[35] 46 U.S.C. 12, 38 Stat. 1193.
[36] 46 U.S.C. 570, R.S. § 4517, 1878.
[37] 46 U.S.C. 569, R.S. § 4516, 1878.
[38] 46 U.S.C. 622, R.S. §§ 4539, 4541, 1878.
[39] 46 U.S.C. 656, 657, 658, R.S. §§ 4559, 4560, 4561, 1878, 38 Stat. 1165.
[40] 46 U.S.C. 662, 664, R.S. §§ 4565, 4567, 1878.
[41] 46 U.S.C. 682–685, R.S. §§ 4580–4583, 1878.
[42] 46 U.S.C. 721, R.S. § 4238, 1878.

arise, it is the consular officer who is authorized to take the necessary steps towards their solution.[43]

The preceding paragraph contains a reasonable sampling of the specific statutory authority over seamen conferred upon United States consuls abroad. As there stated, the statutes do not currently deal with his status generally. Thus, if a situation arises which is not specifically covered by statute, the problem is whether he could legally deal with it. It has been pointed out in Chapter II that by treaty the United States may be granted authority over certain maritime problems not expressly covered by any statute. The same situation could arise in a case where the local officials refrain from taking action as a matter of comity or customary international law. The Foreign Affairs Manual helps to fill this void by authorizing action in more general categories of cases than those defined by statute. For example, in any case of an offense committed outside the territorial jurisdiction of the receiving state or within its territory under circumstances not causing local officials to intervene, the consul is authorized to "assume jurisdiction for the United States Government in every case where local authorities will permit him to do so, either by virtue of treaty arrangements or under comity between nations." [44] This mandate encompasses a host of situations not covered by statute. The manual similarly deals in a general manner with disputes between seamen [45] and removal of the master of a vessel.[46]

On the other side of this same problem, namely the authority in the United States of a foreign consul over seamen on vessels having the nationality of his state, there is very little in the way of United States legislative treatment. The only legislative enactment on the subject deals with judicial assistance to foreign consuls attempting to implement special treaty authority to resolve disputes internal to the vessel.[47] Obviously, treaties and customary international law provide for consular authority over many more areas of maritime commerce than are dealt with in those sections, but much of the necessary and authorized consular activity can be accomplished without the aid of local authorities. As an example, the foreign consul could certainly sign crew members on or off a vessel without any assistance. However, if, for example, the consul were attempting to deal with a passive disobedience

[43] 46 U.S.C. 703, R.S. § 4600, 1878.
[44] § 534. 2–1.
[45] 532.
[46] 528. 2.
[47] 22 U.S.C. 256, 257, 258, 258a, R.S. 4079–4081, 1878, 38 Stat. 1184.

campaign on board a ship of his state without treaty authority to do so, there would be no statutory authority for local officials to lend their assistance. That, of course, does not affect the question of his legal status to deal with such problems. He may have status but be unable to enforce his will upon the parties involved.

Because of the nature of this inquiry, namely the official status of a consular officer in the maritime affairs of his state, the courts have not been called upon to decide the question squarely. Generally, the problem is whether the consul has the authority to perform a particular act. The answer to that question will depend upon treaty interpretation or the court's construction of the customary international law in the area, or a combination of the two. The effect of United States treaties upon this question has already been discussed. In any situation where a court, without the benefit of express treaty provision, decides that a consular officer has an official function in the maritime affairs of his state, or when the court proceeds upon the implicit assumption that he does, this tends to establish an international practice which confers that status upon him.

There is no doubt that a consul is an official of the sending state and that the detailed definition of his status is governed by the law of that state. In the case of *Oscanyan v. Arms Co.*,[48] which was a contract action in which the defense was illegality, it was established that the plaintiff was a consul of Turkey in the United States and had agreed to use his personal influence to persuade a military buying agent of Turkey to place orders with the defendant company. In consideration of this, the defendant promised to pay him a percentage of the total purchase price. The Supreme Court decided that the agreement was against the public policy of the United States because it amounted to a selling to the defendant of the influence of one official of the Turkish government over another. The court assumed that Turkish law governed the status of its consuls, but decided that even if by that law such a contract was not illegal, it nevertheless could not be enforced in courts of the United States.[49] United States law precluding a trustee from taking a beneficial interest in trust property has been held to

[48] 103 U.S. 261 (1880).

[49] In the case of *In re Aubrey*, 26 Fed. 848 (E.D. La. 1885), although the court decided that it had no power to assist the consul by keeping the seamen incarcerated pursuant to his order, it assumed throughout that he was an official of the British government one of whose functions it was to enforce British shipping laws on British seamen in the United States. There was no treaty with Britain out of which the result could have been inferred.

control a United States consul who officiated at a public auction of an American vessel abroad.[50]

In *Harrison v. Vose*,[51] the Supreme Court in construing a United States statute which itself assumed the competence of United States consuls to take official action even in absence of treaty with the receiving state,[52] assumed the competence of consuls to resolve grievances and to give aid and advice to members of the ship's company without regard to whether he was so authorized by treaty.[53] Twice since then the Supreme Court has decided civil cases involving disputes internal to the vessel upon the basis that the consul of the state of the vessel's nationality is the official maritime representative of his government and that his request that the court refuse jurisdiction will normally be respected.[54] To the extent that any local foreign official action is indicated in the dispute, the assumption is that the consul would be the person entitled to take that action.

The lower court decisions are replete with other examples of official consular action not authorized by any treaty. In *Riley v. The Obell Mitchell*,[55] the consul officiated at the auctioning of an American vessel without treaty or statutory authorization. In *American Surety Co. of New York v. Sullivan*,[56] he enforced United States law pertaining to restriction on vessel transfers to foreign flag.[57] During the Spanish civil war, the consul of the Republican government of Spain was assumed to have authority either to take possession of a Spanish vessel as his country's agent in the enforcement of an expropriation decree or to take whatever steps were reasonably necessary to expedite it in the interest of its owners.[58] In *The New City*,[59] the court recognized

[50] *Riley v. The Obell Mitchell*, 20 Fed. Cas. 804 (No. 11839) (S.D. N.Y. 1861).

[51] 50 U.S. 37 (1850).

[52] 2 Stat. 203. The statute required the master of American merchant vessels to deposit the official ship's papers with the consul on arrival in his district, he to have the power to withhold return of them to compel compliance with his orders under certain circumstances.

[53] 50 U.S. 372, 381–382. At one point the Court said: "Those functions [consular] are . . . to exercise jurisdiction in some respects over American vessels and seamen abroad; sometimes of a judicial character . . . ." *Id.* at 382.

[54] *The Belgenland*, 114 U.S. 355, 364–365 (1885); *Ex Parte Newman*, 81 U.S. 152, 168–169 (1871).

[55] *Supra* note 50.

[56] 7 F. 2d 605 (2d Cir. 1925).

[57] In this case, he was held to have exceeded his authority by preventing the vessel's master from leaving the country, but the court throughout assumed that he had the authority to take any steps reasonably necessary to enforce the particular United States statute involved.

[58] *The Navemar*, 102 F. 2d 444 (2d Cir. 1939), reversing 24 F. Supp. 495 (E.D. N.Y. 1938). The particular decision became moot because the revolution was successful and the United States recognized the Franco revolutionary government which promptly rescinded the prior

that it shared concurrent jurisdiction with the British consul – who had already decided the matter adversely to the plaintiff – for the purpose of resolving an internal dispute on a British vessel:

> This court has the power to issue process and grant a hearing upon complaints against foreign vessels found within this state, but in exercising its jurisdiction it proceeds upon the idea that comity towards the nation to which the vessel belongs requires it. The object in each case is to prevent a failure of justice, and it will not officiously interfere in any case after a fair hearing and decision of the matter in controversy has been given by an authorized agency [consul] of the government of the country to which the vessel belongs ....[60]

There are numerous other cases in which the official capacity of consuls in civil maritime cases is recognized, the courts asserting the power to entertain jurisdiction regardless of where the cause of action arose but refusing to do so over the protest of the consul, barring special circumstances dictating the necessity of deciding the case.[61]

There can be little doubt that the treaties, statutes, consular regulations, and decisional law of the United States all combine to establish the United States position that the consular officer is the proper official of his state with authority under international law to exercise the jurisdiction of his government in maritime affairs whenever for any reason such jurisdiction exists. The next step is to determine when that situation pertains.

BASIC TYPES OF JURISDICTION

This section is intended as a survey of general jurisdictional problems. Having determined that a state has jurisdiction in international law over a particular class of acts, then if any action is indicated in a foreign port, it would be performed by the consular officer of that state there.

Since this section is to serve as an analysis of general jurisdictional problems, and the terminology of The American Law Institute in its

government's action in expropriating the vessel and asked the court to dismiss the action seeking possession of the vessel from its owners.

[59] 47 Fed. 328 (D. Wash. N.D. 1891).

[60] *Id.* at 329. *The Falls of Keltie*, 114 Fed. 357 (D. Wash. N.D. 1902), restricted this rule to situations involving no American national. Accord, *Bolden v. Jensen*, 70 Fed. 505 (D. Wash. N.D. 1895).

[61] *The Becherdass*, 3 Fed. Cas. 13 (No. 1203) (D. Mass. 1871); *The Lilian M. Vigius*, 15 Fed. Cas. 520 (No. 8346) (S.D. N.Y. 1879); *The Carolina*, 14 Fed. 424 (E.D. La. 1876); *The Montapedia*, 14 Fed. 427 (E.D. La. 1882); *The City of Carlise*, 39 Fed. 807 (D. Cir. 1889); *Camille v. Couch*, 40 Fed. 176 (E.D. S.C. 1889); *The Topsy*, 44 Fed. 631 (D. S.C. 1890); *The Sirius*, 47 Fed. 825 (N.D. Cal. 1891); *The Karoo*, 49 Fed. 651 (D. Wash. W.D. 1892).

proposed official draft of the Restatement of the Law, the Foreign Relations Law of the United States, is peculiarly appropriate to such analysis, that terminology will be used.[62]

For the purpose of this analysis, jurisdictional acts of a sovereign are classified in two general categories, namely prescriptive and enforcement.[63] The problem which generally arises is whether a state has the legal right to prescribe certain rules of conduct, or having legally prescribed a particular rule, has the right to take steps necessary to enforce it.

A state generally prescribes rules of conduct by legislative act or by executive decree or regulation. The judicial authority to regulate certain types of conduct depends upon the municipal law of the particular state involved. The international legal problem is whether the state has the right to prescribe a particular rule; the domestic, what branch of government has that right.

The threshold question is the authority of the state to make the rule at all. Obviously, if a state has no right to control conduct, it would not have the right to enforce a rule designed to have that effect.[64] Thus, the question of jurisdiction to enforce only arises if the state had the authority to prescribe the rule which it seeks to enforce.[65]

Prescriptive jurisdiction, then, involves the right of a sovereign under international law to require a person to perform an act or the right to require him to refrain from an act. To put it another way, prescriptive jurisdiction is the right to classify an act or failure to act and to attach legal consequences.

The action of a state taken for the purpose of giving effect to the legal consequences attached to conduct involves the exercise of enforcement jurisdiction. The fact that a state has legal authority to prescribe a rule of conduct does not mean that it also has the right to take any action necessary to enforce that rule. It may be that a state has both types of jurisdiction in a particular situation, but the two problems are separate. There may be a sufficient basis for the state to attach legal consequences to an act but not for enforcement of the rule against a particular individual at a certain time.[66]

[62] May 3, 1962. For convenience sake, it will be cited only as *Restatement* hereinafter.

[63] *Restatement* § 6, p. 25.

[64] *Restatement* § 7, p. 26.

[65] Whether an international claim arises out of illegal prescription is beyond the scope of this paper.

[66] The fact that one state has jurisdiction either to prescribe or to enforce does not impose upon any other state the legal obligation to give effect to the rule established pursuant to that authority. Whether it will do so depends upon its municipal law rule of conflict of laws. *Restatement* § 9, p. 31.

BASES FOR EXERCISE OF JURISDICTION

There are certain contacts between a state and a person which are deemed sufficient in international law to justify the state's prescribing rules of conduct binding upon him. Lacking the minimum contact recognized by international law as justifying a state in attaching legal consequence to an act, some other state will generally be entitled to complain if the attempt is made.[67]

One of the most time honored contacts between state and conduct which justifies the exercise of prescriptive jurisdiction is territorial in nature. One of the incidents of sovereignty is the right to govern conduct or status connected in some way with the territory of the state.[68] If an act occurs within the territory of a state or if it has an effect within that territory, no other state can complain if that state attaches legal consequences to it.[69]

The territory of a state is comprised of its land masses, internal waters and their beds, the territorial sea [70] and its bed, and the subsoil below and air space above the described areas.[71] For the purpose of this discussion, it is only necessary to discuss the land mass, internal waters, and territorial seas.[72]

Vessels having the nationality of a state are deemed to be territory of that state for prescriptive jurisdictional purposes.[73] If, therefore, an act occurs or it takes effect either on the land mass, in internal waters, in the territorial seas or on board a ship having the nationality of a

[67] If the prescription itself adversely affects another state. it will have an international claim against the prescribing state. See *Restatement* § 8, Comment b., p. 29. Even if not adversely affected, a state may have an interest in objecting to the rule. A failure to object may be taken as a tacit acceptance of the prescribing state's authority and tend toward the establishment of a customary rule of international law. *Id.*, Comment C, p. 29–30.

[68] I *Oppenheim's International Law* 293–294 (7th ed. 1948).

[69] *Restatement* § 10, p. 35–36.

[70] The breadth of the band of water known as the territorial sea will not be discussed herein. Suffice it to say that there is a substantial amount of disagreement on the breadth that a coastal state can legally claim. The United States claims a three mile breadth, while other states claim varying widths of up to 200 miles. Laws and Regulations on the Regime of the Territorial Sea, United Nations Legislative Series, ST/LEG/Ser. B/6 (U.N., N.Y., 1957).

[71] *Restatement* § 11, p. 37. The state also has exclusive jurisdiction over the sea bed and subsoil of the continental shelf for the purpose of exploitation, but this is not relevant to the instant inquiry. Article 2, Convention on the Continental Shelf, Apr. 29, 1958, U.N. Doc. A/CONF. 13/L. 55.

[72] It does not matter, insofar as this discussion is concerned, whether a state has absolute sovereignty over a particular area or exercises jurisdiction over it pursuant to an agreement. The result is the same, subject to any restrictions imposed by the agreement. See *Restatement* §§ 24 and 25, pp. 76 and 77.

[73] S.S. Lotus, *P.C.I.J.*, Ser. A, No. 10, 24–25. The Court used the term "the State the flag of which it flies," but that was the equivalent of nationality. *Restatement* § 31, p. 91.

state, international law recognizes the right of that state to attach legal significance to the act.[74]

Another recognized basis for the exercise by a state of prescriptive jurisdiction is that the nationality of the actor is that of the prescribing state.[75] This authority is not restricted to conduct occurring in any particular location; wherever the act occurs, a state may ascribe legal consequences to it.[76] For purposes related to the operation of a vessel, an alien serving as a member of her crew may be deemed to have the nationality of his ship.[77]

Up to this point, the discussion has centered upon the question of the prescriptive jurisdiction of a state. As stated before, the existence of jurisdiction to prescribe does not impart also jurisdiction to enforce. Different contacts with a state are required by international law to justify its enforcement of rules of conduct validly prescribed by it. It is a fundamental rule of international law that a state normally cannot take police action within the territory of another state.[78] Thus, if a state prescribes a rule requiring its nationals to return from abroad for military service, it certainly could not legally send an agent into another state to arrest one and bring him back or to punish him for failing to comply.[79] The usual foundation for exercise of enforcement jurisdic-

[74] *Restatement* §§ 17, 18, pp. 49, 52–53.

[75] See the brief discussion of nationality in Chapter III at p. 165. The Comment to Article 5 of the Harvard Research in International Law, Jurisdiction with respect to Crime, states that "The competence of the State to prosecute and punish its nationals on the sole basis of their nationality is universally conceded". 29 *A.J.I.L.* Supp. 519 (1935).

[76] *Restatement* § 30, p. 87.

[77] *Restatement* § 31, p. 91; see Chapter III at p. 88 *et seq.* The nationality of the victim of an act apparently is not recognized as a legal basis for the exercise of jurisdiction to prescribe rules of conduct affecting others. *Restatement* § 30 (2), p. 87. See the discussion of this problem in the S.S. Lotus, *P.C.I.J.*, Ser. A, No. 10, pp 37–39. *Contra*, Art. 4 (b) Convention on Offences and Certain other Acts Committed on Board Aircraft, signed at Tokyo, Sept. 14, 1963, *I.C.A.O.* Doc. 8364 (1963). "A Contracting State which is not the state of registration may not interfere with an aircraft in flight in order to exercise its criminal jurisdiction over an offense committed on board except in the following cases: (b) the offense has been committed by *or against* a national or permanent resident of such state; [emphasis supplied]. There is another recognized basis for the exercise of prescriptive jurisdiction by a state which has not been discussed herein because it has no relevance within the scope of this paper. A state is entitled to attach legal consequences to conduct abroad which threatens its security. *Restatement* § 33, p. 94; see *United States v. Bowman*, 260 U.S. 94, 102 (1922), involving the possibility that a foreigner might be punished in the United States for acts committed broad in a conspiracy to defraud the United States. A seaman might become involved in some situation covered by this principle, but it is unlikely that the problem would in any way be affected by his status as a seaman.

[78] See I *Oppenheim's International Law* 262–263 (7th ed. 1948); Hall, *International Law* 56–57 (8th ed. 1924).

[79] *Restatement* § 7, Comment on Subsection (1), pp. 26–27.

tion is the fact that the enforcement action is taken within the enforcing state [80] or on board a national vessel or aircraft.[81]

CONFLICTS OF JURISDICTION

There will frequently be situations with which two or more states will have sufficient contacts to legally warrant their assuming jurisdiction over one or more of the actors involved. If only one state were to have a relationship with the problem, that state alone would have the rights to exercise authority imposing legal consequences. However, it is not unusual, particularly in maritime matters, for the significant contacts to be so fragmented among two or more states that more than one has jurisdiction.

In a situation where two or more states have concurrent jurisdiction to prescribe or enforce, the problem immediately arises as to how to resolve the obvious conflict among them. In most situations, international law does not provide any rule to determine precedence among them. Thus, generally, in that type of situation, no state need defer to any other and may exercise its jurisdiction as if no other state had an interest.[82] In certain problem areas, this conflict problem has been resolved by customary rules of international law,[83] or by international agreement.[84]

The conflict problem of concurrent jurisdiction may be approached by determining which of the states involved has the strongest or most significant contacts with the problem and assigning to that state a preferred or prior right to take action. Apparently, international law has not developed to a point that a state is required to forego exercise of jurisdiction solely because another state also has basis for a like exercise, nor has it developed any system of priorities. However, individual states have formulated rules for their own conduct which tend to create a hierarchy of jurisdictional bases.[85]

[80] *Restatement* § 20, p. 64. Effective enforcement action may be made possible by use of extradition procedures, but that question is not within the scope of this paper.

[81] *Restatement* § 32, pp. 92–93.

[82] *Restatement* § 37, pp. 105–106.

[83] *Restatement* §§ 54–65, pertaining to jurisdiction over visiting foreign military forces.

[84] See exchange of notes between the United States and Iceland of 21 and 27 Dec, 1962, reciprocally conferring relief from local taxation of earnings from the operations of ships or aircraft (established by documentation and registration) of the other. TIAS 5255, 13 USTIAS 3827.

[85] The Harvard Research in International Law, Part II, Jurisdiction of Crime, Comment to Article 5, 29 *A.J.I.L.* 531 (1935), states, with regard to the conflict of jurisdiction between the state of nationality of the actor and the state where the act occurred: "The widespread

In general, the domestic law of the United States gives precedence to territoriality over nationality as a basis of jurisdiction. This effect is accomplished by statutory construction where such a construction is possible. The courts generally will construe a statute, where its terms admit the interpretation, as being applicable only where both the act and its effects occur within the territory of the United States.[86] Where this technique is possible, it eliminates any problem of conflict of jurisdiction, and therefore of priority of jurisdiction – where the act was done abroad by a national of the United States. Of course, if the situation were reversed, the United States would assert jurisdiction over a foreign national where the act occurred within United States territory. Presumably, since the United States emphasizes the territorial basis of jurisdiction, it would insist that it had the prior right to exercise its authority.

The problem of priority of jurisdiction may, of course, be resolved by treaty.[87]

The ensuing discussion will deal with certain generalized fact situations in which conflicts of jurisdiction might arise. The purpose is to demonstrate the scope of the problem which is posed.[88]

CONFLICTS OF PRESCRIPTIVE JURISDICTION

Locus of the Activity

If a particular activity occurs on a vessel having the nationality of a state, while it is within the territory of that same state, there would not be any territorial basis for any other state to ascribe legal consequence to the activity. If the conduct should later have an effect within another state by virtue of the vessel's arriving there, however, this would give the latter state too a territorial basis for the exercise of prescriptive jurisdiction. The mere happening of an act on board a ship without any contact with any other state would, of course, raise no conflict of jurisdiction problem. Since only the flag state has juris-

inclusion of such limitations [upon the prosecution of a national for an act committed abroad] in national legislation tends to confirm the opinion that jurisdiction based upon nationality is properly regarded as subsidiary to the territorial jursdiction of the State where the crime was committed .... It is believed, however, that these are matters which each State is free to determine for itself."

[86] *Restatement* § 38, pp. 109–113.

[87] See the NATO Status of Forces Agreement of 1951, Art. VII 3, TIAS 2846, 4 USTIAS 1792, 1800.

[88] Specific situations which may depart from the general rules will be discussed in the succeeding chapter.

diction over a vessel on the high seas,[89] no different conclusion is dictated if the activity occurred there.

If the vessel were in the contiguous zone of another state,[90] the right of the littoral state to prescribe rules governing activity on her would depend upon the activity which is to be affected. The convention[91] limits the competence of the littoral state to matters involving customs, immigration, fiscal or sanitary problems.[92] Logic would seem to dictate that vessels entering a port of the littoral state should be treated differently from those which are merely passing through these waters. The competence conferred upon the littoral state by the convention is not limited to any particular types of vessels, nor is a distinction drawn between vessels entering inland waters and those which are not. It appears, therefore, that it applies equally to both categories. However, since a state may wholly bar the vessels of another state from her inland waters – absent treaty obligation to the contrary –, and may therefore condition her permission to enter upon the performance of acts reasonably related to entry, those vessels should be subject to any additional regulation so defined.[93]

Treaty provisions may affect the problem of admitting foreign vessels only upon compliance with conditions. For example, the United States has entered into treaties guaranteeing "freedom of navigation" between her territories and those of other states.[94] Of course, "freedom of navigation" would not likely be construed to mean completely unfettered right of entry. Presumably, either state would be entitled to impose reasonable conditions upon ships of the other which propose to enter. There are other treaty provisions which impose a duty not to discriminate between ships of the other party and national ships or ships of any third state.[95] Both these types of treaties necessarily

[89] U.N. Convention on the High Seas, TIAS 5200, 13 USTIAS 2312.

[90] Art. 24, United Nations Convention on the Territorial Sea and the Contiguous Zone, U.N. Doc. A/CONF. 13/L. 52.

[91] *Id.*

[92] *Id.*

[93] This rationale could also extended to the requiring of certain acts while the vessel is still on the high seas outside the contiguous zone. For example, a state should have the authority to require a vessel which is approaching for the purpose of entry into inland waters to give notice, say 24 hours, in advance of reaching territorial waters. She might also legitimately be required to do some act even in her home port in a foreign state, such as procuring a document from a consul of the prescribing state attesting to health and sanitary conditions there.

[94] See Article XIII 1. of the Treaty of Friendship, Establishment and Navigation with Luxemborg (1962), TIAS 5306, 14 USTIAS 251, 260.

[95] *E.g.* Art. XX, 1954, Treaty of Friendship, Commerce and Navigation with the Federal Republic of Germany, TIAS 2593, 7 USTIAS 1839, 1860.

preclude subjection of vessels of either state to arbitrary conditions upon entry into the other, but merely change the basis for distinguishing them from vessels merely passing through the contiguous zone to another destination.

If a vessel were in the territorial sea of another state, that state would have, under the rules already discussed, a territorial basis for prescribing rules of conduct on board. Here, of course, we have a direct conflict of two territorial jurisdictions, one by virtue of the nationality of the vessel, and the other by her location. Here too, vessels seeking to enter a local port may be treated differently from those which are merely passing through.

The territorial sea is subject to the complete sovereignty of the coastal state, subject to the right of vessels of all states to traverse it in innocent passage.[96] The convention defines the right of innocent passage as inhering in vessels merely passing through and those proceeding to or from inland waters.[97] It deals with the two classes of vessels differently. Subdivision 2 of Article 19 permits the enforcement of local criminal law on ships after leaving internal waters but still in the territorial sea. Of necessity, the littoral state must have the right to prescribe and enforce special rules of conduct applicable to those vessels. Article 20, subdivision 2, precludes local enforcement of rules designed to effectuate civil liability against a ship in innocent passage except for obligations or liabilities incurred by the ship itself in the course or for the purpose of its current voyage through the coastal state's waters. Subdivision 3 of that article permits civil enforcement action against a vessel still in territorial waters after leaving internal waters. No mention is made of vessels preparing to enter the inland waters of another state. However, it would appear that the coastal state could prescribe at least reasonable conditions upon such entry, as discussed in some of the preceding material of this section. At any rate, since the vessel is by hypothesis about to enter, no purpose is served by exercise of jurisdiction at that point. It is universally recognized that civil jurisdiction may be exercised once it has entered.

With regard to priority between the jurisdiction of the littoral state and that of the flag state, the convention seems to give precedence to that of the littoral state. Article 19 states that

[96] Articles 14–23, United Nations Convention on the Territorial Sea and the Contiguous Zone, U.N. Doc. A/CONF. 13/L. 52.

[97] Article 14, subd. 2, *id.*

> The criminal jurisdiction of the coastal State *should not be exercised* on board a foreign ship passing through the territorial sea to arrest any person or to conduct any investigation in connexion with any crime committed on board the ship during its passage ....[98]

Article 20 states that

> The coastal State *should not* stop or divert a foreign ship passing through the territorial sea for the purpose of exercising civil jurisdiction in relation to a person on board the ship.[99]

The use of the term "should" in preference to a word of obligation must have been intended to give priority to the enforcement jurisdiction of the coastal state. The term "may not" is used in the second subdivision of Article 20, clearly giving precedence to the law of the flag state. On the other hand, it would seem more rational to say that, since a foreign vessel has the right to traverse the territorial seas in innocent passage, the coastal state only has the right to prescribe rules of conduct on board which do not unreasonably interfere with that right. This, of course, raises the problem of what rules are reasonable, but certainly the obviously unreasonable could be easily identified.

When a vessel is in the inland waters of another state, there is once more a direct conflict of jurisdiction for the same reason as when in the territorial sea. The only difference is that, barring a treaty provision, there is no right of innocent passage through internal waters of another state.[100] Because the activity is occurring within her territory the local state would seem to have the more vital interest to protect, and therefore logically could be expected to have a prior right to prescribe rules of conduct in this situation. In other words, the flag state should not prescribe a rule in conflict with a local rule.[101]

[98] Emphasis supplied. This section will be considered in more detail in the succeeding chapter.

[99] Emphasis supplied.

[100] Article 4 of the United Nations Convention on the Territorial Sea and the Contiguous Zone envisages the possibility of a right of innocent passage through inland waters where the use of straight base lines cuts off areas which had previously been high seas or territorial waters. This was a codification of the decision in the *Anglo-Norwegian Fisheries Case.* 1951 I.C.J. 116.

[101] This question will be considered in detail in the succeeding chapter. Note: If a member of the ship's company should go off the ship, although there may be a conflict of jurisdiction because of his nationality differing from that of the local state, that conflict is not peculiarly related to his status as a seaman and therefore will not be discussed.

Locus of the Effect of Activity

This section deals with the conflict which arises out of activity located within the territory of one state, the effect of which is felt within that of another. It is clear that a recognized basis for the exercise of prescriptive jurisdiction is that the activity to be controlled has an effect within the territory of the prescribing state.[102] National ships are assimilated to national territory for this purpose.[103] It follows that a state may regulate conduct, wherever occurring, which has effect within her territory or on a vessel of her nationality. Thus, if the activity in question is on board a ship of another state, there is a direct conflict of jurisdiction, and the location of the ship at the time of the incident is not significant except on the question of a possible reconciliation of competing claims te exercise jurisdiction. That would depend upon a balancing of the competing interests of the two states. Presumably, a state would have a more significant claim if the foreign vessel were tied up to a pier in one of its ports than if tied up to a pier in a port of the state of which she is a national or in waters of a third state. The further removed, territorially speaking, the action and the less direct its effects, the less likely that the state will have any vital interest in attaching legal significance to it. As a general proposition, the further removed the act is, the less likely it will have effect in a state. The nature of the activity, of course, bears upon this question.[104]

Nationality of the Actor

In any situation where a national of one state is on board a ship having the nationality of another, there are conflicting bases for the exercise of prescriptive jurisdiction in the two states.

The conflict problem arising out of differences between nationality of actor and ship may, of course, be eliminated by considering any member of the ship's company as having a nationality derived from that of the ship.[105] In *The Ester*,[106] a United States court treated a German national serving on a Swedish ship as having Swedish nationality for the purposes of the employment relationship. This, of course, does not resolve the problem which would have arisen if the case had

[102] *Supra* note 68 and 69.
[103] *Supra* note 73.
[104] The discussion of the locus of the activity, and the provisions of the United Nations Conventions on the law of the sea considered there are relevant to this problem. *Supra* at p. 210 *et seq.*
[105] *Supra* at p. 108.
[106] 190 Fed. 216 (E.D. S.C. 1911).

been before a German court. However, the United States State Department has taken the position that nationals of other states serving in United States vessels acquire American nationality for the purpose of resolving issues arising out of the employment.[107] Additionally, it has refused to intervene with a foreign government for the protection of an American national serving on a foreign ship, saying that he must look to the government of the flag state for protection.[108] The cases in which United States courts took jurisdiction, over the objection of foreign consuls, in cases where an American citizen plaintiff was involved [109] do not really meet this question since they did not deal with the choise of laws question. Having taken jurisdiction of the action, if they had then applied the law of the ship in preference to that of the United States, this would have been a recognition on the priority of the law of the flag over that of the nationality of the plaintiff. These courts felt that they were required on constitutional grounds to provide a forum to a citizen of the United States, but the question of priority of prescriptive rules is another question.

On the question of choice of laws, the case which discusses the problem most fully is *Lauritzen v. Larsen*.[110] That was a case involving the applicability of a United States statute [111] to an injury suffered by a Danish national who had signed on a Danish vessel in New York and was injurid on board while the vessel was in port at Havana, Cuba. The only contacts with the United States were that the seaman had signed on in the United States and thereafter sued in a United States court. In a sense, the Court assumed that it had jurisdiction to prescribe the rules governing the controversy. It took jurisdiction for the purpose of deciding applicable law.[112] However, in thereafter deciding that issue, it held the law of Denmark controlling. In coming to this conclusion, the Court stressed especially the significance of the nationality of the vessel in determining controlling law.

> Perhaps the most venerable and universal rule of maritime law relevant to our problem is that which gives cardinal importance to the law of the flag....
> This Court has said that the law of the flag supersedes the territorial principle,

[107] *Supra* at p. 91.
[108] See IV Hackworth, *Digest of International Law* 885.
[109] *The Falls of Keltie*, 114 Fed. 357 (D. Wash. N.D. 1902); *Bolden v. Jensen*, 70 Fed. 505 (D. Wash. N.D. 1895); *The Troop*, 117 Fed. 557 (D. Wash. W.D. 1902); *The Neck*, 138 Fed. 144 (W. D. Wash. N.D. 1905).
[110] 345 U.S. 571 (1952).
[111] 46 U.S.C. 688, 38 Stat. 1185.
[112] *Supra* note 110 at 574–575.

even for the purposes of criminal jurisdiction of personnel of a merchant ship, because it is deemed to be a part of the territory of that sovereignty [whose flag it flies], and not to lose that character when in navigable waters within the territorial limits of another sovereignty....

It is significanct to us here that the weight given to the ensign overbears most other connecting events in determining applicable law ....

These considerations are of such weight in favor of Danish and against American law in this case that it must prevail unless some heavy counterweight appears.[113]

In *Romero v. International Terminal Operating Company*,[114] the operative facts were similar except that the injury occurred while the vessel was in an American port. Once again preference was given to the law of the flag, the Court noting that the plaintiff had a convenient remedy before the Spanish Consul in New York.[115]

Both *Lauritzen* and *Romero* dealt with situations where the nationality of the plaintiff was the same as that of the ship. However, in *Lauritzen*, the Court did discuss that question briefly under the heading of "Allegiance or Domicile of the Injured." [116] The Court restated the principle of derivative nationality from that of the ship, but admitted that it might be qualified by the interest that a state has in protecting its nationals from becoming dependent upon others for support. Some lower court cases have held that United States law, including statutory law, applies in those situations where an American national is injured while serving on a foreign vessel.[117] Other courts have held that the law of the flag applies.[118]

The cases discussed in the preceding paragraph dealth with the question of priority of prescriptive jurisdiction only in the limited context of a personal injury situation. There are many other situations in which the same problem would arise, and in which the rather vital interest of the state of the forum in protecting its national in a personal injury recovery would not be present. In those situations, the quotation from *Lauritzen v. Larsen* [119] would be entitled to even greater weight.

For the purpose of determining priority of jurisdiction as between the state of the ship and that of the nationality of one of the actors on

[113] *Id.* at 584–586.

[114] 358 U.S. 354 (1959).

[115] *Id.* at 383.

[116] 345 U.S. 571, 586–587.

[117] *Shorter v. Bermuda & West Indies S.S. Co., Ltd.*, 57 F. 2d 313 (S.D. N.Y. 1932); *Gambera v. Bergoty*, 132 F. 2d 414 (2d Cir. 1942) – alien seamen domiciled in the United States.

[118] *The Oriskany*, 3 F. Supp. 805 (D. Md. 1933); *Clark v. Montezuma Transportation* Co., 217 App. Div. 172, 216 N.Y. Supp. 295, (2d Dept. 1926)·

[119] *Supra* at pp. 115–116.

that ship, the location of the ship at the time of the act would not seem to be a particularly material consideration unless it was in a port of the state of which the actor was a national. In *Lauritzen v. Larsen*,[120] the Court said

> The test of location of the wrongful act or omission, however sufficient for torts ashore, is of limited application to shipboard torts, because of the varieties of legal authority over waters she may navigate .... [T]he territorial standard is so unfitted to an enterprise conducted under so many territorial rules and under none that it usually is modified by the more constant law of the flag.[121]

Even if the ship were in the territory of the state of the actor's nationality, it is not generally the location of the ship which is important, but the fact of these two factors coinciding in a court of the same state.[122]

CONFLICTS OF ENFORCEMENT JURISDICTION

A universal requirement for the exercise of enforcement jurisdiction is that the person, thing or activity affected by the state action be either within the territory of the state, in a place not within the territory of any other state, or the agents of the state must be acting with the consent of the state where they take action.[123]

The United Nations Convention on the High Seas clearly prohibits the exercise of enforcement jurisdiction by one state on the vessels of another on the high seas.[124] This provision is clearly inconsistent with the United States statutes authorizing the establishment of "customs-enforcement areas" on the high seas adjacent to the coast of the United States but not more than fifty nautical miles from the outer limits of customs waters [125] and the enforcement there of United States customs laws upon foreign vessels.[126] The treaty rights of foreign states under treaties which enable or permit United States authorities to enforce such laws on the high seas are protected by the act.[127] However, that proviso can have no effect of preserving rights under the Convention on the High Seas, since it in no way enables the

[120] *Supra* note 110.
[121] *Id.* at 583–584.
[122] This question will be considered in more detail in the Succeeding chapter.
[123] *Restatement* § 20, p. 64.
[124] Article 22, 13 USTIAS 2312, 2318–2319.
[125] 19 U.S.C. 1701(a), 49 Stat. 517.
[126] *Id.* 19 U.S.C. 1701(b); 49 Stat. 517, 525. For a discussion of this statute, see Jessup, "The Anti-Smuggling Act of 1935," 31 *A.J.I.L.* 101 (1937).
[127] *Id.* See *The Reidun*, 14 F. Supp. 771 (E.D. N.Y. 1936).

United States to enforce its customs laws on the high seas. However, since the United Nations Convention on the Territorial Sea and the Contiguous Zone [128] provides for a contiguous zone of nine miles into the high seas from the outer limits of the territorial sea of the United States, that treaty together with the statutory proviso might serve to eliminate the conflict *vis-à-vis* states party to it.

On their face, the statutes under consideration raise a possibility of direct conflict with the international legal rights of other states. Apparently, no case has arisen in which the problem was litigated. It is possible that they will be construed in such a way as to avoid such a conflict. In one case where the problem was implicit in the facts – the vessel was seized 14 miles from the coast – the court said in dicta that enforcement was subject to the rules of international law.[129] However, there was a treaty with the flag state, Great Britain, which validated the seizure. Thus, the question was never resolved. The suggestion that a court might find itself limited by international law in interpreting a statute so clearly permitting a violation of international law by United States officials is of rather doubtful validity. At any rate, this is the one area of potential jurisdictional conflict between the United States and foreign nations on the high seas.

In the Contiguous Zone

The United Nations Convention on the Territorial Sea and the Contiguous Zone permits a state to establish a contiguous zone extending not more than twelve miles outward from the baseline from which the territorial sea is measured.[130] Within that zone, the littoral state is authorized to "exercise the control necessary to:

> (a) Prevent infringement of its customs, fiscal, immigration or sanitary regulations within its territory or territorial sea;
> (b) Punish infringement of the above regulations committed within its territory or territorial sea.

Of course, the flag state might also provide for punishment for violation of these same laws. However, since the coastal state manifestly has the greater interest in enforcement of laws of this type, there can be

[128] U.N. Doc. A/CONF. 13/L. 52, Article 24.
[129] *The Pictorian*, 3 F. 2d 145, 146 (E.D. N.Y. 1924).
[130] Article 24., Subdivision 2, U.N. Doc. A/CONF. 13/L. 52.

little question that its right would take precedence over the right of the flag state.[131]

The right to take enforcement jurisdiction within the territory of a state is normally exclusive.[132] However, it is also clear that the flag state may take steps to enforce its laws on board wherever the ship may happen to be, even within the territorial sea or inland waters of another state.[133] Thus, if a ship of one state is within the territory of another, there is a direct conflict of jurisdiction between the two states. The problem then necessarily arises as to which has priority.

In the Territorial Sea, Criminal Jurisdiction

The United Nations Convention on the Territorial Sea and the Contiguous Zone,[134] in Article 19, pertaining to the right of innocent passage, states:

> The criminal jurisdiction of the coastal State should not be exercised on board a foreign ship passing through the territorial sea to arrest any person or to conduct any investigation in connexion with any crime during its passage, save only in the following cases:
>
> (a) If the consequences of the crime extend to the coastal State; or
>
> (b) If the crime is of a kind to disturb the peace of the country or the good order of the territorial sea; or
>
> (c) If the assistance of the local authorities has been requested by the captain of the ship or by the consul of the country whose flag the ship flies; or
>
> (d) If it is necessary for the suppression of illicit traffic in narcotic drugs.
>
> The above provisions do not affect the right of the coastal State to take any steps authorized by its laws for the purpose of an arrest or investigation on board a foreign ship passing through the territorial sea after leaving internal waters.
>
> The coastal State may not take any steps on board a foreign ship passing through the territorial sea to arrest any person or to conduct any investigation in connexion with any crime committed before the ship entered the territorial sea if the ship, proceeding from a foreign port, is only passing through the territorial sea without entering internal waters.

[131] It is, perhaps necessary to point out that, since the convention limits the type of interests which may be protected by enforcement action within the zone, all others are presumably implicitly excluded. *E.g.*, the local authorities would not have the right to stop a foreign vessel in the zone after leaving port for the purpose of arresting and punishing a seaman for a crime committed ashore. See *Restatement* § 21, Comment on Subsection (1)(b), p. 67.

[132] *Restatement* § 20, Comment b., p. 64.

[133] The flag state does not have a right to take any action it chooses to enforce its laws while the ship is within snother state. In criminal matters, for example, the local authorities need only permit the action necessary to restrain the offender. If more than minor disciplinary action is indicated, the offender would have to be shipped home for action. *Restatement* § 49, Comment on Subsection (3), p. 167.

[134] U.N. Doc. A/CONF. 13/L. 52.

It would appear that a vessel which is in the territorial waters of another state, but not in innocent passage, is not affected by this provision at all. The article is included in a section of the convention dealing with innocent passage. Any vessels not in innocent passage would be subject to the customary rules of international law. Since the coastal state would be entitled to exclude such a vessel and to inflict punishment for its being there under those circumstances, it seems clear that the enforcement jurisdiction of the coastal state with regard to any criminal act on board would take precedence over that of the flag state.[135]

It is important to define "innocent passage," then, in order to determine what ships are affected by the provision under consideration. The convention says that:

> Passage means navigation through the territorial sea for the purpose either of traversing that sea without entering internal waters, or of proceeding to internal waters, or of making for the high seas from internal waters.
>
> Passage is innocent so long as it is not prejudicial to the peace, good order or security of the coastal State. Such passage shall take place in conformity with these articles and with other rules of international law.[136]

In the Second Committee of the Hague Codification Conference of 1930, the draft articles produced stated that "Passage is not *innocent* when a vessel makes use of the territorial sea of a Coastal State for the purpose of doing any act prejudicial to the security, to the public policy or to the fiscal interest of that State." [137] It would appear that not every violation of rules of the coastal state controlling navigation in the territorial sea would impair the innocence of the passage. Rationally, the violation, to have such effect, would have to be one which prejudicially affects the peace, good order or security of the coastal state. This would depend upon all the surrounding circumstances.[138]

Once having determined that a vessel is in territorial waters in innocent passage, the question of priority of competing jurisdictions under the convention is reasonably well defined. If the consequences of the act extend to the shore, if it is of a nature to disturb the peace of the country or the good order of the territorial sea, or if the act pertains to an illicit traffic in narcotic drugs, the coastal state is given a clear

[135] See Jessup, *The Law of Territorial Waters and Maritime Jurisdiction* 123–133 (1927).
[136] Article 14, subd. 2, 4.
[137] 24 *A.J.I.L.* Supp. 234, 240 (1930).
[138] See *Restatement* § 48, Comment h., p. 160.

priority over the flag state. The definition of "illicit traffic in narcotic drugs" might present some problem. A particular traffic might be legal under the laws of one or more states having contact with it, but be illegal by the laws of the coastal state. Under these circumstances, it would seem that the traffic would not be "illicit" unless illegal in some way by the law of one of the states having contacts with it, namely the flag state or a state from or to which the narcotics are moving.

Since the convention says that the coastal state "should not" exercise its criminal jurisdiction on board except in the cases described in the preceding paragraph, the provision should at least be construed as giving priority to the enforcement jurisdiction of the flag state in all other cases. Whether the term "should not" imparts exclusive jurisdiction to the flag state in that area is doubtful. The term is ambiguous when considered by itself without reference to the rest of the convention. Since subdivision 5 of the same article [139] uses the term "may not" in reference to a coastal state's taking enforcement jurisdictional steps for an act which occurred before the vessel entered the territorial sea, the inference is that "should not" is intended merely to establish priority.

Additional evidence of the intention to give the flag state's jurisdiction precedence appears in subdivision 1. (c) of Article 19. That provision envisages the possibility that the flag state might invite the intervention of the local authorities in situations where it otherwise "should not" exercise its criminal jurisdiction. If the local jurisdiction were primary, there would have been no need to include that provision.

Ships entering and leaving internal waters of the coastal state are logically treated differently from those passing through. The provisions previously discussed in this section dealt with foreign vessels generally in the territorial sea. Subdivision 2 of the same article deals with the special situation of the vessel in the territorial sea after leaving internal waters.[140] That provision is broad enough to admit the coastal state's criminal enforcement jurisdiction relating to any act, wherever performed and regardless of its nature or effects, provided local law permits or requires it. An alternative and more limited construction is that this provision merely supplements the rules governing all vessels by providing additionally for those acts which occurred while the vessel

[139] Article 19.

[140] "The above provisions do not affect the right of the coastal State to take any steps authorized by its laws for the purpose of an arrest or investigation on board a foreign ship passing through the territorial sea after leaving internal waters."

was in internal waters.[141] The better construction of that subdivision would seem to be that, in the case of vessels leaving inland waters, the jurisdiction of the coastal state is primary as regards all acts which occurred while the vessel was in inland waters, in addition to the areas where it is primary for all vessels. In all other cases, it is secondary.

If an act occurred on board before the vessel enters the territorial sea, the coastal state is prohibited from taking enforcement steps on board if the vessel is passing through without entering inland waters.[142] By inference, enforcement action could be taken if the vessel is there for the purpose of entering inland waters. Of course, the rule it seeks to enforce must be one which it had the jurisdiction to prescribe. Most acts which occur on the high seas would not be within this competence.[143] If the activity which occurred while the vessel was on the high seas was subject to littoral state control because related to the vessel's proposed entry into internal waters, the local jurisdiction should be considered primary and the flag state's secondary. If, however, some different contacts supported the local state's jurisdiction to prescribe,[144] then it would seem more rational that the flag state's enforcement jurisdiction would be considered primary, since that construction would impose the least burden on the flow of commerce.

In the Territorial Sea, Civil Jurisdiction

The question of conflict of civil jurisdiction is being considered independently from criminal because there is a special article of the convention on the territorial sea [145] dealing with that subject:

1. The coastal State should not stop or divert a foreign ship passing through the territorial sea for the purpose of exercising civil jurisdiction in relation to a person on board the ship.
2. The coastal State may not levy execution against or arrest the ship for the purpose of any civil proceedings, save only in respect of obligations or liabilities assumed or incurred by the ship itself in the course or for the purpose of its voyage through the waters of the coastal State.
3. The provisions of the previous paragraph are without prejudice to the right of the coastal State, in accordance with its laws, to levy execution against or to arrest, for the purpose of any civil proceedings, a foreign ship lying in the

[141] On vessels merely passing through, it will be recalled, the coastal state may take jurisdiction with regard to any act which occurred in the territorial waters, but in any case not within the listed exceptions, that jurisdiction was secondary to the flag state's.

[142] Article 19, subdivision 5.

[143] See *supra* at p. 213.

[144] *E.g.*, only that the actor was a national of the coastal state.

[145] *Supra* note 90.

territorial sea, or passing through the territorial sea after leaving internal waters.[146]

In the first subdivision of this article, once again the ambiguous term "should not" is used.[147] That provision is directed only to stopping or diverting a ship for the purpose of exercising civil jurisdiction over a person on board. The following two subdivisions pertain to civil causes against the vessel itself. In the discussion of this term as used in the article pertaining to criminal jurisdiction, it was submitted that it conferred upon the coastal state primary jurisdiction, relegating the flag state to secondary position.[148] It does not necessarily follow that the same result should obtain when dealing with conflicts of civil jurisdiction. The coastal state has a more vital interest in enforcing its criminal law on vessels in its territorial sea than its civil law.[149] In the balancing of the exclusive interest of the coastal state against the inclusive interest of all states, including both the coastal state and the flag state, in an unimpeded flow of commerce, it would be difficult to justify construing this provision as conferring any enforcement jurisdiction, other than upon consent of the traversing vessel, upon the authorities of the coastal state.[150]

The second subdivision deals less ambiguously with actions against the vessel herself. It permits the coastal state to arrest the vessel only for civil obligations incurred by the vessel itself in the course of or for the purpose of the particular voyage through the territorial sea. This would include obligations arising out of contract or tort while in inland waters before entering the territorial sea, or while in the territorial sea.

A problem of construction which could arise is whether a particular act produces an *in rem* liability of the vessel or merely an *in personam* liability of her owner or of the particular actor involved. This would depend initially upon the law of the coastal state. But would the coastal state be permitted by international law to make every transaction, with anyone on board, out of which a civil obligation arises create a lien upon the vessel? For example, suppose a passenger were to purchase a curio ashore and fail to render payment, it would seem strange

146 Article 20.

147 See *supra* at p. 48.

148 *Supra* at p. 121.

149 See *Restatement* § 50, Comment on Subsection (2), pp. 172–173.

150 This is the conclusion of the reporters in the *Restatement*. *Id.* It should be noted that the suggestion is that the authority is unnecessary if the ship is passing through the territorial sea to or from internal waters since the authority could be exercised in any event while the ship is there. Of course, if the vessel is not in "innocent" passage, the cosatal state has jurisdiction for all purposes. *Supra* at note 135.

indeed if this transaction should be deemed to create a liability of the vessel justifying its arrest in territorial waters after leaving port. The better construction is that only those transactions arising out of the operation of the ship or the conduct of the ship's business would be admitted to raise an obligation of "the ship itself".

The third subdivision of article nineteen seems either redundant or irrational. The preceding subdivisions are said to be without prejudice to the right to arrest a foreign ship in the territorial sea after leaving internal waters. If the meaning of that provision is that there is a right to arrest for enforcement of a civil obligation incurred while in the internal waters, that authority has already been conferred by the preceding subdivision. If it means that the mere fact of having been in internal waters makes the vessel subject to civil arrest for the enforcement of liability arising out of a transaction occurring at any time or place, no matter how remote, it goes much too far in protecting the exclusive interest of the coastal state. The construction dictated by sound policy is that it is merely redundant.[151]

In Inland Waters

When a vessel of one state is in the inland waters of another, it and the people on board are subject to the enforcement jurisdiction of the local authorities because it is within the territory and the power of the host state. Since a vessel in distress enters as of right,[152] it is logical that it should not be subjected to local jurisdiction to the same extent as vessels which legally could be prevented from entering. Obviously, the coastal state would not have the right to prevent the entry or punish the vessel or personnel for having entered, nor could it punish for any act reasonably necessary or incidental to the entry.[153] Complementary to the right to enter and do any acts reasonably dictated by the entry would be the right to depart without interference when the emergency is over. It would also seem to follow that the vessel should be exempt from the exercise of local criminal enforcement jurisdiction relating to any acts likely to be restricted in their effect to the vessel.[154] It is submitted further that the vessel and the people and cargo on board

[151] Inferentially, this is the view of the *Restatement*. See § 50, Comment d. on Subsection (1), p. 50.

[152] See *The Eleanor*, Edw. 135 (1809) – "distress ... must be at all times a sufficient passport for human beings ...."; *Restatement* § 51, Comment a., p. 174.

[153] See *North Atlantic Fisheries Tribunal of Arbitration*, Per. Ct. Arb., Scott, *Hague Court Reports* (1916) 146, 180.

[154] *Restatement* §§ 51, 52, 53.

should not be subject to the enforcement of any civil obligation during its stay exept those incurred during the time that it is there. There does not appear to be any valid policy reason for subjecting a vessel which has been forced into port by circumstances beyond her control to local civil jurisdiction. This would be one more consideration unnecessarily imposed upon her master in deciding whether to enter and could interfere with a decision otherwise dictated by the facts and more consistent with safety of life and property.

The formulation of the rule applicable to vessels entering in distress is much too broadly stated in Jessup, *The Law of Territorial Waters and Maritime Jurisdiction:*

> There is one condition under which a foreign vessel in territorial waters may claim as of right an entire immunity from the local jurisdiction. The condition is that such presence in territorial waters be due to *force majeure*. If a ship is driven in by storm, carried in by mutineers, or seeks refuge for vital repairs or provisioning, international customary law declares that the local state shall not take advantage of its necessity.[155]

Assuming, for example, that a local resident was murdered on board, or the Master refused to pay for repairs to the vessel which were accomplished during the current voyage, the local authorities certainly should have the right to enforce their law in resolving these claims. If local residents had no civil recourse against the vessel, it might not be able to procure the very supplies and services essential to relieve the distress.

Vessels other than those which enter in distress are subjected to a very different regime. There can be not doubt that both the flag and the local sovereign have an interest in maintaining order on board. Therefore, both should have criminal enforcement jurisdiction related to activity located there. The question, then, resolves itself to which has primary jurisdiction in a particular type of situation. Situations have been classified generally into those the effect of which are likely to be limited to the ship and those which are not. In the former, the flag state has primary jurisdiction; in the latter, local legal processes have precedence.[156]

If the effects of an act actually extend to the shore, that would conclusively place it within the primary cognizance of the coastal state.

[155] P. 194 (1927). Professor Jessup was treating the question of vessels in port as well as in the territorial sea.

[156] See *Restatement* § 53.

If it affected someone not a member of the ship's company (or non-national passenger), its effect will almost certainly be carried or felt ashore and thus bring it within the orbit of the primacy of local enforcement jurisdiction. Finally, if it is of a type which is so serious as to cause anxiety, fear or deep moral indignation in the local populace, it must be of a type the effects of which are likely to be felt ashore.

Since the question is whether the act is likely to have an effect ashore, the question of whether a particular act is of a type which would disturb the peace of the port should depend upon the standards of the local society rather than those of the flag state. Thus, it should initially be determined by the local authorities,[157] and their decision should not be subject to question unless it is celarly inconsistent with the usage of civilized states.[158]

With regard to those acts the effect of which are likely to be felt ashore, the local authorities have primary jurisdiction. All others will come within the primary jurisdiction of the flag state.[159] The treaties of the United States have usually followed this general line of demarcation in balancing the competing interests of the two states. For example, the 1948 Consular Officers Convention with Costa Rica [160] states:

> A consular officer ... shall ... have the right to exercise exclusive jurisdiction over controversies arising out of the internal order of merchant vessels of the sending state and over matters pertaining to the enforcement of discipline on board whenever any such vessels shall have entered the territorial waters of the receiving state within his consular district.

[157] See Dana's Wheaton, Section 95, note 58; II Moore, *Digest of International Law* 292.

[158] In this area as in others where the actions of governments come into conflict, there must be some internationally accepted standard to control state conduct. Otherwise, the international rule may be nullified by the domestic legal action of a particular state. Other areas similarly governed by an international standard are the treatment to which aliens are entitled and the credit required of one state to the conferral of nationality by another. See Cutler, "Treatment of Foreigners," 27 *A.J.I.L.* 227 (1933), and the *Nottebohm Case,* 1955 I.C.J. 4.

[159] The concurrent nature of the jurisdiction of the two states arose in the case of *United States v. Flores,* 289 U.S. 137, 155–157 (1933), although the court was not required to decide the question of priority. Note that a problem inherent in the federal system of the United States arises at this point. If a ship of a foreign state is within the internal waters of a state of the United States, all acts on board her would normally be subject to that state's enforcement jurisdiction. Federal law would be controlling on state activity because of the Constitutional power to control maritime affairs, but absent Congressional action requiring the state to defer to the law of the ship, state authorities might not consider themselves free to defer to that law because of a rule of customary international law. However, if that rule of international law were contained in a treaty with the flag state, it would be binding automatically as being Constitutionally the supreme law of the land.

[160] TIAS 2045, 1 USTIAS 247.

Notwitstanding the provisions of paragraph 1 [preceding quotation] ... a consular officer shall not, except as permitted by the laws of the receiving state, exercise jurisdiction in any case involving an offense committed on board a merchant vessel of the sending state, which offense would be punishable under the law of the receiving state by a sentence of imprisonment for a period of at least one year, or by penalties in excess thereof.[161]

In this particular treaty there is no express reference to acts which affect persons other than of the ship's company or for some other reason reach beyond the confines of the vessel,[162] but it is doubtful that such acts would be considered as "arising out of the internal order" of the vessel. The Costa Rica treaty deals specially with crimes of a type likely to disturb the peace of the port, it will be noted, by giving primary jurisdiction to the coastal state in cases where local law provides a severe penalty.[163] Nevertheless, the intent to accomplish the same result is clear.[164]

The reconciliation of the conflicting interests in the exercise of civil enforcement jurisdiction could rationally follow the same line as suggested for the allocation of criminal enforcement jurisdiction. Provided a controversy involves only the internal relationships of the vessel, the local authorities should have little interest in becoming involved. The interests of commerce would, of course, best be subserved by the flag state's having as comprehensive a right as possible to resolve conflicts involving its vessels. The vessel's business would more likely be expedited if the consular officer took initial action to resolve a dispute on board, leaving ultimate resolution, perhaps, in accordance with the law of the flag state, to be resolved by its judicial authorities upon return of the vessel. On the other hand, the local authorities have an interest in resolving disputes in which local residents are involved. On the face of it, then, the rule allocating civil jurisdiction to the respective states should be the same, namely that if the controversy is limited to persons on board the vessel, the jurisdiction should be left to the flag state; otherwise, local authorities would be free to resolve the conflict.[165]

161 Art. X, 1(a), 2, *id.* at 270–272. This general allocation of authority has been followed since the very early treaties of the United States. See Treaty of 1827 with Sweden and Norway, Art. XIII, 8 Stat. 346, 352.

162 See Article 22 (2) (b) of the 1951 Convention on Consular Officers with U.K., TIAS 2494, 3 USTIAS 3426, 3443.

163 Incidentally, this section conclusively adopts the standards of the local society as to what acts are of a type which are likely to disturb the peace of the port whether or not those standards are consistent with any international standard.

164 This problem will be dealt with in detail in the succeeding chapter.

165 See *Restatement* § 53, Reporters' Note 2, p. 181.

The treaty provision set forth in the preceding material is broad enough to support the rule stated in the preceding paragraph. However, since the passage of the Seamen's Act of 1915, treaties of the United States have consistently contained provisions preserving the primary right of the coastal state to taken cognizance of disputes involving seamen's contracts of service and wage claims. For example, the treaty with Costa Rica [166] says:

> A consular officer ... shall have jurisdiction over issues concerning the adjustment of wages of members of the crews of vessels of the sending state which shall have entered the territorial waters of the receiving state within his consular district and the execution of contracts relating to such wages. Such jurisdiction shall not in any case, however, exclude the jurisdiction conferred on the competent authorities of the receiving state under existing or future laws.[167]

Since "existing or future laws" might well make local jurisdiction obligatory upon the courts, this type of treaty provision has the effect of rendering local civil enforcement primary in the area referred to. In all other areas of civil controversy restricted to the vessel, the flag state's jurisdiction would apparently have precedence.[168]

[166] *Supra* note 160.
[167] Art. X, 1. (b), 1 USTIAS 272.
[168] See Article 22 (1), of Treaty with United Kingdom, *supra* note 162, which contains a provision having similar import. A more detailed treatment of this problem will be undertaken in the succeeding chapter.

CHAPTER V

CONSULAR AUTHORITY SPECIFICALLY DEFINED

A particular situation concerning activity on board or involving a vessel may give rise to possible criminal liability of one or more of the persons involved, as well as potential civil liability, and may also raise questions of administrative control of the problem. In Chapter IV it was attempted to clarify the areas of possible conflict generally between the jurisdiction of a state where a vessel happens to be and that of the state of the vessel's nationality. The suggestion is that whenever official action by the flag state is indicated, the consul is the most likely official of the flag state to carry it into effect.

Of course, the master of the vessel, too, is an official of the flag state, and will in many situations be armed with the necessary authority and ability to take any steps necessary, at least of an interim nature, to resolve a problem. However, if a consular officer is available, he would normally have a supervening authority over that of the master. Additionally, in the nature of things, many conflicts will involve the master as a party, and in such a situation, a third party's decision becomes practically essential.

Generally, in the situations considered in this chapter, the action taken, although it may be of an adjudicative nature, will ultimately be subject to review by the judicial or administrative authorities of the flag state. This is a question determined by the laws of that state, however, and its law might provide that consul's decision is final. Once it is determined as between the two states that the flag state will take jurisdiction, it is essentially a question for its domestic law to what extent the action taken by any official will be subject to review. That is a problem which involves the interests of the parties and the flag state, but in no way the interests of the receiving state.

It would be untrue to say, however, that once the receiving state has conceded jurisdiction to the flag state, it has no further interest in the matter. The very corrective action by the consular officer or master of the ship might be so inconsistent with the basic mores of the local populace as to interfere with their tranquility. For this reason, particularly in criminal matters, the interests of the local sovereign might dictate that the consul do only what is reasonably necessary to preserve order on board and expedite the vessel's departure, leaving any final execution of punishment to be carried out either on the high seas or in the territory of the flag state on the ship's return.[1]

Once it is determined that the flag state has jurisdiction to take enforcement action in a civil matter, it necessarily follows that the contacts between the problem and the state must be sufficient to dictate the application of its law.[2] In any case, therefore, where the consul takes action, he does so in pursuance of the law of his own state and enforces the provisions of that law.[3]

UNITED STATES TREATY PROVISIONS

Many treaties to which the United States is a party contain general provisions concerning consular authority which are equally applicable to civil or criminal jurisdictional problems.[4] A typical provision of this type is the one contained in the 1923 treaty of Friendship, Commerce and Consular Rights with Germany.[5]

> A consular officer shall have exclusive jurisdiction over controversies arising out of the internal order of private vessels of his country ....[6]

[1] *Cf. Restatement* § 49, Comment on Subsection (3), p. 167. This section deals with the same problem when a vessel is in innocent passage. The rationale would seem to be even more appropriate in the case of a vessel tied up to a dock in port. § 534. 2–6 and 2–7 of the *U.S. Foreign Affairs Manual* distinctly limits consular action in serious criminal matters to investigation, detention and return to the U.S. for trial.

[2] Choice of laws problems do not arise in criminal matters. A state which prosecutes a person for a criminal act always applies its own penal laws. See *Restatement,* Conflict of Laws §§ 427, 611 (1934).

[3] Choice of laws problems do arise where the local authorities take jurisdiction of a civil matter. It may be that the motivation of a court in exercising its discretion and assuming to decide a controversy was to assure that a particular plaintiff is afforded a remedy. However, it by no means follows that it will apply local law. The flag state may well be the only state with any significant contacts with the transaction. Under these circumstances the local authorities would apply the law of the flag state. These questions are beyond the scope of the present inquiry. Having considered the factors which may induce the assumption of jurisdiction, I shall consider the choice of laws problem to the extent necessary to give a clear picture of consular authority.

[4] Many of these same treaties additionally contain special provisions dealing expressly with one branch or the other of consular authority. Those provisions will be considered hereinafter.

[5] 44 Stat. 2132.

[6] Article XXII, *id.* at 2152. This article is expressly caused to survive by Article XXVIII of the treaty of 1954. 7 TIAS 1839, 1868.

Identical or substantially similar provisions are contained in eleven other recent treaties.[7] Similar provisions are to be found in treaties going back into the early history of the United States.[8] With slightly different wording, a similar result was effected in another series of earlier treaties:

> The consuls ... shall have the right ... to sit as judges and arbitrators in such differences as may arise between the captains and crews of the vessels belonging to the nation whose interests are committed to their charge ....[9]

There can be no doubt that the intention of the parties to these treaties was to reserve to the consular authority of the flag state exclusive authority to decide controversies, whether civil or criminal, which have no effect external to the ship. Even the most recent treaty provisions on the subject make a like allocation of authority between officials of the flag state and local officials. The treaty of 1948 with Costa Rica speaks of the consular officer's "right to exercise exclusive jurisdiction over controversies arising out of the internal order of merchant vessels of the sending state",[10] while the treaty of 1951 with the United Kingdom refers to "any matter concerning the internal management of the vessel." [11] The treaty of 1951 with Greece is not quite as clear on the subject, stating:

> Consular officers ... shall at their request be accorded by the local authorities such assistance as they may need for carrying out, in accordance with the applicable local laws and regulations, their duties with respect to the maintenance of discipline and order aboard vessels ....[12]

Probably the term "order" would include civil jurisdiction, and by implication the consular officer would presumably have jurisdiction over the internal order of the vessel, defined by the law of the sending state. However, it is somewhat of a departure from usual practice to require the consul to carry out his duties "in accordance with the applicable local laws and regulations." That clause is open to a construction which would admit emasculation of any rights the consul might have. Such construction would be inconsistent with the general

[7] Appendix A, #'s 119, 121, 122, 123, 124, 126, 130, 131, 136, 138 and 145.
[8] Appendix A, #'s 112, 108, 107, 96, 93, 92, 91, 89, 86, 84, 82, 81, 79, 56 and 50.
[9] Sweden, 1827, Art. XIII, 8 Stat. 346, 352. Similar provisions are found in treaties, Appendix A, #'s 24, 30, 36, 40, 41, 44, 46, 55, 61, 70 and 71.
[10] Art. X, 1 TIAS 247, 270–272.
[11] Art. 22 (1), 3 TIAS 3426, 3443. An identical provision is consined in treaty with Ireland. Art. 23 (1), 5 TIAS 949, 992 (1952).
[12] Art. XXII (5), 5 TIAS 1829, 1897–1899.

tenor of the treaty, however, since it would result in the parties not being bound, at their own election, in the future. A more reasonable construction would be that the local authorities are not required to render aid if they are required to do any act outside their authority as defined by local law. Under those circumstances, the consul would not be deprived of his authority, but would have to restrain his demands for aid to those permissible under local law. That construction would make the treaty consistent with the other recent treaties on the subject which have been concluded by the United States.[13]

The only recent treaty which constitutes any substantial departure from the established United States treaty practice in this area is that with Muscat and Oman of 1958. In the protocol, it says:

> Without prejudice to the right of the administrative and judicial authorities of the receiving state ... to enforce the laws of the receiving state applicable to vessels of any state in its ports and territorial waters, it is the intention of the Parties that a consular officer shall have jurisdiction over controversies ... on board vessels of the sending state in the territorial waters of the receiving state ....[14]

It is probable that the term "territorial waters" was intended as a generic term encompassing all waters under the sovereignty of the respective parties, including inland waters. Otherwise, the consul would have very little authority, since most controversies on board ship at least manifest themselves while the vessel is in port. Those which are restricted to the territorial sea would not in the usual course come to his attention at all. The more difficult problem, however, is that the section apparently admits of the establishment of local law to govern all types of controversies on board ships of the other party while in port. This is inconsistent with the otherwise ubiquitous provision reserving matters involving the vessel's internal order to the authority of the consul, who applies the applicable law of the flag state. Perhaps it could be construed in a manner similar to that suggested for the clause in the United Kingdom convention.[15]

In addition to the type of treaty clause which expressly confers authority on consular officers to exercise control over the internal

[13] See *In re Labrasciano*, 38 Misc. 415, 77 N.Y. Supp. 1040 (Surr. Ct., Westchester, 1902) construing a similar provision (Art. IX, Treaty of 1853 with Argentine Confederation, 10 Stat. 1001, 1009, through most-favored-nation clause in Treaty of 1871 with Italy – Art. XXIV – 17 Stat. 845, 856.) to merely provide for conformity with local procedural law.

[14] Subdivision 3, (b.), 11 TIAS 1835, 1843–1844.

[15] *Supra* p. 131.

operation of his country's ships, it has been common to incorporate into treaties dealing with consular affairs clauses conferring rights defined by those granted to any third country. A typical clause is that contained in the treaty of 1887 with Peru:

> To protect more effectually the commerce and navigation of their respective citizens ... agree to admit ... consuls who shall enjoy ... all the rights, privileges, and immunities, of the consuls ... of the most favored nation ....[16]

The clause is changed to "rights, prerogatives and immunities" in numerous other treaties,[17] and "privileges, exemptions and immunities" in others.[18] With regard to the jurisdictional authority, if any, conferred on consular officers by these various clauses, there does not seem to be any good reason to construe them differently because of the different wording, nor would "privileges",[19] "privileges and powers",[20] or "privileges, powers and exemptions" [21] require any different conclusion. It would seem that all those clauses as a class either do or do not import the special consular authority over maritime matters granted by the parties to third states. The question is one of construction. Is the authority of a consular officer to resolve internal disputes on board merchant vessels of his country a "right", privilege", "prerogative" or "power" which he enjoys as representative of the commercial interests of his state? If so, then clauses of this type import that authority from treaties with other states. It seems clear that any one of these terms has a generic meaning broad enough to encompass the kind of authority under discussion. That fact alone, of course, is not determinative of the issue.

The Supreme Court of the state of California considered this type of treaty provision in the case of *In re Clausen's Estate.*[22] In that case, the consul of Denmark claimed the right to receive for distribution the assets of the estate of a deceased Danish national by virtue of the most-favored-nation provision contained in the United States treaty of 1826 with Denmark – "Consuls ... shall enjoy ... the rights, privileges, and

[16] Art. XXX, 25 Stat. 1444, 1459. Similar provisions will be found in the treaties with: Peru, 1870, Art. XXXII, 18 Stat, 698, 713, and Denmark, 1826, Art. 8, 8 Stat. 340, 342.

[17] Appendix A, #'s 75, 65, 54, 49, 48, 45, 39, 33, 29, 28 and 25.

[18] Appendix A, #'s 135, 78, 74, 69, 58 and 53.

[19] Orange Free State, 1871, Art. V, 18 Stat. 749, 750.

[20] Dominican Republic, 1867, Art. XXVI, 15 Stat. 473, 487–488; Swiss Confederation, 1850, Art. VII, 11 Stat. 1, 5; Hawaiian Islands, 1849, Art. X, 9 Stat. 178, 181–182; Austria, 1829, Art. X, 8 Stat. 398, 400.

[21] Sardinia, 1838, Art. XV, 8 Stat. 512, 518.

[22] 202 Calif. 267, 259 Pac. 1094 (1927).

immunities, of the Consuls ... of the most favored nation ...." –[23] which he claimed imported the decedent estates provision of the treaty of 1923 with Germany.[24] The court held that the Danish consul was not entitled to the benefit of that particular provision of the German treaty. This result was reached by reasoning that the right claimed as encompassed within the generic term "rights" or "privileges", namely the right to distribute decedents' estates, was not one within the scope of the subject matter dealt with in the treaty with Denmark, nor was it of the type generally afforded under treaties of that type at that time. In other words, the question is resolved by determining the intent of the parties. The Danish treaty dealt solely with subject matter totally unrelated to decedents' estates, and this type of authority was not at that time commonly conferred on consuls. Thus, it could not have been intended to encompass it within the most-favored-nation clause.[25] This seems to be an emminently well reasoned decision.[26]

The converse of the reasoning in *In re Clausen's Estate* is that any authority which is within the scope of the subjects dealt with in the controlling treaty or customarily included in that type of treaty at the time of its conclusion would be imported from third state treaties dealing with similar subject matter. As has been shown in the earlier materials in this chapter, authority to resolve disputes internal to vessels of the consul's state was and is one of the most common provisions contained in treaties of this type; and in nearly all of them, treaty resolution of maritime jurisdictional conflicts is a topic considered. The titles of most of them include the term "Commerce" or "Navigation" or both, and this would tend to fix the scope of subject matter dealt with. It is clear, therefore, that these clauses should be construed to import the benefit of the grant of any consular authority over any maritime matters included in treaties with third states. This, of course, greatly increases the number of states with which the United States should be obligated to permit consular control of matters of internal economy of national ships.[27]

[23] Art. 8, 8 Stat. 340, 342.

[24] Art. XXIV, 44 Stat. 2132, 2153–2154.

[25] 202 Calif. 271, 259 Pac. 1095.

[26] In view of the court's construction, it never reached the question of reciprocity; in other words, whether Denmark would confer the same right on United States consuls as did Germany under the 1923 treaty. That is a question which could best be raised in a Danish court or in diplomatic correspondence between the two governments.

[27] On the question of importing consular authority from treaties with third states because of most-favored-nation clauses, see also *In re Labrasciano's Estate, supra* note 13.

In addition to those treaties which by one type of phraseology or another expressly confer upon consuls the authority granted to consuls of the most favored nation, the United States has also concluded agreements which mutually confer upon the parties certain categories of rights not couched in terms of consular authority granted to third states. In the treaty of 1875 with Belgium, for example, the following provision will be found:

> In all that relates to duties of customs and navigation, the two high contracting parties promise, reciprocally, not to grant any favor, privilege, or immunity to any other State which shall not instantly become common to the citizens and subjects of both parties respectively ....[28]

A similar provision is to be found in the treaty of 1870 with Peru,[29] except that it refers to "any favor, privilege, or immunity whatever, in commerce and navigation," and in the treaty of 1864 with Hayti.[30] Some of these same treaties also contain provision conferring most-favored-nation authority upon the consuls of the respective parties.[31] In the treaties containing both types of clauses, there is, of course, no difficulty in importing consular maritime authority from treaties with third states. In these treaties, however, where an article such as the one quoted from the treaty with Belgium stands alone, a problem of construction arises. Does a clause which confers any "favor", "privilege", or "immunity" in "navigation" granted to a third state include a grant of consular authority over seamen? Does the addition of the term "commerce" to "navigation" affect that question? And would the grant of consular authority be one which benefited "the citizens and subjects of both parties"; or is it not included because it benefits the state itself, and its citizens only indirectly?

It appears clear from the meaning ordinarily attributed to the terms "navigation" and "commerce" that either might be interpreted broadly enough to encompass the resolution of disputes arising among the members of a ship's company. Of course, either term could be so restrictively construed as to exclude such problems. The Supreme Court has said that the obligation of treaties should be construed

[28] Art. XII, 19 Stat. 628 [72], 631–632 [75–76]. This article goes on to make the right conditional upon the other party paying the same price as the third state did for the concession, but this aspect of the article is not immediately pertinent to the problem under consideration.

[29] Art. III, 18 Stat. 698, 700.

[30] Art. II, 13 Stat. 711, 712. Similar articles are found in treaties, Appendix A, #'s 95, 74, 73, 69, 65, 54, 53, 49, 48, 47, 45, 43, 39, 37, 35, 33, 29 and 23.

[31] *Supra* notes 17 and 18.

liberally to effectuate the apparent intentions of the parties.[32] Additionally, and for the same purpose, if a treaty provision, fairly construed, admits of two interpretations, one restricting and the other enlarging its scope, the more liberal construction is to be preferred.[33]

In the case of *Jordan v. Tashiro*,[34] the Court construed the terms "commerce" and "trade" used in the treaty of commerce and navigation with Japan [35] to include the operation of a hospital in California as a protected activity by Japanese nationals in the United States. The Court said:

> While in a narrow and restricted sense the terms "commerce," or "commercial," and "trade" may be limited to the purchase and sale or exchange of goods and commodities, they may connote, as well other occupations and other recognized forms of business enterprise which do not necessarily involve trading in merchandise .... And although commerce includes traffic in this narrower sense, for more than a century it has been judicially recognized that *in a broad sense it embraces every phase of commercial and business activity and intercourse.*[36]

The Court stated in the course of its opinion that it felt impelled by controlling principle to give the treaty "a liberal rather than a narrower interpretation." [37]

Certainly, that interpretation of the treaty provisions under consideration which defines the terms "favor", "right", "privilege" or "exemption" in "navigation" or "commerce" to encompass the grant of authority to resolve maritime disputes in a like manner as the most-favored-nation would be the more liberal construction available on that question. Even in absence of authority on the question, it seems clear on principle that the grant to another nation of the right to resolve a class of maritime disputes on its national vessels without the intervention of local authorities is a "favor" in either "commerce" or "navigation", and this construction comports with the most natural meaning of the terms used. There can be little question that the maritime commerce of a state, and the interests of those persons engaged in it, are better subserved by an understanding that prevents interference with it except by officials of the flag state. A vessel's departure and its operation in port are much more likely to be expedited

[32] See *Tucker v. Alexandroff*, 183 U.S. 424, 437 (1901); *Wright v. Henkel*, 190 U.S. 40, 57 (1902).

[33] *Asakura v. Seattle*, 265 U.S. 332, 342 (1923).

[34] 278 U.S. 123 (1928).

[35] 1911, 37 Stat. 1504.

[36] Emphasis added. 278 U.S. 129–130.

[37] *Id.* at 128.

if all disputes await final settlement in the home port, only essential interim measures being taken locally by an official with this idea in mind.

The Supreme Court has also dealt with this problem of construction more directly. In *Dainese v. Hale*,[38] the Court was considering Article I of the treaty of 1862 with Turkey.[39] That provision stated that

> All rights, privileges, or immunities, which the Sublime Porte now grants, or may hereafter grant to, or suffer to be enjoyed by the subjects, ships, commerce, or navigation of any foreign power, shall be equally granted to and exercised and enjoyed by the citizens, vessels, commerce, and navigation of the United States of America.

The Court, in construing that article, said:

> If, therefore, it be true, as laid down by writers and public documents, that the subjects of other Christian nations have and enjoy in Turkey the right to have their civil controversies decided by their own ministers and consuls, it would seem clear, that under the treaty of 1862 ... the same right is guaranteed to citizens of the United States.[40]

It follows from this language that the most-favored-nation clause in commercial treaties does import grants of consular powers over maritime matters to third states.[41]

The International Court of Justice has considered the effect of a treaty clause between Greece and the United Kingdom which guaranteed most-favored-nation treatment in matters of "commerce and navigation".[42] The majority of the court only found it necessary to decide that Greece had an arguable position in the claim that the clause imported administration of justice provisions from treaties with third states. However, the four dissenting judges concluded that the class of benefits imported by the most-favored-nation clause was restricted to matters of commerce and navigation, those being the specific subjects dealt with by the article in question. Therefore, it did not operate to import provisions in treaties with third states concerning the administration of justice. This was in answer to the argument of Greece that

38 91 U.S. 13 (1875).
39 12 Stat. 1213.
40 91 U.S. 13, 18 (1875).
41 The fact that the particular clause construed was contained in a treaty which was not reciprocal is not material to its interpretation on this point. It would, of course, bear upon the position of the United States on the question of whether most-favored-nation clauses are conditional. See note 26 *supra*.
42 *The Ambatielos Case*, 1953 I.C.J. 10.

the clause imported rights granted by Britain to nationals of third states to invoke certain procedures in British courts. These rights and procedures in the local courts to enforce claims were claimed to be favors in "commerce and navigation". The dissenting judges denied this, stating: "in the whole of the Treaty this matter [administration of justice] is the subject of only one provision, of limited scope ... concerning free access to the Courts, and that Article contains no references to most-favored-nation treatment." [43] It is fair to say that the problem considered by the Court was not exactly analogous to the question of incorporating consular maritime dispute settlement by a most-favored-nation clause dealing with "commerce and navigation". When the consul decides an internal dispute on one of his state's ships, his decision has direct economic effect upon the commerce of his state. In this case, the problem involved the procedure for resolving a claim for breach of contract damages arising out of commercial activity which itself had terminated. Thus, the effect upon the commerce of Greece was more remote. It is submitted, however, that the dissenting opinion was nevertheless in error in its reasoning. The contract involved the "commerce" of Greece, and the procedures for its resolution must necessarily have some effect upon it. Therefore, the benefits of treaties with third states involving resolution of such disputes should have been incorporated by the most-favored-nation clause.[44]

On the question of whether consular settlement of internal disputes is a right which "citizens ... shall enjoy", as opposed to one from which only the state is entitled to benefit,[45] it seems that *Dainese v. Hall* [46] also puts that problem at rest. The language from the decision which is set forth in the text [47] assumes implicitly that these are rights enjoyed directly by the citizens who are intended to benefit. Since all rights under treaties are presumptively for the immediate legal benefit of the states signatory to it, the use of the phrase "citizens ... shall enjoy" these rights rather than "Parties ... shall enjoy" is without significance. It is submitted that the language referred to merely

[43] *Id.* at 34.

[44] The I.C.J. decision in the Anglo-Iranian dispute (1952 I.C.J. 110) that the most-favored-nation clause in the U.K. – Persia treaty did not import the right of Denmark to prosecute an action against Iran in the International Court of Justice is not relevant, since it depended upon a construction of Iran's declaration accepting compulsory jurisdiction, which was held to exclude controversies arising out of treaties concluded prior to the declaration.

[45] See Art. III, Convention with Peru-Bolivia of 1836, 8 Stat. 487, 488.

[46] *Supra* note 38.

[47] *Supra* at p. 137.

refers to the fact that the effect of the commitment comes to bear upon the day to day activities of citizens. The parties to the treaty bargained for a benefit to be conferred upon their citizens engaging in particular pursuits. It appears, therefore, that the only reasonable interpretation of these provisions, and the one indicated by Supreme Court decisions is that they require the importing of grants to third states of specific consular authority over maritime affairs.[48]

The relatively recent development which has the greatest potential for affecting the international pattern of consular authority over seamen is the General Agreement on Tariffs and Trade.[49] There are 82 states party to the convention.[50] Thus, any effect which its provisions may have will of necessity be quite widespread.

The General Agreement on Tariffs and Trade includes several clauses dealing with commerce which guarantee mutual most-favored-nation treatment among the parties. For the purposes of the particular problem under discussion, the first one of importance is as follows:

> Goods (including baggage), and also vessels ... shall be deemed to be in transit across the territory of a contracting party when the passage ... with or without trans-shipment, warehousing, breaking of bulk, or change in the mode of transport, is only a portion of a complete journey beginning and terminating beyond the frontier of the contracting party across whose territory the traffic passes. Traffic of this nature is termed in this Article "traffic in transit."
>
> There shall be freedom of transit through the territory of each contracting party, via the routes most convenient for international transit, for traffic in transit to or from the territory of other contracting parties. No distinction shall be made which is based on the flag of vessels, the place of origin, departure, entry, exit or destination, or on any circumstances relating to the ownership of goods, of vessels or of other means of transport.
>
> With respect to all charges, regulations and formalities in connection with transit, each contracting party shall accord to traffic in transit to or from the territory of any other contracting party treatment no less favourable than the treatment accorded to traffic in transit to or from any third country.[51]

[48] The treaty with Siam of 1937 uses much more specific terms than the other treaties concluded by the United States. There, the language is: "In all that concerns the entering, clearing, stationing, loading and unloading of vessels" the parties are entitled to most-favored-nation treatment. This language may not be broad enough in meaning to include a grant to a third state of consular authority over seamen, although it is at least open to argument that even such a clause should be interpreted to include such grants. Art. 11, 53 Stat. 1731, 1737.

[49] 1947, 61 Stat. Pt. 5, 6.

[50] Treaties in Force, 1 Jan. 1965.

[51] Art. V, 1, 2, 5, 61 Stat. Pt. 5, A 21, A 22. Paragraph 7. of the same article excludes aircraft from the connotation of the word "vessels." The most-favored-nation clauses in Article I, 1, (61 Stat. Pt. 5, A 12) and Article II, 1 .(a) (61 Stat. Pt. 5, A14), are evidently intended only to import third state benefits in importation and exportation which are of direct financial benefit to the competitive position of these goods.

The previous discussion of the effect of most-favored-nation clauses in commercial treaties – the importing of grants of consular authority over seamen to third states – applies equally to the construction of this provision. It would appear that if a third state were granted the right to exercise consular authority over a segment of the activities on board its "vessels in transit", the same grant would become common to all other parties to the agreement. Otherwise, the other parties' vessels in transit would be accorded treatment less favorable rather than "no less favourable" as dictated by the treaty.

An important problem of construction of most-favored-nation clauses which can be of vital consequence, particularly in the case of such clause appearing in a multilateral convention such as the General Agreement on Tariffs and Trade is whether a right which becomes available to state "A" as against "B" because of a grant of that right by "B" to "C" is also available to "B" against "A". Nearly all modern commercial treaties are reciprocal, in that each party grants to the other the same rights, and this is the form in which GATT has been drawn. However, suppose that state "A", a party to GATT, were to grant a commercial favor to state "X", not a party to GATT. That concession would become available to all the other parties to GATT by virtue of the most-favored-nation clause. But, if "A" did not have the right to demand a reciprocal and equal privilege from each of these other states, the result could be to place "A" at a commercial disadvantage. Of course, the same problem exists if "A" had bilateral most-favored-nation agreements with each of the same number of states as make up the membership of GATT. This problem of reciprocity is just another way of stating the controversy that has frequently arisen between the United States and other states as to whether these clauses are conditional or unconditional. Or, to put it another way, is the state which demands, pursuant to a most-favored-nation clause, the benefit of a grant to a third state required to pay the price which the third state paid, by making the right mutual?

There is no doubt that the earlier position of the United States on the question of whether most-favored-nation clauses were conditional was consistently in favor of that construction.[52] Some – perhaps most –

[52] *Bartram v. Robertson*, 122 U.S. 116 (1886); *Whitney v. Robertson*, 124 U.S. 190 (1888). That case involved benefits of lower rates for duties on imports. However, the Court was prepared to give the benefit provided it was mutual. See statement of Mr. Adams, Sec. of State, Dec. 23, 1817, V American State Papers, For. Rel. 152 – "one nation cannot enjoy as a gift that which is conceded to other nations for a full equivalent." *Contra*, Speed, 11 Op. Atty. Gen. 508.

of the treaties had clauses expressly conditional in form,[53] whereas others did not expressly state whether they were conditional.[54] However, apparently the interpretation of a clause not expressly conditional was the same as those containing such language. For both types, the United States positition was that they were conditional.[55]

In 1923, the United States initiated a policy of concluding commercial treaties containing most-favored-nation clauses expressly unconditional in form.[56] The clauses referred to in the treaties with Germany and Siam [57] deal only with import duty consessions to third states. These same treaties also contain most-favored-nation clauses pertaining to consular powers which are conditioned upon reciprocity.[58] The term "reciprocally used in the treaty with Germany and the expression "on condition of reciprocity" with Siam could be construed merely to mean that each party is entitled to all the rights the other grants to third states, but that construction would make those expressions redundant. The clauses containing them are themselves mutual in form without reference to the term under consideration. Additionally, the clauses are included in treaties containing the other clauses expressly unconditional. Therefore, the only reasonable construction is that, with regard to consular authority, the right to benefits granted third states is dependent upon offering those same benefits in return. In view of past practice of the United States of construing clauses as conditional which are silent on the question, and the subsequent change to expressly unconditional clauses, presumably, today, any clause which is not expressly unconditional would be interpreted as being conditional.

Most recent commercial treaties of the United States include most-favored-nation clauses neither expressly conditional nor unconditional.[59] They are frequently coupled with clauses expressly covering the question of consular authority over seamen, and to that extent dis-

[53] See Convention with Chile, 1832, Art. II, 8 Stat. 434.

[54] See treaty with Guatemala, 1849, Art. II, 10 Stat. 1.

[55] See instruction to American diplomatic officers, dated 18 August, 1923, Diplomatic serial 211, MS Dept. of State, file 611. 0031/197a, V Hackworth, *Digest of International Law* 272–273.

[56] *Id.* at 271. *E.g.*, Treaty of 1923 with Germany. Art. VII, 44 Stat. 2132, 2137; Treaty of 1937 with Siam, Art. 8, 53 Stat. 1731, 1736.

[57] *Id.*

[58] Art. XVII, 44 Stat. 2147–2148; Art. 11, 14, 53 Stat. 1738.

[59] See treaty with Germany, 1954, Art. XX, 1, TIAS 3593, 7 USTIAS 1839, 1868.

pense with this problem of interpretation.[60] Some, however, are still concluded with most-favored-nation clauses alone.[61]

The United Nations convention on consular relations, which was concluded in 1963,[62] raises this problem of construction of the most-favored-nation clause. It defines the consular function as including, *inter alia*, "exercising rights of supervision and inspection provided for in the laws and regulations of the sending state in respect of vessels having the nationality of the sending state ...." [63] and "conducting investigations into any incidents which occurred during the voyage, and settling disputes of any kind between the master, the officers and the seamen insofar as this may be authorized by the laws and regulations of the sending state".[64] These provisions must be related to Article 72 [65] which states: "In the application of the provisions of the present Convention the receiving state shall not discriminate as between states." This latter clause has the same effect as the more typical most-favored-nation clauses, and raises the same question as to whether a state is required to grant another party to that convention any consular authority over maritime affairs it has granted to a third state, also a party, without insisting upon a reciprocal grant.

Lord McNair says that "the new policy [of using unconditional most-favored-nation clauses] of the United States does not apply to most-favored-nation provisions contained in Consular Conventions; in consular matters 'most-favored-nation treatment is conditioned upon reciprocal treatment being accorded by the country invoking the provision'." [66] It is certainly true that the most-favored-nation clauses pertaining to consular authority have consistently either been expressly reciprocal or have not dealt with the question at all. In view of past practice of the United States concerning construction of such clauses and the practice of making some expressly unconditional and some expressly reciprocal, the most likely interpretation of one silent

[60] See Art. XXVIII of treaty with Germany, *id.*, which causes Art. XXIII of the treaty of 1923 to survive. 44 Stat. 2132, 2147–2148, 1951, Art. XXII, 5 TIAS 3057, 5 USTIAS 1829, 1897–1899.

[61] See treaty with Korea, 1956, Art. XIX, 3 TIAS 3947, 8 USTIAS 2217, 2230; Nicaragua, 1956, TIAS 4024, 9 USTIAS 449, 464.

[62] U.N. Doc. A/CONF. 25/12, 57 *A.J.I.L.* 995.

[63] Art. 5(K), *id.* at 998.

[64] Art. 5(1), *id.*

[65] *Id.* at 1020.

[66] *The Law of Treaties* 276 (1961). He cites as authority for that conclusion a reference in V Hackworth, *Digest of International Law* 274, 275. This is rather ancient authority, but I have been able to find no other more recent. He goes on to say that United Kingdom practice in respect of Consular Conventions appears to be the same. *Id.*

on the subject is that it is also implicitly subject to the condition of reciprocity.[67]

It appears that the courts are required to enforce rights arising from most-favored-nation clauses without any implementing legislation if the treaty is of a self executing type.[68] It also seems clear that they should be held to be conditional unless expressly unconditional in nature. Whether, however, a United States court should take evidence on the question of whether the other party to the treaty has or is prepared to grant the favor in return is a different problem. It would seem that by demanding the benefit from the United States she must have admitted the right of the United States to a reciprocal benefit, else she would be demanding treatment more favorable than that accorded the most-favored-nation. Thus, the United States has the right, and any failure to effectuate it thereafter would constitute the basis for an international claim, but that problem would not be an issue for the court in the initial action.

Assuming that grants of authority to consuls of third states do not automatically and without reciprocity inure to the benefit of the other party to a treaty containing a most-favored-nation clause, it is nevertheless true that that state is by virtue of the clause entitled to equal treatment and therefore in a position to demand the right upon offering the equivalent.[69]

Notwithstanding all the many difficult problems of construction and application incident to most-favored-nation clauses, the United States still regularly uses them in furtherance of a policy of liberalizing trade conditions by every means available. Since 1951, no less than twelve treaties containing one type or another of these clauses have been concluded, in which they constitute the only treatment of the question of consular maritime authority.

The clause most frequently found states that:

> Vessels of either Party shall have liberty ... on equal terms with vessels of any third country, to come with their cargoes to all ports, places and waters of such other Party open to foreign commerce and navigation. Such vessels and cargoes shall be accorded in all respects national treatment and most-favored-nation treatment within the ports, places and waters of such other Party ....[70]

[67] See Mr. Buchanan, Sec. of State, to Chev. Hulseman, Austrian chargé d'affaires, May 18, 1896, M.S. Notes to German States, VI, 130; II Moore, *Digest of International Law* 301.

[68] *John T. Bill Co. v. United States*, 104 F. 2d. 67, 73 (CCPA. 1939).

[69] Memorandum of the legal Adviser of the Dept. of State (Hackworth), Oct. 30, 1931, MS. Dept. of State, file 711. 6521/192, V Hackworth, *Digest of International Law* 274.

[70] Similar provision is to be found in the treaties with Viet-Nam, 1961, Art. XI, 3., TIAS 4890, 12 USTIAS 1711; Denmark 1961, Art. XIX, 3., TIAS 4797, 12 USTIAS 908, 925–930;

The treaty of 1960 with Pakistan [71] includes only a clause guaranteeing "Nationals and companies ... national ... and most-favored-nation ... treatment with respect to all matters relating to importation and exportation." [72] This might be construed to include only such matters as import duties having direct effect on the flow of goods.

Another clause which is sometimes found is one guaranteeing that "Nationals ... shall be accorded ... treatment no less favorable than that accorded nationals of any third country or that required by international law." [73] The international law standard of treatment of aliens is also found in the treaty of 1956 with Nicaragua in a clause not containing the most-favored-nation standard of treatment.[74] The question involved here would be whether use of the term "nationals" without reference to navigation or commerce would include special favors conferred in the maritime area.

In two recent treaties consular representatives are guaranteed the right to "enjoy the privileges and immunities accorded to officers ... of their rank ... by general international usage and ... shall be treated, subject to reciprocity, in a manner no less favorable than ... any third country", and to "exercise all functions, subject to reciprocity, which are in accordance with general international usage." [75] The treaty with Costa Rica of 1948 confers not only the specific rights granted by the convention but also any additional granted to any third state.[76]

So, it appears that the efforts of the State Department are still being directed to liberalization on the basis of equality of treatment on a broad plane by the use of the most-favored-nation clause. This

Muscat and Oman, 1958, Art. X, 3., TIAS 4530, 11 USTIAS 1835, 1840 – This treaty is supplemented by a protocol which expressly deals with the question of consular authority over seamen. Korea, 1956, Art. XIX, 3, TIAS 3947, 8 USTIAS 2217, 2230; Nicaragua, 1956, Art. XIX, 3., TIAS 4024, 9 USTIAS 449, 464; The Netherlands, 1956, Art. XIX, 2., TIAS 3942, 8 USTIAS 2043, 2074; Iran, 1955, Art. X, 3., TIAS 3853, 8 USTIAS 899, 907–908; Japan, 1953, Art, XIX, 3., TIAS 2863, 4 USTIAS 2077–2078; Israel, 1951, Art. XIX, 3., TIAS 2948, 5 USTIAS 550, 570; Ethiopia, 1951, Art. XIV, 2., TIAS 2864, 4 USTIAS 2134, 2145.

[71] TIAS 4683, 12 TIAS 110.

[72] Art. XIV, 5., *id.* at 118. Similar provisions are found in the treaties with Germany, 1954, Art. XIV, 4., TIAS 3593, 7 USTIAS 1839, 1855; Korea, 1956, Art. XIV, 5., TIAS 3947, 8 USTIAS 2217, 2228; Nicaragua, 1956, Art. XIV, 5., TIAS 4024, 9 USTIAS 449, 460; The Netherlands, 1956, Art. XIV, 5., TIAS 3942, 8 USTIAS 2043, 2070–2071; Iran, 1955, Art. IX, 2., TIAS 3853, 8 USTIAS 899, 907.

[73] Germany, 1954, Art. III, 1., TIAS 3593, 7 USTIAS 1839, 1842. A similar provision will be found in the treaty with Korea, 1956, Art. III, 1., TIAS 3947, 8 USTIAS 2217, 2220.

[74] Art. III, 1., TIAS 4024, 9 USTIAS 449, 452.

[75] Iran, 1955, Art. XIII, 1., TIAS 3853, 8 USTIAS 899, 909–910; Ethiopia, 1951, Art. III, 1., TIAS 2864, 4 USTIAS 2134, 2137–2138.

[76] Art. 1 , 2., TIAS 2045, 1 USTIAS 247, 255.

clause, as has been shown, when used in a commercial treaty in the form described will nearly always import grants to third states of consular authority over seamen. Thus, considering the modern widespread use of the clause, consular authority has undoubtedly been nearly stabilized along the lines indicated at the beginning of this chapter.

Customary International Law

It will be recalled that a number of the recent treaties of the United States define the authority of the consul in terms of international law and international usage.[77] Such treaty provisions raise a question of construction, namely, what is the controlling rule of international law, or what is the prevailing international practice? The same problem might arise *vis-à-vis* a state with which the United States has no controlling treaty.

It is possible to argue that the very fact of so many similar treaty provisions on the subject, substantially all of which give the consul authority over internal matters of the vessel, tend to create a customary rule of international law.[78] There is such a widespread use of clauses identical in substance, and which have even wider application by virtue of most-favored-nation clauses, that it would be difficult to imagine any treaty which has greater claim to universality.

Notwithstanding the rather broad network of treaties to which the United States is party, which include provisions allocating authority over internal matters of vessels to the consul of the state of which the vessel is a national, the United States has nearly always taken the position that absent such a controlling treaty provision, the matter is one of comity rather than international law.[79] This has been the position of the courts of the United States in numerous cases. The position is that, absent treaty commitment, the courts of a state have jurisdiction even over disputes which solely involve the internal operation of the ships, but will not exercise it over the objection of the consul unless special facts make it necessary in order to do justice.[80]

[77] *Supra* note 75.

[78] Oppenheim says: "Universal International law is created only when all or practically all the members of the Family of Nations are parties to these treaties." I *Oppenheim's International Law* 27 (6th ed. 1947).

[79] See IV Hackworth, *Digest of International Law* 878–879.

[80] *The Belgenland,* 114 U.S. 355, 363–364 (1884); *Wildenhus's Case,* 120 U.S. 1, 11–12 (1886); *Patterson v. Bark Eudora,* 190 U.S. 169, 177–178 (1903). The question of the circumstances which render it unjust not to take jurisdiction will be considered in a later portion of this chapter.

The State Department's most recent regulations concerning consular duties in maritime matters also assume the primary jurisdiction of the local authorities even where a matter exclusively involves the vessel and its company. With regard to civil controversies, the only regulation permits the consul to investigate[81] and arbitrate the matter.[82] In the area of disciplinary or penal offenses, the regulations are more explicit.

> When an offense is committed aboard a merchant vessel in the port or territorial waters of a nation other than the nation of registry, but does not involve the peace of the port, such offense is usually left by local governments to be adjusted by officers of the vessel and the diplomatic or consular representatives of the nation of registry. In the case of vessels of the United States, the right to protection against intervention by a foreign government in this class of cases is safeguarded in many areas by a treaty of friendship, commerce and navigation or by a consular convention between the United States and the foreign government concerned. Even where no treaty or convention exists, the local foreign government will usually refrain from intervening in such cases on the basis of comity between nations.[83]

Consuls are required to accept this but to discourage local officials from assuming jurisdiction in any case of a criminal act involving solely members of the crew,[84] no distinction being made between acts which do and those which do not disturb the "peace of the port". The assumption, of course, is that the foreign officials may legitimately intervene in all cases, but might not do so out of comity, particularly if the United States consul takes an interest in the matter.

STATUTES OF THE UNITED STATES

The only United States statutes which deal directly with the subject of allocation of jurisdiction over the internal affairs of vessels to consular officers are those which provide for judicial assistance to foreign consuls in the carrying out of their treaty related authority.[85] Perhaps the implication of this is that Congress recognizes no consular authority over those matters unless they are guaranteed by treaty. At any rate, there would be no statutory authority for the federal courts to lend assistance to a foreign consul in absense of such a treaty with his state.

[81] 22 C.F.R. 83.5; 7 *Foreign Affairs Manual* § 532. 1.

[82] 22 C.F.R. 83.6; 7 *Foreign Affairs Manual* § 53 2.2.

[83] 22 C.F.R. § 83.8 (b); 7 *Foreign Affairs Manual* 533. 2–2. The reference to "diplomatic" representatives having authority in these matters is to recognize the fact that diplomatic officers sometimes perform consular duties and that the consuls are generally under the administrative control of the embassy.

[84] 7 *Foreign Affairs Manual* § 534. 2–2.

[85] 22 U.S.C. 256, 257, 258, 258a; R.S. 4079, 4080, 4081 (1878), 36 Stat. 1163.

There are other statutes which authorize United States consuls abroad to assume rather broad powers over disputes on board United States vessels within their districts. However, none deals directly with the question of whether the consul performs these duties as of right or merely by sufferance.[86]

CRIMINAL JURISDICTION

Treaty Provisions

It will be recalled that most treaties pertaining to the subject of consular authority to which the United States is a party include clauses which draw the line between local and flag state authority in such a way that controversies arising out of the internal order of the vessel are left to the flag state, and all others are subject to the primary jurisdiction of the territorial authorities. In all cases which are allocated primarily to one or the other, however, the authority can be surrendered or deferred to the state having secondary authority. This is not likely to happen in any situation where a United States consular officer has primary jurisdiction by virtue of a treaty provision.[87]

Many of these treaties go on to define what types of criminal acts are included within the general category described as "internal" to the vessel. The treaty of 1951 with the United Kingdom provides a good example of this type of treaty clause.[88]

> (1) Except at the request or with the consent of the consular officer, the administrative authorities of the territory shall not concern themselves with any matter concerning the internal management of the vessel. The judicial authorities ... may, however, exercise any jurisdiction ... [they] possess under the law ... with regard to disputes as to wages and contracts of service .... The administrative and judicial authorities will not interfere with the detention in custody on the vessel ... for disciplinary offenses, provided ... lawful under the law of the sending state and not accompanied by unjustifiable severity or inhumanity.
>
> (2) Without prejudice to the right of ... [local] authorities ... to take cognizance of crimes or offenses ... on board ... in the ports or in the territorial waters ... and which are cognizable under the local law or to enforce local laws applicable to vessels ... it is the common intention ... that ... [local] authorities ... should not, except at the request or with the consent of the consular officer,

[86] The statutes referred to will be considered in detail *post.*

[87] See *supra* p. 146.

[88] TIAS 2494, 3 USTIAS 3426.

(a) concern themselves with any matter ... on board ... unless for the preservation of peace and order or in the interests of public health or safety, or

(b) institute prosecutions in respect of crimes or offenses ... on board ... unless ... of a serious character or involve the tranquillity of the port or ... committed by or against persons other than the crew.[89]

It seems that the negotiators of this treaty intentionally created an ambiguity regarding the extent of of consular authority. The term "should not" concern themselves with the matters defined in subdivision (a) or institute prosecution in the situation set forth in subdivision (b) accomplishes that objective admirably, particularly when coupled with "shall not" used in the general provision in paragraph (1). The question is, is it a treaty violation if local authorities do in fact take jurisdiction of a controversy internal in every way to the vessel, or is it merely a violation of international etiquette or comity? Perhaps the most rational construction would be that "should not" really means "shall not". It is difficult to imagine what interest the local sovereign could have that would dictate interference under the conventionally defined circumstances.

The initial clause of paragraph (2) appears to give either local government authority to make and enforce any law to vessels of the other not only while in port but while in territorial waters. Such a meaning would be clearly inconsistent with the United Nations Convention on the Territorial Sea and Contiguous Zone.[90] On the other hand, it would be possible to construe this provision to be restricted by the contents of paragraph (1). In other words, the local establishment is authorized to determine for itself which situations on board are not exclusively internal to the vessel. Such a construction would place a duty upon them to make a determination, incident to the law making process, that a particular rule does not interfere in purely internal matters. The question then would be whether they acted in good faith in prescribing and enforcing the rule in question, or whether such determination could not have been made because clearly without factual basis.

Unless it be assumed that the parties intended to assume no obligations under this article, the construction suggested in the preceding paragraph is the only one entitled to serious consideration. The territorial authorities would then be precluded from interfering with any matter

[89] Art. 22, *id.* at 3443. Identical provisions are found in the treaty of 1950–1952 with Ireland. TIAS 2984, Art. 23, 5 USTIAS 949, 992–995.

[90] Ch. IV, pp. 112 *et seq.*

which, according to their own good faith and rationally founded determination, was purely internal.

The provisions of subdivisions (a) and (b), then, refine the definition of acts internal to the vessel, permitting interference for the "preservation of peace and order", to protect the "public health or safety", to prosecute for "crimes or offenses ... of a serious character" or "involve the tranquillity of the port" or are "committed by or against persons other then the crew."

The protocol to the treaty of 1958 with Muscat and Oman [91] provides that local authorities may "take cognizance of crimes or offenses which disturb the peace of the port" and "enforce the laws of the receiving state applicable to vessels of any state in its ports and territorial waters".[92]

The term "peace of the port" is the equivalent of "the tranquillity of the port" used in the treaty with the United Kingdom. The problem also exists here of whether the local government can arbitrarily determine the rules applicable on foreign vessels in its ports and territorial waters. At least with regard to territorial waters, such an interpretation is not to be favored because inconsistent with the United Nations Convention on the Territorial Sea and Contiguous Zone.[93] Although there is in this treaty no equivalent of paragraph (1) of the United Kingdom treaty, there seems to be no reason why the protocol should not be construed in a like manner.

The Consular Convention of 1948 with Costa Rica provides as the only refinement of the consul's exclusive authority over the internal affairs of vessels of his state's nationality that he shall not

> except as permitted by the laws of the receiving state, exercise jurisdiction in any case involving an offense committed on board a merchant vessel of the sending state, which offense would be punishable under the law of the receiving state by a sentence of imprisonment for a period of at least one year, or by penalties in excess thereof.[94]

This clause apparently places it in the authority of the receiving state to determine in which types of situations it will intervene. The local government need only make that class of acts punishable by imprisonment for a period in excess of one year. It thus accomplishes an ob-

[91] TIAS 4530, 11 USTIAS 1835.
[92] *Id.* at 1843–1844.
[93] *Supra* note 90.
[94] Art. X2., TIAS 2045, 1 USTIAS 247, 272.

jective which could logically flow from construction of the "peace of the port" doctrine.[95] In this treaty too, however, there is a latent ambiguity. The first paragraph of the same article commences by conferring upon the consul "the right to exercise exclusive jurisdiction over controversies arising out of the internal order of merchant vessels of the sending state" "except as herinafter provided". The question is whether it is reasonable to assume that the parties really intended that that provision could be completely nullified by the receiving state's arbitrarily classifying any act as criminal and punishable by imprisonment for a period in excess of one year? If not, it should be construed similarly to the United Kingdom treaty.

In 1923 the United States concluded a consular convention with Germany which provided that the consular officer would have

> exclusive jurisdiction over controversies arising out of the internal order of private vessels of his country, and shall alone exercise jurisdiction in cases, wherever arising, between officers and crews, pertaining to the enforcement of discipline on board ....
>
> When an act ... constitutes a crime according to the laws of that [local] State, subjecting the person guilty thereof to punishment as a criminal, the consular officer shall not exercise jurisdiction except insofar as he is permitted to do so by local law.[96]

It will be noted that in this provision, too, it is apparently within the contractual right of a party to determine in what types of situation it will be empowered to assert criminal jurisdiction on board. In these treaties, this can be done, it would seem, by designating the activity as a "crime".

Prior to the German treaty of 1923, United States consular conventions followed two general forms, one of which gave the consul exclusive charge of the internal order of merchant vessels, without reservation, and the other of which refined this by reserving for the local authorities situations which might disturb the peace of the port or in which persons not members of the ship's crew were involved. An

[95] See Ch. IV, p. 125.

[96] Art. XXIII, 44 Stat. 2132, 2152–2153, preserved by Art. XXVIII of treaty of 1954, 7 TIAS 1839, 1867. Similar provisions were incorporated into treaties with Cuba, 1925, Art. XII, 44 Stat. 2471, 2477–2478 (except that there is no like provision envisaging the possibility that local law may permit consular jurisdiction even in case of serious crimes.); Honduras, 1927, Art. XXII, 45 Stat. 2618, 2635; Latvia, 1928, Art. XXIII, 45 Stat. 2641, 2649–2650; El Salvador, 1926, Art. XXI, 46 Stat. 2817, 2833–2834; Norway, 1928, Art. XXII, 47 Stat. 2135, 2152–2153; Poland, 1931, Art. XXV, 48 Stat. 1507, 1530–1531; Finland, 1934, Art. XXV, 49 Stat. 2659, 2677–2678; Liberia, 1938, Art. X, 54 Stat. 1739, 1756–1757; Mexico, 1942, Art. X, 57 Stat. 800, 812–813–814 (except does not exclude local jurisdiction); Philippines, 1947, Art. XI, 62 Stat. 1593, 1599–1600.

example of the former was the treaty of 1853 with France. The provision there was as sfollows:

> ...consuls ... shall have exclusive charge of the internal order of the merchant vessels of their nation, and shall alone take cognizance of differences which may arise, either at sea or in port, between the captain, officers, and crew, without exception .... The local authorities shall not, on any pretext, interfere in these differences ....[97]

The latter group stated that the

> ... consuls ... shall have exclusive charge of the internal order of the merchant-vessels of their nation, and shall have the exclusive power to take cognizance of and to determine differences of every kind which may arise, either at sea or in port, between the captains, officer, and crews .... Neither any court or authority shall, on any pretext, interfere in these differences, except in cases where the differences on board ship are of a nature to disturb the peace and public order in port, or on shore, or when persons other than the officers and crew of the vessel are parties to the disturbance.[98]

The former provision seems to give the consul broader powers than the latter. However, in both types, the question necessarily will arise as to whether a particular act involves the internal order of the vessel. The latter clause merely attempts to clarify the distinction between those acts which are and those which are not restricted to the vessel and its crew. Probably both would be construed to have the same effect.

It is apparent from a comparison of the earlier treaty clauses with those concluded more recently that there is a trend toward language which tends to diminish the authority of the consul or at least creates ambiguity as to his powers. The use of language which appears to place it in the power of the local government to restrict his authority by legislation expressly applicable on board foreign vessels, or defining acts as of a class subjected by the treaty to local control, at least creates an additional ambiguity and gives a state which is intent upon

[97] Art. VIII, 10 Stat. 992, 996. Similar clauses will be found in the conventions with Italy, 1868, Art. XI, 15 Stat. 605, 609–610; Belgium, 1868, Art. XI, 16 Stat. 757, 761; and the Austro-Hungarian Monarchy, 1870, Art. XI, 17 Stat. 821, 827–828.

[98] Treaty with Germany of 1871, Art. XIII, 17 Stat. 921, 928. Similar provisions are found in the treaties with New Granada, 1850, Art. III, 8, 10 Stat. 900, 903 (except that it does not use the term "exclusive"); Salvador, 1870, Art. 33rd 8th, 18 Stat. 725, 743–744 (also gives consul exclusive jurisdiction when a national of sending state not a crew member is involved); The Netherlands, 1878, Art. XI, 21 Stat. 662, 668; Italy, 1878, Art. XI, 20 Stat. 725, 729–730; Belgium, 1880, Art. XI, 21 Stat. 776, 781; Italy, 1881, Art. I, 22 Stat. 831, 832; Roumania, 1881, Art. XI, 23 Stat. 711, 714; Spain, 1902, Art, XXIII, 33 Stat. 2105, 2116–2117; Greece, 1902, Art. XII, 33 Stat. 2122, 2129; Sweden, 1910, Art. XI, 37 Stat. 1479, 1485.

vitiating the effect of the treaty clauses an argument to strengthen its claim to legality.

Customary International Law

Whether treaty provisions allocating to the consular officer authority over matters internal to vessels of his state are a codification of customary international law or by their universality have effected the development of a customary rule, the right is generally treated as being part of general international law.[99]

The courts of the United States have from time to time, in situations where no treaty provision was involved, assumed that the dividing line between local and consular authority lay between conduct which did and that which did not affect the peace of the port. In *Murphy v. New York & Cuba S.S. Co.*,[100] the court held that a passenger who was leaving an American vessel in a Cuban port was not a "member of the ship's company" amongst whom "internal discipline is a matter for the law of the sovereignty of the ship." [101] The inference is that if the passenger had not been leaving the vessel, the controversy [102] should have been subject to the authority of United States officials.[103]

The language in *Wildenhus's Case* [104] clearly shows that that court, although dealing with a controversy governed by a treaty containing a typical jurisdiction allocation provision,[105] assumed the existence of a similar customary rule:

> From experience, however, it was found long ago that it would be beneficial to commerce if the local government would abstain from interfering with the internal discipline of the ship, and the general regulation of the rights and duties of the officers and crew towards the vessel or among themselves. And so by comity it came to be generally understood among civilized nations that all matters of discipline and all things done on board which affected only the vessel or those belonging to her, and did not involve the peace or dignity of the

[99] See Colombos, *The International Law of the Sea* 294 *et seq.* (1962); I Hyde, *International Law, Chiefly as Interpreted and Applied by the United States* 396–397 (1922).

[100] 273 Fed. 305 (C.A.D.C. 1921).

[101] *Id.* at 310. There was no treaty jurisdictional provision.

[102] Being between two passengers as to whether one had stolen something from the other.

[103] The statement of the court was dicta, since it merely supported the court's holding that the passenger was not entitled to recover from the shipowner upon the theory that the captain was obliged to intervene with the local authorities and prevent them from exercising jurisdiction over the plaintiff. The court held that the captain had done all that could reasonably be expected under the circumstances, and at any rate a passenger leaving a vessel was not a member of the ship's company entitled to the benefit of the rule.

[104] 120 U.S. 1 (1887).

[105] Treaty with Belgium, 1880, Art. XI, 21 Stat. 776, 781.

country, or the tranquillity of the port, should be left by the local government to be dealt with by the authorities of the nation to which the vessel belonged as the laws of that nation or the interests of its commerce should require. But if crimes are committed on board of a character to disturb the peace and tranquillity of the country to which the vessel has been brought, the offenders have never by comity or usage been entitled to any exemption from the operation of the local laws for their punishment, if the local tribunals see fit to assert their authority.[106]

It will be noted that the court attributed the usage described to "comity" rather than a binding rule of international law. This has rather consistently been the position of governmental authorities in the United States, the theory being that since a sovereign has the right arbitrarily to exclude foreign vessels from its ports, it is a necessary corollary that it also has the right to impose any conditions it wishes upon the permission to enter.[107] In *Patterson* the Court stated that there was "implied consent" to consular control over internal matters which arose out of admission of the vessel without contrary conditions being imposed.[108] In *Cunard S.S. Co. v. Mellon* [109] the Court, in refusing to enjoin enforcement of the criminal sactions of the prohibition laws against foreign vessels in United States ports, expressly stated that any exemption from local jurisdiction over the internal affairs of a vessel rested solely in the discretion of the territorial sovereign.[110]

In view of commonly used treaty provisions requiring mutual admission of vessels upon the basis of national and most-favored-nation treatment [111] and the numerous most-favored-nation clauses which carry their effect even further afield in international relations, in very few situations would any state have truly arbitrary right to exclude or condition the right of entry of foreign vessels. Any such authority would be limited by rights granted other states and even by international custom and usage.[112] At any rate, whether by law, comity or usage, matters internal to the vessel will generally be conceded by local authorities to the consular authority.

It is difficult to determine whether the State Department attributes the rule exempting internal affairs of merchant vessels from local

[106] *Supra* note 104 at 12.
[107] *See Patterson v. Bark Eudora*, 190 U.S. 169, 178 (1903).
[108] *Id.*
[109] 262 U.S. 100 (1923).
[110] *Id.* at 124. The Court cited with approval the language in *Patterson, supra* note 108, recognizing an unlimited local jurisdiction over foreign vessels in port and ascribing the exemptions normally accorded them to comity.
[111] *E.g.*, Art. XIX 3, treaty of 1951 with Israel, TIAS 2948, 5 USTIAS 550, 570.
[112] See *supra*, p. 144.

authority to comity or to a customary legal rule. In response to a general abstract question addressed to the Department by the British Ambassador, the reply was clearly framed in terms of comity.[113] However, the Department has protested the exercise of jurisdiction over controversies of this kind in terms implying a binding rule of international law.[114] In this case, the protest was made to Great Britain, with which nation there was no controlling treaty law.[115] The current Foreign Affairs Manual places the restriction on local authority squarely on the basis of comity.[116] At any rate, the Department has been consistent in its position that the existence of the rule or usage does not depend upon a pertinent treaty provision.[117]

The only United States legislation which directly relates to the question of consular authority over seamen on vessels of their states refers only to such rights guaranteed by treaty.[118]

Definition of the Consul's Area of Competence

Whether the problem of the limits on consular authority over criminal acts on board vessels of his state depends upon treaty, custom and usage or comity, it will be necessary to determine the types of acts over which he is likely to exercise authority. There are few treaties which go any further than a general statement to the effect that internal matters are exclusively within his cognizance.[119] The problem dealt with in this section, therefore, is the definition of the types of acts which do or do not "affect the peace of the port" and therefore come within the primary jurisdiction of local authorities.[120]

It will be recalled that some treaties refine the limits of consular authority over criminal acts somewhat more definitively that others by stating that if its effects reach the shore or it involves a person not a

[113] II Hackworth, *Digest of International Law* 209; see also the Ass't Sec. of State (Carr) to the Atty. Gen., Nov. 24, 1926, MS Dept. of State, file 195.8/813.

[114] See Mr. Fish, Sec. of State, to Mr. Schenck, March 12, 1875, II Moore, *Digest of International Law* 295–297.

[115] See also Acting Sec. of State (Wilson) to Ambassador Dudley, Nov. 4, 1909, MS. Dept. of State, file 17753/3, II Hackworth, *Digest of International Law* 217–218, also a situation involving a state with which no controlling treaty existed.

[116] Vol. 7, § 533.2–2.

[117] If a treaty provision did exist on the subject, it would of course be the controlling law between the parties.

[118] 22 U.S.C. 256–258a, R.S. §§ 4079–4081, 36 Stat. 1163.

[119] See *supra* at p. 147 *et seq.*

[120] It should be recalled initially that if the act occurred anywhere else except in the territorial or inland waters of the state where the vessel is located, the local authorities will probably have no authority over the perpetrator regardless of the nature of the act. See Chapter IV at p. 114.

member of the ship's crew, local authorities may intervene.[121] Even in absence of such a treaty provision, those acts would not be internal to the vessel and are therefore not within the primary authority of the consul. Thus, the question resolves itself to a defining of the types of acts which although strictly localized on the vessel, are of such a nature that mere knowledge by the local populace of their occurrence would tend to disturb their tranquillity.

Perhaps the first question should be whether actual knowledge ashore of acts on board which are likely to cause disturbance of the local tranquillity is necessary to justify interference by local authorities. The problem would of course not even arise if someone ashore did not learn of the act. However, if the knowledge were restricted to law enforcement officers, it surely would not follow that any disturbance is likely to result. The problem was posed in *Wildenhus's Case* [122] and decided in favor of local jurisdiction even when the circumstances were such that actual knowledge ashore was highly improbable. In that case the act (homicide) occurred below decks, and although no disturbance ensued ashore and none was probable, the court held that the local authorities acted properly in prosecuting the perpetrator.[123] The converse is that the mere fact of local knowledge of the occurrence of an inconsequential crime internal to a ship will not justify the exercise of local jurisdiction.[124]

As for the type of act which by its nature "involves the peace of the port", *Wildenhus's Case* [125] set one of the extremes. A charge of murder was held within local jurisdiction.[126] The Department of State has taken the position that a charge of manslaughter committed on board an American vessel in a Mexican port also involves the peace of the

[121] *Supra* at pp. 147–148.

[122] *Supra* note 104.

[123] "It is not alone the publicity of the act, or the noise and clamor which attends it, that fixes the nature of the crime, but the act itself. If that is of a character to awaken public interest when it becomes known, it is a 'disorder' the nature of which is to affect the community at large, and consequently to invoke the power of the local government whose people have been disturbed by what was done." *Id.* at 18. The State Department has taken a similar position: "[T]he killing of one human being by another was 'a disorder of such a nature as to cause, or be likely to cause a breach of the peace or serious trouble in the port or on shore.'" Sec. Knox to Minister Riano, no. 22, Dec. 7, 1910, MS. Dept. of State, file 711.5211/–, II Hackworth, *Digest of International Law* 211–212.

[124] See *Ex parte Anderson*, 184 Fed. 114 (D.Me. 1910), involving physical chastisement of a crew member by an officer on the dock.

[125] *Supra* note 104.

[126] In a similar situation, the Supreme Court of Mexico declined local jurisdiction. *Case of Antoni*, Hudson, *Cases and other Materials on International Law* 630 (1929).

port.[127] This case is significant, since Mexico had already evinced her willingness to surrender the man to the jurisdiction of the United States. The State Department is avowedly interested in securing the exercise of United States jurisdiction over all possible situations occurring on board American vessels even in foreign ports.[128] However, when it came to the necessity of securing such exercise by conceding that manslaughter did not involve the peace of the port, they were not prepared to set such a precedent.

At the other end of the spectrum, a theft on board ship by one member of the ship's company from another apparently does not involve the peace of the port.[129] Nor would an assault, at least one that did not result in very serious injuries, even though succeeded by imprisonment on board of the victim.[130] As for assaults of a more serious nature, the State Department on one occasion instructed a United States consul to request of French officials that an assailant be surrendered to United States jurisdiction if the assault – a shooting on board resulting in the serious wounding of the master of an American ship – was not of such a nature as to disturb the peace of the port. The man was turned over to the consul and returned by him to the United States for trial.[131] Apparently, the Department and French authorities were able to agree that even an assault with such serious consequences need not by its very nature involve the peace of the port.[132] A problem not posed the particular situation was whether the result might have been different had the matter actually been known amongst the local populace. The French authorities, at least, would probably consider this to be an immaterial consideration. They had previously declined jurisdiction in two cases of assault by American seamen on board their own vessels, one of which resulted in a "severe wound". In both cases, both the American consul and local authorities claimed exclusive jurisdiction; and in both the consular authority was sustained by the French appellate court.[133] The State Department took a similar stand

[127] Acting Sec. of State (Wilson) to the Mexican Ambassador (Crespo), no. 29, Aug. 31, 1911, MS. Dept. of State, file 812.858, II Hackworth, *Digest of International Law* 219–220.

[128] 7 *Foreign Affairs Manual* (1961) §§ 534.2–1, 534.2–2.

[129] *See Murphy v. New York & Cuba Mail S.S. Co.*, 273 Fed. 305 (C.A.D.C. 1921).

[130] *Ex parte Anderson*, 184 Fed. 114 (D. Me. 1910).

[131] The Acting Sec. of State (Polk) to Consul Wallace, May 8, 1919, MS. Dept. of State, file 195.8/158, II Hackworth, *Digest of International Law* 212.

[132] Whether the result was accomplished by comity or by international law is not clear. However, the instruction to the consul suggested that his request be directed to the discretion of the French authorities. That would appear to be consistent with the United States position that all surrenders of jurisdiction by local authorities are discretionary and therefore result from considerations of comity rather than law.

[133] Wheaton, *Elements of International Law* 153–154 (3rd ed. 1846).

vis-à-vis Mexico in a situation involving an assault which resulted in hospitalization ashore of the victim. The action of the consul in successfully requesting jurisdiction was approved.[134] In that case, since the man was hospitalized ashore, there was clearly knowledge ashore of the act complained of. Nevertheless, it was held to be within the jurisdiction of the consul because not disturbing the peace of the port.

A fact situation with a curious twist was involved in *The Wind.*[135] That case involved a taking and holding, by members of one union to the exclusion of another, of a Norwegian vessel by force inconsistently with the wishes of the owner-libellant. He had previously sought and procured an adjudication by the Norwegian consul at Philadelphia ordering the crew to leave the vessel. This order could not be enforced by the local courts because of a peculiarity of United States law.[136] Libellant, therefore, with the blessings of the consul sought an order of the United States District Court giving it possession of the ship. The defense was that the court had no jurisdiction because of the treaty provision giving "exclusive jurisdiction" to the consul. The majority agreed with the respondents that the court had no jurisdiction to grant the remedy. This, then, amounts to a holding that this type of non-violent mutiny is a controversy "arising out of the internal order" of the vessel, and inferentially at least, does not affect the peace of the port.[137]

In a case involving mutiny on board an American ship in a Mexican port by seamen of Mexican nationality, in which the local authorities insisted upon the right to prosecute, the State Department was successful in convinving the Mexican officials that the offense did not involve the tranquillity of the port, and therefore that United States officials should have jurisdiction. The Department stated that even if members of the ship's company were injured as a result of the mutiny,

[134] Director of Consular Affairs (Carr) to Mr. Hostetter, Mar. 6, 1911, M.S. Dept. of State, file 195.8/5, IV Hackworth, *Digest of International Law* 880.

[135] 22 F. Supp. 883 (E.D. Pa. 1938).

[136] Judicial assistance could only be granted to consular officers of states which reciprocally offered the same to the United States. *Id.* at 885. 22 U.S.C. 256 *et seq.*, R.S. 4079–4081.

[137] It is submitted that the dissenting opinion was sound on the question of the effect of the treaty provision in question. Judge Dickenson held that, even conceding that this was a matter arising out of the internal economy of the ship, the term "exclusive jurisdiction" really meant primary jurisdiction. The United States, he insisted, retained secondary jurisdiction which it could exercise with the consent or upon the request of the consul. *Id.* at 885–886. In Petition of Georgakopoulos, 81 F. Supp. 411 (E.D. Pa 1948), the court held that a similar situation was one within the "exclusive charge" of the Consul of Greece under the treaty with that state, and therefore that it would enforce his award against the seamen. Greece had reciprocal judicial assistance provision, so the United States court was statutorily authorized to enforce his decree. 22 U.S.C. 256, R.S. 4079.

it would not follow that it was of a nature to disturb the peace of the port.[138]

Possessory offenses as defined by local law, committed on board a foreign ship in port should not, it is submitted, be considered of a nature likely to disturb the peace of the port. However, in narcotics cases at least, the State Department has taken the position *vis-à-vis* Germany that the local courts do have primary jurisdiction.[139] Narcotics possession, of course, presents a special problem not common to all possessory crimes. The manufacture and traffic in narcotic drugs has been subjected to international conventional control.[140] Since, presumably, Germany is as much interested in preventing illicit traffic in narcotics as is the United States – both countries being party to the convention – it would appear that both should seek the most expeditious means of suppressing it. As a general rule, the most effective way would be for local authorities to exercise their jurisdiction to the fullest, even on vessels of other states. The interest in a free flow of commerce is in this type of situation balanced by the same vital international interest that produced the convention, namely the suppression of the very type of act involved. Although this type of act has not become an international crime of the piracy type, there is sufficient analogy to justify the action of the United States authorities in this matter.

There is sufficient analogical justification for the distinction between possession of narcotics and other possessory crimes in the United Nations Convention on the Territorial Sea and the Contiguous Zone. The littoral state is authorized to exercise its criminal enforcement jurisdiction on board a vessel in innocent passage through its territorial sea when "necessary for the suppression of illicit traffic in narcotic drugs." [141] This is the only crime which is specifically excepted from the general exclusion of such vessel from local action. If that action is justified on a vessel passing through in innocent passage, how much more justified when the vessel is in port and will therefore probably not be delayed by the action.

Possession of a weapon, for example, without a license inconsistently with a local penal statute, it is submitted, is not at all similar to posses-

[138] 1921, MS. Dept. of State, file 196.32/294, 196.32/322, IV Hackworth, *Digest of International Law* 880.

[139] 1922, MS. Dept. of State, file 311. 6221, II Hackworth, *Digest of International Law* 223.

[140] Multilateral convention of 1912, 8 *L.N.T.S.* 187; Convention of 1925 on Traffic in Opium and Drugs, III Hudson, *International Legislation* 1589; Convention of 1931 on Narcotic Drugs, 48 Stat. 1543.

[141] Art. 19, 1. (d), U.N. Doc. A/CONF. 13/L. 52.

sion of narcotics. There is no widely effective international convention in force for suppression of traffic in such implements, and there certainly is no international consensus that their possession is an evil *per se*. It is submitted that such possessory acts generally should be considered as involving the internal economy of the vessel and therefore should be left to the consular authority. The United States Supreme Court has come down squarely against this proposition in *Cunard S.S. Co. v. Mellon*,[142] involving possession of alcohol on board foreign vessels in American ports inconsistently with the prohibition laws. In that case, however, the Supreme Court was faced with enforcement of a statute duly enacted by Congress which was clearly applicable on board ships of foreign registration in United States waters. It did not constitute a conclusion by the Court that the statute was consistent with international law or usage, although there is language subject to that interpretation.[143]

Closely related to the question of possession of narcotics is that of their use. It would seem to follow as a matter of course that if the local authorities are justified in exercising jurisdiction over their possession, they are also warranted in prosecuting for their use. The Supreme Court of the Philippines has so held.[144] In *United States v. Look Chaw*,[145] the same Court in dicta said that mere possession of prohibited narcotics would not be within local jurisdiction. However, the use of narcotics has not been subjected to international conventional control as has the traffic, including of necessity possession. Therefore, perhaps there is not as cogent a reason for exercise of jurisdiction by the local authorities. It is clear that there should be, in common sense, a less vital interest in the use of narcotics on board than in their possession for possible trafficing. The use is less likely to have an effect ashore than is the trafficing. However, it is doubtful that United States authorities would readily admit that this is a matter which should be left to the authority of the flag state, particularly in view of the uniformly severe treatment of narcotics offenses – including use – in the various jurisdictions of the United States.

An occasional treaty will contain a provision precluding local interference with detention of seamen on board for disciplinary infractions.[146]

142 262 U.S. 100 (1923).
143 *Id.* at 125 *et seq.*
144 *People v. Wong Cheng*, 46 Phil. 729 (1922).
145 18 Phil. 573 (1910).
146 Convention on Consular Officers with the United Kingdom, 1951, Art. 22 (1), TIAS 2494, 3 USTIAS 3426, 3444; Ireland, 1950–1952, Art. 23, TIAS 2984, 5 USTIAS 949, 992–995.

Others require that the consul be granted assistance by the local authorities in the performing of his functions.[147] Some expressly require the arrest of seamen by local officers on demand of the consul.[148] Statutes of the United States provide for imprisonment of seamen at the request of a consul in order to effectuate his decision, made pursuant to a treaty with the United States, provided certain prerequisites may be shown.[149] Others authorize United States Consuls to seek local assistance in like circumstances abroad when they see fit.[150] All of these provisions involve different aspects of the same problem, namely the right or restriction upon the right of local authorities to interfere in the detention on board of a seaman while the vessel is in port.

The biggest percentage of United States treaties dealing with problems of consular authority do not contain any express provision on the question either of local assistance to the consul in confining the seaman or of refraining from interference with such confinement. However, a large number of them do, as discussed previously, include provisions giving the consul authority over the internal affairs of the vessel; and customary international law appears to accomplish the same result in absence of treaty. The question, then, is whether there is a duty on the part of local authorities not to interfere with disciplinary detention of seamen on board, and if so, the definition of that duty.

Assuming initially the right of the consul in all cases, either as a matter of customary international law or as a matter of comity or usage, to control matters of internal discipline on board, it would seem to follow as a matter of course that there is a concomitant reciprocal duty on the part of the host state to respect that right and all its incidents, including disciplinary detention.[151]

Whether it also involves a reciprocal duty to give assistance in arresting and detaining the man is a more difficult question. The United States judicial assistance statute [152] is expressly limited in its scope not only to states with which the United States has a treaty which obligates local authorities to grant assistance, but is further restricted to states within that class which have been designated by

[147] See, *e.g.*, Treaty of 1951 with Greece, Art. XXII (5), TIAS 3057, 5 USTIAS 1829, 1897–1899; Treaty of 1923 with Germany, Art. XXIII, 44 Stat. 2132, 2152–2153.

[148] *E.g.*, Treaty of 1878 with Italy, Art. XI, 20 Stat. 725, 729–730.

[149] 22 U.S.C. 258a, 36 Stat. 1163.

[150] 46 U.S.C. 703, 38 Stat. 1167.

[151] The Acting Sec. of State, (Wilson) to Ambassador Dudley, Nov. 4, 1909, MS. Dept. of State, file 17753/3, II Hackworth, *Digest of International Law* 218.

[152] 22 U.S.C. 258a, 36 Stat. 1163.

the President as having provided reciprocal legislation benefitting the United States.[153] In other situations, the federal courts would have no statutory authority to grant aid to the consul in carrying out his functions. If the application for assistance were made to federal executive officers, they would probably have to decline because the same statute implicitly precludes them from acting.

If state authorities were to intervene and give assistance to the consul, this would raise serious constitutional questions as to the legitimacy of state action in an area of federal supremacy where Congress has preempted the area. In *Dallemagne v. Moisan*,[154] the arrest was made by state police on the request of the French consul. On *habeas corpus*, the seaman claimed his discharge on the ground that the arrest violated California law and that it was impermissible because Congress had pre-empted the field from state authority by passing the judicial assistance statute. The Court held that California law had not been violated, but agreed that the arrest was invalid on the second ground. However, the discharge was not granted because the *habeas corpus* application was made to the very court [155] which had jurisdiction under the federal act to grant the assistance improperly requested of the state authorities. Thus, since France had provided effective legal machinery to effectuate United States consular decisions (the vessel flying the French flag), the defect in the arrest could be corrected by that court and the confinement continued legally. Presumably, if the application had been made to any other court, the relief must have been granted, since the defect could not be corrected in that court. Seamen should henceforth seek discharge in *habeas corpus* by application to the courts of the state where they are being held.

Failing applicability of the federal judicial assistance statute, therefore, no one in the United States has a legal right to arrest or detain a seaman at the request of a consular officer. Thus, we have the difficult situation of the consul having the right to arrest and imprison the man on board but possibly not the effective power to do so.

The limits to the right of the consul to imprison on board correspond with the limits of the duty of local authorities not to interfere with his action. The limits of his authority are generally defined by the requirement that the situation with which he is dealing must concern

[153] A question of the operation of this statute in a problem context may be seen in *The Wind*, 22 F. Supp. 883 (E.D. Pa. 1938).

[154] 197 U.S. 169 (1905).

[155] United States District Court.

the internal order of the vessel. The problem is to reduce this general limitation to more specific dimensions. This may be considered by reference to the kind of act or situation which resulted in the confinement, the nature of the confinement, and who has the right to determine the limits in the first two classifications.

The situations in which the consul has exclusive authority to confine are limited in the same way that his authority generally is limited. If no effect external to the ship results from the act, the matter is within his primary competence. Thus, it must involve only members of the ship's company and must include no act of a nature which threatens the peace of the port. Of course, if the local authorities do not claim jurisdiction, or if they waive it on request of the consul, he would have authority to confine on board either as punishment or as a means of preventing the seaman's escape pending the vessel's departure.

As for the limitations upon the methods and incidents of imprisonment, this would depend upon whether they are of a nature which is likely to disturb the tranquillity of the populace if they should come to the notice of people ashore. In other words, the consul too is not permitted to "disturb the peace of the port" even for the purpose of maintaining order on board. The treaty with the United Kingdom expresses this restriction "... [local] authorities will not interfere ... [with the detention] provided ... lawful under the law of the sending state and is not accompanied by unjustifiable severity or inhumanity.[156] Even in absence of such a provision, however, there can be no doubt that the consul must not violate humanitarian standards by his actions controlling the internal affairs of a vessel. The question is, by whose standards is this to be judged, those of the local populace or those of the consul and his state; and who will make the determination, local authorities or the consul?

Since the question is whether a particular act of the consul in detaining a seaman is likely to disturb the tranquillity of the port, this must depend upon the sensitivity of the local populace to any method chosen. This determines the upper limits of severity which is available to him in dealing with any situation. No objection could be raised that his methods are too mild, since this could not jeopardize local tranquillity provided the offender was not likely to escape and do harm ashore.

It would seem to follow that it should not be within the province of

[156] *Supra* at note 89.

the consul to determine whether a particular situation is one under his authority, or a particular method of restraint violative of social mores. Of course, he will in the nature of things make an initial determination when called upon to act by the ship's officers. However, he would presumably refuse to act in the first place if he thought it was beyond his authority. In addition, once the question of his authority is raised, it is clear that local judicial authorities are more competent to determine whether local feelings are likely to be outraged by an act either of the seaman or of the consul in dealing with him. The State Department has taken that position:

> These tribunals [state and federal courts] ... are bound ... to entertain every complaint in which is presented a *prima facie* case of violation of the local laws, and it consequently becomes necessary ... that the judge should hear the evidence before he is able to determine whether the case is one of mere discipline connected with the ship, or whether it is of such a nature as to involve a disturbance of the public order in port or on shore .... No doubt is entertained, however, but that ... their decisions [will] be always rendered with a due regard for the obligations of the Government under its treaty stipulations with foreign powers. [157] In all such cases it must necessarily be left to the local authorities whether the procedure shall take place in the United States or in Sweden, to determine if in fact there has been such disturbance of the local order or tranquillity ....[158]

Incidental to the right of the local authorities to determine whether a particular activity is likely to affect local peace and order is the right to take all reasonable steps to investigate the matter, including investigation on board the vessel.[159] Of course, the writ of *habeas corpus* is a legitimate judicial process for use in determining these facts. It is not likely to be utilized unless the detained seaman seeks judicial review of the legality of his detention. If the local authorities claim jurisdiction over an individual, the proceeding would likely be commenced by an arrest. Then, *habeas corpus* would be used not to test the legality of detention on board but of detention ashore. The question would then be whether local authorities were in violation of a provision of local or international law (possibly incorporated into and therefore a part of local law).

Questions concerning the handling of desertions from ships involve problems of consular authority, but the act concerned is one which is clearly within the primary jurisdiction of local authorities. The act is

[157] Mr. Frelinghuysen, Sec. of State, to Baron Schaeffer, Austrian min., Nov. 13, 1883, For. Rel. 1883, 30; II Moore, *Digest of International Law* 302.

[158] Mr. Evarts, Sec. of State, to Count Lewenhaupt, Swed. and Nor. min., July 30, 1880, MS. Notes to Swed. and Nor. VII 204, II Moore, *Digest of International Law* 316.

[159] See Cushing, 8 Ops. Att'y Gen. 73 (1856) and Dana's Wheaton, Section 95, note 58.

one which, in its very nature, involves an effect ashore. However, many of the earlier treaties of the United States provided for the arrest of deserters by local authorities on request of the consul. Similar provisions are still common in treaties not involving the United States.[160] This class of provision in treaties to which the United States was a party was emasculated by the Seamen's Act of 1915 which expressly forbade arrest for desertion.[161] Today, that Congressional policy has been fully implemented, modern treaties of the United States containing no such provision, nor are United States consular officers permitted to request the arrest of deserters from American ships.[162]

As indicated in Chapter II, the policy Congress effectuated by the Seamen's Act of 1915 was to encourage foreign seamen to desert in United States ports and to provide United States seamen with a relatively safe weapon in their fight for better employment conditions. Subsequently, however, a countervailing policy expressed itself in United States immigration laws. There is an obvious conflict between the policy of encouraging desertions and that of controlling immigration. Only two years after the act which was designed to encourage desertion of foreign seamen, provision was made for their possible arrest and deportation by administrative action.[163] In 1926, the whole area was codified.[164] At that time, it was provided that a report by the master of a desertion would constitute *prima facie* evidence of a failure to comply with the rules providing for detention aboard and ultimate carrying away of seamen who arrived on the vessel.[165]

Currently, United States law very adequately discourages desertions by seamen from foreign vessels in United States ports. The master or agent of the ship is required under penalty of fine to supply reports to the immigration authorities of any illegal landing by a crew member.[166] Additionally, it is made a criminal act punishable by up to $ 500 fine and six months in prison for an alien seaman to stay in the United States in excess of the time prescribed by statute.[167] That act

[160] See *e.g.*, Consular Convention of 1954, U.K. – Italy, Art. 28 (1), U.K.T.S. No. 51 of 1960.

[161] See Chapter II at p. 150.

[162] See The Director of Consular Service (Carr) to Consul General Robertson, No. 320, Nov. 7, 1917, MS. Dept. of State, file 196.3/29; II Hackworth, *Digest of International Law* 253.

[163] Act of Feb. 3, 1917, Ch. 29, Sec. 34, 39 Stat. 896. See also the Act of May 26, 1924, Ch. 190, Sec. 19 and 20, 43 Stat. 164.

[164] See 44 Stat. 141–143.

[165] Title 8, Consolidated Laws, § 167 (b), 44 Stat. 142.

[166] 8 U.S.C. 1281, 66 Stat. 219.

[167] 8 U.S.C. 1282 (c), 66 Stat. 221.

also envisages the possibility of turning the man over to the commanding officer of his vessel for deportation.[168] In view of these provisions of the immigration laws, perhaps a Congressional review of the policy precluding treaty obligations to arrest and turn over foreign seamen would be in order.

To this day there is no legal authority for a United States Consul to instigate the arrest of American seamen deserters abroad. They are in fact informed by the Foreign Affairs Manual that arrest for desertion has been forbidden by act of Congress.[169] The exclusive criminal penalty such a deserter can suffer under United States law is forfeiture of effects left on board and of wages and emoluments then earned.[170] Arrest or imprisonment not being mentioned, it would be an unauthorized act for a consular officer to seek his arrest. Of course, foreign immigration laws may have the same effect as those of the United States, and presumably the deserting seaman would in fact be arrested and returned to his vessel or otherwise placed at the disposal of the United States consul persuant to local law.

The authority of American consuls concerning desertions is set forth in the Foreign Affairs Manual.[171] He is authorized to investigate reported desertions in light of existing United States law on the subject.[172] If he determines that the master's claim of desertion is legally accurate, he is authorized to certify the master's formal statement to that effect. Otherwise, he is only permitted to authenticate the statement.[173] Presumably, such a certificate would, if in proper form and following a proper investigation, be evidence of the factual conclusions therein.[174] Authenticated copies of official records of the consul's office are admissible in evidence,[175] and if they contain otherwise admissible evidence, will be evidence to prove the facts contained in them.[176] If these records are of an official hearing and determination by the consul pursuant to law, fair and unbiased, the fact conclusions are entitled to great weight in any subsequent judicial proceeding.[177]

[168] 8 U.S.C. 1282 (b), 66 Stat. 221.

[169] Vol. 7, § 529.6.

[170] 46 U.S.C. 701, R.S. § 4596, 38 Stat. 1166.

[171] Vol. 7, § 529–529.9.

[172] *Id.* at § 529.4–1.

[173] *Id.* at § 529.4–2.

[174] *Cf. The W. F. Babcock*, 79 Fed. 92 (S.D. N.Y. 1897); rev'd on other grounds, 85 Fed. 978 (2d Cir. 1898).

[175] 28 U.S.C. 1740, 62 Stat. 947.

[176] *Cf. Suey Fong v. Dulles*, 169 F. Supp. 537 (E.D. Wis. 1958); *Nieto v. McGrath*, 108 F. Supp. 150 (S.D. Tex. 1951).

[177] *Cf. The Sachem*, 59 Fed. 790 (S.D. N.Y. 1894).

To the extent that a United States consul's action amounts to an administrative determination that the seaman is guilty of crime, the issues would probably be subject to trial *de novo* in a court before any final punishment could be inflicted. Of course, in the meantime, he may very possibly be under restraint, but this would be in the nature of remand by a magistrate after a preliminary arraignment, whether accompanied by a hearing into *prima facie* guilt or not. None of the statutes defining consular authority in the area of crimes purports to make his action a final determination of guilt. At any rate, such a statute would probably be invalid because depriving a person of life liberty or property without due process of law.[178] It appears, therefore, that such a seaman would be entitled at least to judicial review of the consular determination; and, since the statutes apparently place the consul in a purely intermediate position as regards any final determination of guilt, any court to which the question was posed would probably require a trial *de novo* of all the facts. In a situation, such as alleged desertion, where the consular determination may have civil as well as criminal effects, the court would have to review at least the criminal aspects of the matter. The problem of judicial review in civil matters will be considered *post.*

It was suggested in the proceding paragraph that the scope of judicial review in criminal matters would probably be by trial *de novo.* That suggestion is not affected by the Administrative Procedure Act.[179] Since consular authority over seamen involves the "foreign affairs function",[180] of the United States, only section 10 [181] of the Act is by its terms applicable to this type of problem. The fact that that section provides for judicial review of the decision disposes of the constitutional problem discussed in the preceding paragraphs. The question, then, is to consider the effect to be given to the consular determination in the subsequent judicial proceeding. It is submitted that the consul's determination is a criminal matter, being generally of a type analagous to police and arraignment proceedings prior to trial in regular criminal prosecutions, is not the type of determination intended to have any final effect under section 10 (e).[182] Therefore it is submitted, the courts should accord no weight whatever to the consul's decision as a decision.

[178] See *Ng Fung Ho v. White,* 259 U.S. 276, 284–285 (1922); cited with favor, *United States v. Minker,* 350 U.S. 179, 187–188 (1955).

[179] 5 U.S.C. 1001–1011, 60 Stat. 237–244 (1946).

[180] 5 U.S.C. 1003 (1), 1004 (4), 60 Stat. 238, 239.

[181] 5 U.S.C. 1009, 60 Stat. 243.

[182] 5 U.S.C. 1009 (e), 60 Stat. 243.

The facts should be determined completely anew using records of the proceeding before the consul as evidence where relevent.

CIVIL JURISDICTION

Treaty Provisions

Generally, the same type of treaty provisions which control the right of consular officers to resolve controversies involving criminal acts on board ship applies also to civil controversies. His authority in civil matters is justified by the same policy considerations as those which led to the establishment of a criminal jurisdiction. If there is no overriding local interest in the exercise of jurisdiction by local authorities, the common international interest in the free movement of commerce would require that the law of the flag state administered by an official of that state should control. Thus, it is not surprising to find the same treaty provisions controlling both types of controversies.

A typical provision which by its terms applies to both civil and criminal controversies is to be found in the treaty with Germany of 1923.[183] It provides that the consul shall have

> exclusive jurisdiction over controversies arising out of the internal order of private vessels of his country and shall alone exercise jurisdiction in cases, wherever arising, between officers and crews, pertaining to the enforcement of discipline on board ... also ... jurisdiction over issues concerning ... wages and ... contracts ... [of services] provided the local laws so permit.[183a]

The first part of this clause is clearly broad enough to relate to both types of controversies. This construction would appear to be borne out by the later language which first deals with criminal type acts and then with a particular type of civil controversy. The question might arise as to whether the mention of specific types of controversies, both civil and criminal, might not exclude by inference any other types, but such a construction would render the initial general grant of authority meaningless. At any rate, it appears that the courts are prepared to

[183] 44 Stat. 2132.

[183a] Art. XXIII, *id.* at 2152. Similar provisions are found in the treaty with Esthonia, 1925, Art. XXII, 44 Stat. 2379, 2387; Cuba, 1926, Art. XII, 44 Stat. 2471, 2477; Honduras, 1927, Art. XXII, 45 Stat. 2618, 2634; Latvia, 1928, Art. XXIII, 45 Stat. 2641, 2649; El Salvador, 1926, Art. XXI, 46 Stat. 2817, 2833; Norway, 1928, Art. XXII, 47 Stat. 2135, 2152; Poland, 1931, Art. XXV, 48 Stat. 1507, 1530; Finland, 1934, Art. XXV, 49 Stat. 2659, 2677; Liberia, 1938, Art. X, 54 Stat., 1739, 1756; Mexico, 1942, Art. X, 57 Stat. 800, 812; Philippines, 1947, Art. XI, 62 Stat. 1593, 1599.

give it its natural interpretation. In the *Koenigin Luise* [184] the court held the German treaty of 1871 applicable to a dispute between an ex-crew member of a German vessel who was suing the vessel in contract for having left him behind in Europe. Although the court might have held the treaty inapplicable because libellant was not at the time of the suit a member of the crew (and therefore it was not a dispute "between officers and crews"), it nevertheless dismissed the libel on the ground that the jurisdiction of the consul was exclusive under the treaty.[185] Such a treaty provision was also held to bar a tort action for personal injuries in a United States court.[186]

The Second Circuit Court of Appeals has held that a tort action against the American owner of a Honduran vessel is not a "controversy arising out of the internal order" of a vessel, which would be under the exclusive jurisdiction of the Honduran consul under the treaty between that state and the United States.[187] The court seemed to feel that an action against the owner of the vessel in tort could not have arisen "out of the internal order" of the vessel. It is submitted that since the injury occurred on board the vessel as a result of the alleged negligence of a fellow employee, it could not have arisen out of anything else. The court devotes only two sentences to this point [188] and cites *Uravic v. Jarka* [189] as authority. That case involved an American longshoreman working on board a German vessel in New York harbor. Since he was not a member of the ship's company, it was clearly a case not solely involving the internal order of the ship. Therefore, the case has no applicability to the proposition for which it was cited. The Supreme Court itself recognizes this distintion in the last paragraph of its decision:

> If it should appear that, by valid contract or special circumstances, seamen on a foreign ship should not be protected by the statute, it will be time enough to consider the exception when it is presented.[190]

[184] 184 Fed. 170 (D. N.J. 1910).

[185] *Cf. The Neck*, 138 Fed. 144 (W.D. Wash. 1905). It is true that the *Koenigin Luise* construed the treaty of 1871 rather than the one currently in force with Germany. However, the only material difference for the purpose of this discussion is that the old treaty did not reserve primary jurisdiction to the local courts in cases of wage and contract disputes as does the current one.

[186] *The Welhaven*, 55 Fed. 80 (S.D. Ala. 1892); *The Ester*, 190 Fed. 216 (E.D. S.C. 1911). The fact that the action was joined with one for wages is not significant, since the court declined jurisdiction as to both claims.

[187] *Gerradin v. United Fruit Company*, 60 F. 2d 927 (2d Cir. 1932); treaty at 45 Stat. 2634.

[188] *Id.* at 930.

[189] 282 U.S. 234 (1931).

[190] *Id.* at 241.

It is submitted, therefore, that language of this type in treaties applies to all civil controversies arising out of the internal order of the vessel, and not solely to those pertaining to wage and employment contract dispute.

In those situations where an American citizen is the plaintiff, although the treaty provision is properly construed as nevertheless conferring jurisdiction on the consul, some courts have taken the position that its implementation to deprive an American citizen of a decision by an American court would be unconstitutional.[191] The argument runs that the Constitution of the United States confers upon the federal government exclusive authority over all cases of admiralty and maritime jurisdiction.[192] If the federal courts' jurisdiction is exclusive, it follows that no other forum can decide the matter, including a consular officer of a foreign state. Other courts have held that such provisions are not unconstitutional even when applied to American seamen.[193]

It is probably true that the constitutional provision referred to was intended merely to allocate governmental powers as between the states and the federal government.[194] Certainly, its language is not such as to exclude even state court jurisdiction. The pertinent language is "The judicial Power [of the United States] *shall extend* ... to all Cases of admiralty and maritime Jurisdiction ...." [195] That does not seem to constitute an exclusive grant of power, and Congress, shortly after the inception of the Constitution, implicitly took that position in passing an implementing statute.

> ... the district courts ... shall have, exclusively of the courts of the several States ... exclusive original cognizance of all civil causes of admiralty and maritime jurisdiction ... *saving to suitors, in all cases, the right of a common law remedy, where the common law is competent to give it* ....[196]

The Supreme Court has construed the "saving to suitors" clause as constitutionally conferring concurrent jurisdiction on the courts of the

[191] *Cf. The Falls of Keltie*, 114 Fed. 357 (D. Wash. N.D. 1902), involving general international law rule embodied in most treaties; *Bolden v. Jensen*, 70 Fed. 505 (D. Wash. N.D. 1895), same.

[192] Art. 3, § 2, cl. 1.

[193] *The Albergen*, 223 Fed. 443 (S.D. Ga. 1915); *The Welhaven*, 55 Fed. 80 (S.D. Ala. 1892).

[194] *The Koenigin Luise*, 184 Fed. 170, 173 (D. N.J. 1910); *The Albergen*, 223 Fed. 443, 444 (S.D. Ga. 1915).

[195] Emphasis supplied.

[196] 1789, Ch. 20, Sec. 9, 1 Stat. 76–77; emphasis supplied.

states in *in personam* actions based on an Admiralty conflict.[197] Apparently, then, neither Congress nor the Supreme Court construes the Constitution to make federal admiralty jurisdiction mandatory. This would seem to be a complete answer to any contention that the treaty provisions in question would be unconstitutional as applied to United States nationals employed on foreign flag vessels. With the constitutional problem out of the way, there seems to be no good reason why they should not be applied indiscriminately to all crew members of foreign ships including nationals of the United States. The Supreme Court is committed to the proposition of derivative nationality – of a seaman from his vessel – for purposes of the employment.[198] It follows that a crew member is entitled to no different treatment purely upon the basis of an actual nationality differing from that of his vessel.

Most of the earlier treaties contained no provision similar to the one in the German treaty [199] reserving primary jurisdiction in matters of wage and employment contract disputes to the local authorities.[200] The root of the change lies in the Seamen's Act of 1915 [201] which provided *inter alia* that certain wage provisions contained therein should apply on foreign as well as American vessels.[202] Section 3 of the same act [203] has been held applicable to foreign crews without express statutory mandate.[204] The court cited as authority *Strathearn S.S. Co. v. Dillon,*[205] which dealt with a section by its own terms applicable to foreign seamen. In order to assure Senate approval of treaties concluded thereafter, as well as effectiveness in the courts of the United States, it was necessary to specify that local authorities should enjoy a prior right to decide cases involving wage disputes. Since wage disputes in-

[197] *Leon v. Galceran,* 78 U.S. 185 (1870) The wording of the statute currently controlling is: "The district courts shall have original jurisdiction, exclusive of the courts of the States, of: (1) Any civil case of admiralty or maritime jurisdiction, saving to suitors in all cases all other remedies to which they are otherwise entitled." 28 U.S.C. 1333, 62 Stat. 931, amended 63 Stat. 101. Apparently, this change of language has no effect upon the prior law that the action may be brought in a state court. See *Madruga v. Superior Court of California,* 346 U.S. 556, 560, n. 12 (1954); *cf. Cline v. Price,* 39 Wash. 2d 816, 239 P. 2d 322 (1951).

[198] *In re Ross,* 140 U.S. 453, 472–474 (1891).

[199] *Supra,* p. 167.

[200] See treaty with France, 1853, Art. VIII, 10 Stat. 992, 996 [114, 118]. This one carefully excluded any possibility of local interference "particularly in reference to the adjustment of wages and the execution of contracts." Similar clauses are contained in the treaties, Appendix A, numbers 22, 24, 30, 36, 40, 41, 44, 46, 55, 61, 70, 71, 79, 81, 82, 84, 86, 89, 91, 92, 96, 107, 108 and 112.

[201] 38 Stat. 1164–1185.

[202] Sec. 4, 16, 18, *id.* at 1165, 1184, 1185.

[203] *Id.* at 1164.

[204] *The Fletero v. Arias,* 206 F. 2d 267 (4th Cir. 1953), *cert.* denied, 346 U.S. 897 (1953).

[205] 252 U.S. 348 (1920).

variably involve employment contract questions, and *vice versa*, the treaty provisions were phrased broadly enough to give the local authorities priority in all conflicts involving wages and employment contracts. Throughout the United States treaties dealing with this subject matter, that is the only restriction on the exclusiveness of the grant of civil authority to consular officers.

All the most recent United States treaties on the subject contain provisions similar in import to that in the treaty with Germany.[206] Only the treaty with Muscat and Oman tends to diminish consular authority generally beyond the specific area of wage and contract disputes. The language there is:

> Without prejudice to the right of the administrative and judicial authorities of the receiving state ... to enforce the laws of the receiving state applicable to vessels of any state in its ports and territorial waters, it is the intention of the Parties that a consular officer shall have jurisdiction over controversies, including wage and contract disputes ....[207]

This language could be contrued as authorizing either party to promulgate laws authorizing any kind of local jurisdiction over foreign merchant vessels in its territorial waters. The only express limitation is that such rules must be applicable to the vessels of any state. At least the United States would be restricted by that requirement, in its freedom, by treaty undertakings with many other states.

The treaty with the United Kingdom contains the usual general provision coupled with the restriction in wage and contract cases.[208] Additionally, there is a provision that the consul "may take measures for the enforcement of the shipping law of the sending state" and "make arrangements for the repatriation and the treatment ... of the master or ... crew ...." [209] The general grant of power contained in the first paragraph of the article would provide some of that authority. Presumably, the "shipping law" of the United States would include all statutes, administrative orders and common law rules concerning rights and duties pertaining to maritime affairs. Not all of these would relate to matters "concerning the internal management of the vessel."

[206] See treaty with Costa Rica, 1948, Art. X, TIAS 2045, 1 USTIAS 247, 270–272; Greece, 1951, Art. XXII, TIAS 3057, 5 USTIAS 1829, 1897–1899.

[207] Protocol, § 3 b), 1958, TIAS 4530, 11 TIAS 1835, 1843–1844.

[208] 1951, Art, 21(3), 22(1), TIAS 2494, 3 USTIAS 3426, 3442–3443, 3444. Similar provision is contained in the treaty with Ireland. 1952, Art. 22(3), TIAS 2984, 5 USTIAS 949, 992.

[209] Art. 21(4)(5), *id.* There are similar provisions in the treaty with Ireland. Art. 22(4)(5),

However, insofar as seamen and their civil rights and duties are concerned, most of them would.

To the extent that the "shipping laws" of the sending state do not deal with matters internal to the vessel, this provision constitutes an increase in the authority of the consul as defined by general international law. For example, there can be little doubt that the *Shipping Act of 1916* [210] would come within the scope of "shipping laws". That act makes it a misdemeanor punishable by a fine not exceeding $ 25,000 for each offense for a common carrier by water operating to or from a United States port to, *inter alia*, grant a "deferred rebate" to a shipper of goods.[211] This act applies to foreign as well as United States carriers. Assuming that the United States consul in Britain were to seek access to a British steamship operator's business records for the purposes of a prosecution under the act: would the British government be required to assist him in carrying out his design, as they are arguably required to do under Article 20(2) [212] of the treaty? To change the facts, suppose it was an American operator whose business records were sought either on board ship or ashore? It is submitted that this clause must be construed consistently with the general international law in the area. As a general rule, the consul's authority in maritime matters is limited to situations in which only the sending state and one of its ships are involved. If any other person or state has an interest, he will have no authority. Therefore the most feasible construction of this provision is that the consul is entitled to take steps to enforce the shipping laws of his state only as they apply solely to vessels of his state and their crews.

The Pan American Consular Convention raises problems similar to those raised by the United Kingdom Consular Convention discussed in the preceding paragraph. Article 10 of that convention says:

> Consuls shall exercise the functions that the law of their state confers upon them, without prejudice to the legislation of the country where they are serving.[213]

That language apparently authorizes the receiving state, by legislation, to negate any specific power of the consul, but in absence of such legislation, similar problems of interpretation arise.

[210] 39 Stat. 733, 41 Stat. 996, 46 U.S.C. 812.

[211] A deferred rebate is a return of part of the freight paid, at some time after the service for which it was paid is performed.

[212] 3 TIAS 3426, 3442, Ireland treaty 21(2), 5 TIAS 949, 990–991.

[213] 1928, 47 Stat. 1976, 1978.

The United Nations Convention on Consular Relations [214] presents a problem similar to that posed in the preceding materials. Consular functions listed in the convention include "exercising rights of supervision and inspection provided for in the laws and regulations of the sending state in respect of vessels having the nationality of the sending state",[215] and "without prejudice to the powers of the authorities of the receiving state, conducting investigations into any incidents which occurred during the voyage, and settling disputes of any kind between the master, the officers and the seamen insofar as this may be authorized by the laws and regulations of the sending state".[216] In this latter subdivision, as in the Pan-American Consular Convention, it will be noted, local jurisdiction is guaranteed primary status.[217]

Employment Contract Questions

Although the United States position since 1914 has consistently been that local authorities have primary jurisdiction in disputes involving seamen's wages and contracts of employment, and this attitude has been reflected in the treaties of the United States which deal with that subject,[218] nevertheless, there is here a vast area for the exercise of consular authority where local officials do not act.

It will be recalled that United States treaties express the priority of local jurisdiction when there is a dispute or an issue between members of the ship's crew concerning wages and contracts of employment.[219] The consul frequently performs functions which involve no disputes of any kind. For example, supervision of the signing of articles and activities in no way involve the primary authority of local officials recognized in the treaties. There seems to be little reason for local authorities to object to the performance of functions of this type, and indeed there may be no local official with authority to perform them for foreign vessels.

United States statutes require masters of American vessels to sign on crew members abroad before a consular officer, and require him to

[214] U.N. Doc. A/CONF. 25/12, April, 1963; 57 *A.J.I.L.* 995 (1963).

[215] Art. 5k, 57 *A.J.I.L.* 995, 998.

[216] Art. 5L, *id.*

[217] The provision in these treaties authorizing consular action only consistently with local law should not be construed to permit arbitrary emasculation by law makers of the general authority grant. See *supra* at p. 148 *et seq.*

[218] *Supra* at 170.

[219] *E.g.* the treaty with Germany of 1923, Article XXIII, 44 Stat. 2132, 2152.

apply all applicable statutes of the United States in doing so.[220] The Foreign Affairs Manual effectively incorporates all statutory controls upon United States Shipping Commissioners concerning the signing on of seamen.[221] The consul, in effect, functions as a Shipping Commissioner abroad.

In any area of consular competence, in the shipping of seamen, where United States law requires the exercise of official authority by consular officials, it is unlikely that there could be any legitimate complaint arising out of a reciprocal exercise by foreign consuls in the United States.[222]

United States statutes controlling the content and formalities of seamen's articles have been held inapplicable to the articles of foreign vessels concluded in United States ports unless expressly made applicable.[223] Presumably, then, the law of the flag would control, including provisions requiring consular application of that law.[224]

Under some circumstances, the law of the flag probably would not control. The *Grivas* and *Evangelinos* cases [225] suggest that if the foreign registration is purely nominal, some other law might apply provided that courts of that state would apply it if the question arose there. It is submitted that this merely means that the vessel may have a nationality other than that of the state of registry, in which case the law of the state of nationality, including its conflict of laws rules would apply. If it could not be established what its applicable conflict rule was, the presumption that the law of the ship's nationality controls will not have been rebutted, but the court will have to resolve the dispute by application of some kind of presumption.

Monteiro v. Sociedad [226] demonstrates that the law of the vessel's nationality may be applied to one cause of action even though local statutes require United States law to be applied to the other. It would appear logical to extend that holding to the point of permitting litiga-

[220] 46 U.S.C. 570, R.S. § 4517. For failure to comply, he is subject to fine, and the vessel may be held for its payment. 46 U.S.C. 571, *id.*

[221] Vol. 7, §§ 525–525.8–2.

[222] In *The Karoo*, 49 Fed. 651, 652. (W.D. Wash. 1892), the court assumed the authority of a British consul in such matters notwithstanding that there was no treaty with Britain conferring it.

[223] *Ktistakis v. Liberian S.S. Star*, 304 F. 2d 356 (4th Cir. 1962).

[224] *Cf. Monteiro v. Sociedad Maritima San Nicolas*, S.A., 280 F. 2d 568, 570–571 (2d Cir. 1960), *cert.* denied, 364 U.S. 915 (1960); *Evangelinos v. Andreavapor Cia. Nav.*, S.A., 291 F. 2d 624 (2d Cir. 1961); *Grivas v. Alianza Compania Armadora*, S.A., 276 F. 2d 822 (2d Cir. 1960).

[225] *Id.*

[226] *Supra* note 224.

tion of the cause of action controlled by local law and remitting the other causes to the foreign consul for determination. This would appear to be necessary to avoid conflict with a treaty provision such as the one involved in that case if one claim came within the "exclusive jurisdiction" of the consul and the other within the concurrent jurisdiction with the local authorities.[227] If the consul's jurisdiction is exclusive with regard to a particular claim, it would certainly be a violation of the treaty to decide it in the local courts, regardless of the fact that another claim which is litigable there is joined with it.

At the other end of the employment contract relationship, namely discharge from the vessel in a foreign port, the consul is once again the official of the flag state who determines issues which have arisen during the voyage.[228] It is to be expected that there will be more controversies between master and seamen at the time of discharge that at any other time. For one thing, the reason for the seeking of the discharge frequently results from some disagreement, and most dissension which occurs during the course of the relationship will be either amicably adjusted or will culminate in a controversy at the time of discharge. Therefore, as would be expected, there are statutes of the United States designed to provide for a resolution of these problems.

It is illegal for the master of an American vessel to discharge a seaman abroad without the consent of a consular officer of the United States.[229] In addition, the consul is expressly charged with the judicial function of determining, upon application for discharge, whether the man is entitled to it because he "has completed his shipping agreement, or is entitled to his discharge under any Act of Congress or according to the general principles or usages of maritime law as recognized in the United States ...."[230] Although this section does not explicitly require or authorize any hearing, it would appear essential for him to conduct some sort of investigation in order to determine the facts upon which to predicate his decision. In fact, the courts have recognized this need. In *The Sachem*[231] the court invalidated a consular discharge on the ground that it had been granted upon the application

[227] See discussion, *id.* at 571–574.

[228] *Supra* at p. 173.

[229] 46 U.S.C. 677, R.S. § 4576 (1878), makes him liable for a fine of $ 400 per person signed on but not brought back to the United States unless, *inter alia,* he has been "discharged in a foreign country with the consent of the consul or vice consul there residing, certified in writing, under his hand and official seal ...."

[230] 46 U.S.C. 682, R.S. § 4580 (1878) .

[231] 59 Fed. 790 (S.D. N.Y. 1894).

of the master without participation of the seaman. The court said:

> Where a hearing has been had on the merits, on the demand of the master, or the seamen, and a proper record preserved of the consul's decision and judgment, discharging the seaman, it is ordinarily entitled to full credence, notwithstanding the contradictions made by the seaman afterwards, such as I have not infrequently had in previous cases. In the present case, there was no hearing, no judgment, and no record .... Such a forced discharge, with no hearing on the merits ... is inhumane and opposed to the policy and the statutes of this country [citing the statute under consideration] and it is no defense that it was abetted ... by the irregular action of the consular office.[232]

Another statute provides:

> Upon a complaint in writing, signed by the first and second officers or a majority of the crew of any vessel, while in a foreign port, that such vessel is in an unsuitable condition to go to sea because she is leaky or insufficiently supplied with sails, rigging, anchors, or any other equipment, or that the crew is insufficient to man her, or that her provisions, stores, and supplies are not or have not been during the voyage sufficient or wholesome, thereupon, in any of these or like cases the consul shall cause to be appointed three persons [as qualified by 46 U.S.C. 654, and who are authorized and required to go on board and investigate and report to the consul, who will decide after considering the report whether the complaint is justified.] ....[233]

The consul is also required to determine, consistently with the report of the inspectors, whether the vessel was sent to sea deficient, as charged, through neglect or design. If he so determines, he is required to discharge those seamen who request it and exact one-month's penalty wages over the amount actually due or transportation home.[234]

The statute quoted in the preceding paragraph confers rather broad powers upon consular officers abroad. There is an endless variety of possible conflicts which could culminate in its implementation. In *The Rolf*,[235] for example, the consul determined that the ship was unseaworthy because improperly manned, in that the mate was brutal. In *The Fullerton*,[236] it was an anchor chain that did not fit the windlass, and in The *Jacob Luckenbach*,[237] a damaged bottom. Its implementation requires the consul to conduct an investigation, and in this case, the statutes in part specify the investigation that must be conducted.

[232] *Id.* For examples of cases in which hearings were actually conducted, see *The T. F. Oakes*, 36 Fed. 442 (D. Cir. Ore. 1888); *The Oregon*, 254 Fed. 752 (E.D. N.Y. 1918) and *Uriarte v. United States*, 14 F. 2d. 164 (E.D. N.Y. 1926).

[233] 46 U.S.C. 656, R.S. § 4557 (1878).

[234] 46 U.S.C. 658, R.S. § 4561 (1878), 23 Stat. 54.

[235] 299 Fed. 52 (9th Cir 1924).

[236] 167 Fed. 1 (9th Cir. 1908).

[237] 36 F. 2d 381 (E.D. La. 1929).

In order to determine whether there was design or neglect involved in the sending of the vessel to sea in an unseaworthy condition, it is doubtless necessary in most cases to conduct a hearing of sorts. It is true that the preceding section [238] provides that the consular appointed inspectors shall take whatever evidence is necessary for them to prepare their report, but in view of the fact that the consul is not bound by the report, he too may find it necessary to procure evidence upon which to base a decision.

Another statutory provision is:

> Whenever on the discharge of a seaman in a foreign country by a consular officer on his complaint that the voyage is continued contrary to agreement, or that the vessel is badly provisioned or unseaworthy, or against the officers for cruel treatment, it shall be the duty of the consul or consular agent to institute a proper inquiry into the matter, and, upon his being satisfied of the truth and justice of such complaint, he shall require the master to pay to such a seaman one month's wages over and above the wages due at the time of discharge, and to provide him with adequate employment on board some other vessel, or provide him with a passage on board some other vessel bound to the port from which he was originally shipped, or to the most convenient port of entry in the United States, or to a port agreed to by the seaman.[239]

It requires the consul to "institute a proper inquiry". Of course, the "inquiry" need not be conducted with the formalities and technicalities of a trial,[240] but it will in many situations be necessary to take testimony or at least statements of witnesses. The terms of this statute appear to provide an even broader scope for consular decision making than those previously discussed. However, it was probably unnecessary to specify his authority in detail as was done, since presumably the general language of section 682 would cover the whole spectrum of possible reasons for demanding a discharge.[241]

The Foreign Affairs Manual [242] prescribes in great detail the duties of consuls related to discharge of seamen. They provide for inquiry into the facts.[243] He is even authorized, in a grave emergency, on his own initiative, to remove the master of a ship who is "seriously ill or disabled, insane, or guilty of gross misconduct." [244]

[238] 46 U.S.C. 657, R.S. § 4560 (1878).

[239] 46 U.S.C. 685, 30 Stat. 760.

[240] See *The Golden Sun*, 30 Fed. Supp. 354, 357 (S.D. Cal. 1939).

[241] 46 U.S.C. 682, 23 Stat. 54 – "has completed his shipping agreement, or is entitled to his discharge under any Act of Congress or according to the general principles or usages of maritime law recognized in the United States ...."

[242] Vol. 7 (1961), §§ 526–528.4.

[243] §§ 526.2, 526.3–2, 526.3–6, 526.3–8, 526.9–3, 526.9–5, 526.9–6.

[244] § 528.2.

In this area, as in any other where the United States asserts a competence in its consuls abroad, there is every reason to assume that no objection could legitimately be raised to a similar claim by foreign consuls in the United States. The courts have on occasion recognized such competence.[245] In the *Mattes* case,[246] the court, applying British law, invalidated a discharge because the master failed to get the sanction of a British consul who was available in the port of discharge.

Destitute Seamen

One of the frequent problems associated with the discharge of seamen abroad is what may be done to relieve their plight in case they are or thereafter become destitute. This is a matter of concern to the flag state for humanitarian reasons. However, economic considerations have dictated a more paternalistic concern for the welfare of seamen than for destitute nationals who are not seamen. The state has a well defined interest in "preserving this important class of citizens for the commercial service and maritime defence of the nation." [247] In fact, this is one problem area in which all concerned have a community of interest, the shipowner in order that he may have always readily available a supply of skilled labor to man his ships, the foreign state involved so that the seaman does not become a public charge, and the seaman for obvious reasons. Thus, this is one area where, although there is a technical legal possibility of conflict between the sending and receiving states over the performance of the consular function, the probability of such conflict is negligible.[248] The officials of the receiving state will be eager for him to perform his duty efficiently, and the seaman himself will not likely solicit any intervention by them. Historically, the function of relieving distressed seamen has been performed by consular officers with little or no inter-state conflict.[249]

[245] *Mattes v. Standard Transp. Co.*, 274 Fed. 1019, 1022 (S.D. N.Y. 1921); see also *The Havenside*, 14 F. 2d 851 (E.D. N.Y. 1926).

[246] *Id.*

[247] See Story, J., in *Harden v. Gordon*, 11 Fed. Cas. 480, 483 (No. 6,047) (D. Cir. Me. 1823).

[248] The Harvard Draft Convention on the Legal Position and Functions of Consuls puts the matter as follows: "National regulations often contain provisions authorizing consuls to take measures for the relief and assistance of seamen, such as accepting money from them for remittance home ... furnishing them money if sick, shipwrecked, destitute, or abandoned by their vessel ... or furnishing them transportation home .... It is difficult to see why a receiving state should object to such action by the consul ...." 26 *A.J.I.L.* Supp. 285. Perhaps it is for this reason that treaties seldom refer to the problem.

[249] See Stuart, *American Diplomatic and Consular Practice*, ch. 16 (New York, 1936); Comment to Article 4(1.) I.L.C. "Alternate Draft Article on Consular Intercourse and Immunities," 55 *A.J.I.L.* 235 (1961).

United States statutes provide consular officers with rather substantial authority to provide seamen with relief under varying circumstances. In case of shipwreck, a seaman is deemed destitute and entitled to treatment and transportation as such.[250] The same is true of a seaman who is discharged because of illness or injury incapacitating him for service.[251] The fact that they are not in fact destitute is immaterial.[252]

In addition to the two special situations mentioned in the preceding paragraph, a general statute provides:

> It shall be the duty of the consuls and vice consuls, from time to time, to provide for the seamen of the United States, who may be found destitute within their districts, respectively, sufficient subsistence and passages to some port in the United States ... at the expense of the United States ....[253]

This statute has been held applicable to alien seamen on American vessels,[254] regardless of whether they signed on in a United States port.[255] The statute, it should be noted, does not require that the destitute seaman found within the consular district be recently off a vessel or even that he always sail on American vessels. However, it would be difficult to classify him as a seaman if he has not worked on board ship for an unreasonable length of time; and he would hardly be an American seaman if he sailed solely on foreign vessels. The test seems to be whether he has given up the calling, and this would depend upon all the circumstances of the case.[256]

On the question of whether the man applying for relief is destitute, it would appear necessary that the consular officer examine into the facts and make that determination in the first instance, and in absence of clear error on his part, his decision would probably be final.[257] A finding of destitution is predicated upon a finding that the seaman has exhausted his own resources.[258]

[250] 46 U.S.C. 593, R.S. § 4526 (1878), 48 Stat. 395.

[251] 46 U.S.C. 683, R.S. § 4581 (1878), 23 Stat. 55, 30 Stat. 759, 38 Stat. 1185.

[252] See note from The Acting Sec. of Commerce (Sweet) to Mr. Lansing, Feb. 5, 1919, MS. Dept. of State, file 196.7/748, IV Hackworth, *Digest of International Law* 917.

[253] 46 U.S.C. 678, R.S. § 4577 (1878). Masters of American merchant ships are required to carry back destitute seamen at the request of consular officers. 46 U.S.C. 679, R.S. § 4578 (1878), 23 Stat. 55.

[254] *Cf. The Santa Elena,* 271 Fed. 347 (D.C. N.Y. 1920).

[255] 1 Comp. Gen. 583–584; IV Hackworth, *Digest of International Law* 915–916. Transportation has not been provided under these circumstances, however. *Id.*

[256] See 2 Comp. Gen. 317, 318.

[257] 7 *Foreign Affairs Manual* § 543.1–1, 2 Comp. Gen. 317.

[258] *Id.* at § 543.1–2. The *Foreign Affairs Manual* thereafter defines in great detail the authority of consuls to give aid to distressed seamen.

In the context of providing for the resolution of controversies concerning the right to a discharge, United States statutes have provided the consular officer with authority to determine nearly any kind of controversy which would likely arise out of the employment contract. Controversies over whether there has been a deviation from the contract voyage, whether the vessel is properly provisioned and seaworthy in all respects, and whether the officers have been guilty of cruel treatment of seamen are all subject to his determination.[259] The provision concerning whether "the voyage is continued contrary to agreement", for example, could be interpreted to be general enough to give him authority to decide any controversy pertaining to obligations and rights arising from the employment contract, including, it is submitted, the underlying collective bargaining contract.[260] The phrase "continued contrary to agreement" need not be construed to mean contrary in point of time alone. If the voyage continues during any continuing breach of the contract, it is being continued contrary to the agreement. It would appear, therefore, that nearly any claim of breach of employment contract might be brought to the consul in the form of a request for discharge.

EFFECT OF CONSULAR DECISIONS

It will be recalled that in the area of crimes the consul's decision making is in the nature of police and pre-trial judicial activity. It is his duty to quell disturbances, effect arrests, decide whether a *prima facie* case can be proved against anyone, take steps to secure evidence necessary to the prosecution's case, and to send the accused and the results of his investigation, evidentiary and otherwise, back to the United States for the anticipated trial. All this has a practical effect upon the outcome of the trial and upon the immediate rights of the defendant, but the decisions of the consul incident to this acitivty have no direct legal effect. This is because the consul is not authorized to take action which, if undisturbed, will leave the rights of the parties permanently legally changed.

Only in the case of charged desertion does the consul's action in a sense change the legal *states quo* between the parties. He is empowered to investigate and preliminarily determine that the seaman is or is not

[259] 46 U.S.C. 685, R.S. § 4583 (1878), 23 Stat. 54, 30 Stat. 760.

[260] The fact that it is unlikely that such a dispute would be submitted to him is not material to this inquiry.

a deserter, and to certify a positive conclusion for the master, which results in a confiscation of the seaman's wages and effects. If the seaman does not challenge that decision in a subsequent judicial proceeding, he will have been permanently deprived of his property.

For the sake of consistency, it would be wholly rational to argue that the consular decision which results in depriving the seaman of his wages and effects is not a criminal penalty at all, but merely a resolution of an existing or potential civil conflict between the seaman and his employer as to whether the employer has breached the employment contract in failing or refusing to pay earned wages and whether he has committed a tort in retaining the property. Assuming this argument to be sound, it leaves the conclusions concerning the effect of consular decisions in criminal matters unimpeached. However, it raises the question of the legal effect of those decisions upon the ultimate civil rights of the parties.

At one extreme, it is possible to argue that the consul's decision is *res judicata* as between the parties, or at least raises a collateral estoppel as to issues necessarily decided by him. At the other, that it has no legal effect in any subsequent proceeding.

There is a division of authority on the question of whether *res judicata* applies under any circumstances to decisions of administrative tribunals.[261] The sound view appears to be that it does operate in that area provided and to the extent that the underlying policy justifications for its usual application exist.[262]

Assuming that *res judicata* can apply to an administrative determination, there are certain prerequisites which must exist before it is applicable to any kind of decision. One requisite to the operation of the doctrine is that the prior adjudication be a final one.[263] The same is true of collateral estoppel,[264] so the discussion henceforth will be equally appropriate to both. The fact that the problem involves a prior administrative determination rather than a judicial one is not material – it must have been a final determination or the doctrine does not apply.[265] Thus, if the consul's decision was not final on the merits of the issues raised in the subsequent action, neither *res judicata* nor collateral estoppel is pertinent.

261 See 2 Davis, *Administrative Law Treatise* ch. 18. (4 vol. 1958).

262 *Id.*

263 *Restatement*, Judgements § 41 (1942); Developments in the Law – *Res Judicata*, 65 Har. L. Rev. 818, 835 (1952).

264 *Restatement*, Judgements § 68(1) (1942).

265 See Schopflocker, "The Doctrine of *Res Judicata* in Administrative Law" [1942] *Wis. L. Rev.* 198, 215–218.

Whether a consular decision is "final" depends initially upon the statute which authorizes the particular action involved. If it expressly or by construction makes his determination final, it will be conclusive between the parties thereafter.

The statutory scheme which goes further than in any other area towards making the consul's decision final is that which governs resolution of seamen's claims that the vessel is unseaworthy, and that they are therefore entitled to their discharge.[266] Those statutes provide that a judge in a domestic port [267] or the consul abroad[268] shall appoint, upon complaint of the first and second officers or majority of the crew, three persons to survey and report whether the vessel is seaworthy, and considering that report, determine whether the vessel is in fact seaworthy. No provision is made for an appeal from that determination, and wage forfeiture is provided for the seaman's failure to sail the ship from a domestic port after judgment that she is seaworthy. Nothing is said about such a refusal to sail from a foreign port, but presumably this would constitute a desertion, thereby working a like penalty.[269]

The question arises as to whether either the seaman or his employer could question the judgment concerning seaworthiness in a later action, *e.g.* by the seaman in a suit to recover the forfeited wages or the wages he would have earned to the end of the voyage. One court has said in dicta: "If they in good faith believed it was unsafe for the ship to go to sea, they might have demanded a survey which, if fairly made by competent persons, would be treated by the court as conclusive ...." [270] Another held that the question of seaworthiness could not be relitigated in a subsequent trial by jury in an action seeking to recover the lost wages.[271] The survey was not conducted pursuant to the statute because no statutory demand had been made for one. However, the shipowner got one without demand, which was held binding because the crew had neglected to seek the remedy available to them. The decision is perhaps justified by the language of the act involved:

> If after judgment that such vessel is fit to proceed on her intended voyage, or after procuring such men, provisions, stores, repairs, or alterations as may be

[266] 46 U.S.C. 653–660, R.S. §§ 4556–4563.

[267] 46 U.S.C. 653, R.S. § 4556.

[268] 46 U.S.C. 656, R.S. § 4559.

[269] 46 U.S.C. 701 First., R.S. § 4596 (1878), 38 Stat. 1166.

[270] *The C. F. Sargent*, 95 Fed. 179, 181 (D. Wash. N.D. 1899) What would be the position if a number were involved insufficient to demand a survey is not raised.

[271] *Heino v. Libby, McNeill & Libby*, 116 Wash. 148, 205 Pac. 854 (1921).

directed, the seamen, or either of them, shall refuse to proceed on the voyage, he shall forfeit any wages that may be due him.[272]

This appears to leave little scope for arguing that the decision is not final. The section applicable to consular action abroad contains no such statements, but by analogy and through use of the desertion statute, the result would probably be the same.

In addition to questions of unseaworthiness, and the consul's decision upon such claim, and duplicating parts of that area to a large extent, is the statutory function of the consul in discharging seamen abroad. United States statutes authorize the consul to discharge seamen and to collect wages and extra wages under certain circumstances.[273] Assuming that a subsequent proceeding involved questions necessarily determined by the consul at that time, the question arises as to the effect of his decision upon the subsequent action. The Supreme Court has held that a consul's decision is a prerequisite to the recovery of the extra wages prescribed by the act.[274] It would follow from that his decision upon that question should have at least the effect of a trial court judgment on the question of the right to the penalty wages. Such determination might be subject to review in a later court proceeding by the shipowner seeking to avoid payment of the penalty or by the seaman in attempting to enforce it, but in absence of such review or if the review confirms the consular decision, it should be conclusive on the issues necessarily determined by him in arriving at his decision. For example, if the grant of extra wages were predicated upon a finding of cruel treatment of the seaman by the officers, the employer should not be in a position thereafter in any other proceeding to relitigate the issue of cruelty. To that extent, it should have exactly the same effect as a determination on the issue of unseaworthiness as discussed in the preceding paragraphs. In both these areas, the consul's decision upon the precise question relegated to him by the statutes is entitled to the weight of a trial court judgment.[275] It would seem to follow that the issues necessarily determined between the parties are thereafter at rest.[276]

If a desertion is alleged to have occurred under circumstances not

[272] R.S. § 4558, 30 Stat. 764.

[273] *Supra* at pp. 175–177.

[274] *McCrea v. United States*, 294 U.S. 23 (1934); 46 U.S.C. 685, R.S. § 4583 (1878), 23 Stat. 54, 30 Stat. 760.

[275] In the case of unseaworthiness, it is arguably not even subject to review. *Supra* at p. 182.

[276] *See Commissioner of Internal Revenue v. Sunnen*, 333 U.S. 59 (1948).

involving an application of the statutes previously discussed in this section, the consul may nevertheless become administratively involved. However, there is no direct statutory authority for him to determine whether there has been a desertion unless a question within the scope of the statutes arises. Generally, if the seaman comes before the consul at all, the consular authority under one of them will be invoked by his explanation of his conduct. An inquiry would follow, and a determination be made which would have the effect discussed in the prior materials herein. In any other circumstances, the consul's action would involve only evidence supplied by the master or derived from the consul's own efforts. The results of such an *ex parte* proceeding should certainly have no binding effect upon the seaman, whatever estoppel effect they may have upon the employer. It is submitted that in any such proceeding in which the seaman does not participate the issues between the parties remain legally unresolved, and the records of the consular proceedings could have only evidentiary value in any later proceeding. The seaman may be estopped from proving matter which he could statutorily have raised by complaint to the consul,[277] and the consular decision at the instance of the master inconsistent with it be given effect, but not otherwise.

In those situations in which the consul's decision is determined not to be final on any particular issue between the parties, the question arises as to the scope of the power of a court to review matters raised before him. It may be that a trial *de novo* is required as in subsequent criminal prosecutions; [278] a court would review trial court proceedings on appeal; [279] or the court may be considering it in a collateral proceeding in which there are issues common to both proceedings.

In a situation wherein either party for any reason is entitled to a trial *de novo* of the issues previously determined by the consul, the decisions by him will have no direct controlling legal effect in the subsequent action. However, it may have some evidentiary value in determining contested issues of fact in the later proceeding. By statute:

> Books or records of account or minutes of proceedings of any department or agency of the United States shall be admissible to prove the act, transaction or occurrence as a memorandum of which the same were made or kept.[280]

[277] See *Heino v. Libby, McNeill & Libby, supra* note 271.

[278] *Supra* at p. 180.

[279] *Supra* at p. 183.

[280] 28 U.S.C. 1733 (a), 62 Stat. 946 (1948). Another statute makes authenticated copies "of all official entries in the books or records of any such office [consular] ... admissible equally with the originals." 28 U.S.C. 1740, 62 Stat. 947 (1948).

The question is what is the effect of fact conclusions by the consul?

In *United States v. McCoy*,[281] the Postmaster General's determination, pursuant to special statute, that the defendant contractor was in default under his contract with the government was held to be *prima facie* evidence of the accuracy of that conclusion. This authority is not conclusive on the question of the effect of a consul's decision, particularly in view of the fact that different statutes were under consideration. However, the basic problem is the same, namely the evidentiary effect to be given an administrative decision in a subsequent judicial action in which the same facts were subject to determination *de novo*.[282] A similar result was reached in *Franklin v. Skelly Oil Co.*[283] In that case, the court said:

> The exception [to the hearsay exclusionary rule in favor of admissibility of reports by a public official acting in the scope of his statutory duties] has been extended to include reports, findings and conclusions of public officials concerning causes and effects when made in pursuance of authority to conduct inquisitions and hearings in the public interest.[284]

There is one area of law which can be considered by analogy to support the conclusion that the reviewing court may consider factual conclusions of the consul as evidence of those facts. Appeals in admiralty are trials *de novo*.[285] However, conclusions of fact by the trial court are accorded great weight in the appellate court without rehearing the evidence which supports them.[286]

In *The Golden Sun*, the court said that "The consul's certificate giving the ground for discharge is *prima facie* evidence of the existence of just cause.[287] Apparently, no claim was made that his decision was entitled to the effect of a trial court judgment on disputed fact issues. This court gave it only *prima facie* effect, whereas it is more likely that, because of the statute involved, it is entitled to even greater weight.[288]

[281] 193 U.S. 599 (1903).

[282] In *United States v. Dumas*, 149 U.S. 278 (1892), it had been held that the prior administrative determination was final.

[283] 141 F. 2d 568 (10th Cir. 1944).

[284] *Id.* at 572. This is consistent with Rule 516, American Law Institute, Model Code of Evidence (Phila., A.L.I. 1942). See also Wigmore on Evidence § 1638 (3rd ed. 1940).

[285] *Reid v. American Express Co.*, 241 U.S. 544 (1915).

[286] *Kilgust v. United States*, 191 F. 2d 69 (2d Cir. 1951).

[287] 30 F. Supp. 354, 356 (S.D. Calif. 1939). *Accord, The Oregon*, 254 Fed. 752 (E.D. N.Y. 1918). *Contra, E.A. McMillin v. Androscoggin Pulp*, 291 Fed. 134 (S.D. Me. 1923).

[288] See *supra* pp. 183. See also *Ennis v. Waterman S.S. Corp.*, 49 F. Supp. 685, 688 (1943), which treated the seaman's failure to seek a consular determination on the alleged cruelty of the officers as strong evidence of the falsity of that claim.

In those situations where the issues decided by the consul are not final on the one hand nor subject to consideration *de novo* on the other, they are subject to judicial review to the same extent that other administrative decisions are. Section 10 of the Administrative Procedure Act makes these decisions subject to judicial review and states:

> So far as necessary to decision and where presented the reviewing court shall ... hold unlawful and set aside agency action, findings, and conclusions found to be (1) arbitrary, capricious, an abuse of discretion ... (5) unsupported by substantial evidence in any case ... otherwise reviewed on the record of an agency hearing provided by statute ....[289]

It will be a rare situation which will be held to be "arbitrary, capricious" or "an abuse of discretion", so the result is that most consular decisions will be disregarded only if they are not supported by substantial evidence as disclosed by the records of the prior proceedings before the consul. Apparently, the substantial evidence test governed these questions prior to the passage of the act.[290]

In *Universal Camera Corp. v. National Labor Relations Board,* the Supreme Court said in an attempt to define the meaning of the statutory term that a reviewing court can set aside the administrative decision "when it cannot conscientiously find that the evidence supporting that decision is substantial, when viewed in the light that the record in its entirety furnishes, including the body of evidence opposed to the ... [agency's] view." [291] This would seem to mean that if the evidence disclosed by the record of the proceedings before the consul is such that a trial court considering the same evidence would be justified in refusing to direct a jury verdict, his decision will not be disturbed.[292]

It may be assumed that whether the "substantial evidence" test is used by the court reviewing a consular officer's decision, or the matter is tried *de novo,* the factual conclusions being given "great weight" or considered "*prima facie* evidence", the result will be the same. However, great practical significance exists in the distinction between the two approaches. If there is a trial *de novo,* new evidence may be offered by either party on any issue, even though previously decided by the

[289] 5 U.S.C. 1009, 60 Stat. 243 (1946).

[290] See *Consolidated Edison Co. v. National Labor Relations Board,* 305 U.S. 197, 229 (1938); *National Labor Relations Board v. Columbian Enameling & Stamping Co.,* 306 U.S. 292, 300 (1938).

[291] 340 U.S. 474, 488 (1951).

[292] See 4 Davis, *Administrative Law* § 29.02 (4 vol. 1958).

consul. If, on the other hand, the court may only disregard the decision if unsupported by substantial evidence, no new evidence could be considered on previously determined issues unless the court made an initial determination that because of the lack of evidentiary support for the decision, it was free to determine the issue anew. The question of whether the consular decision is supported by substantial evidence could be determined on motion for summary judgment supported by the record of the proceedings before the consul. Thus, the litigation might be disposed of without the taking of any evidence in the judicial action.

APPLICATION OF UNITED STATES LABOR LAWS TO FOREIGN VESSELS

Closely related to the question of whether the United States will in fact take jurisdiction of an employment dispute on a foreign flag vessel is the proper construction of the labor laws of the United States. There seems to be some question as to whether such a question involves a matter within the exclusive jurisdiction of the consular officer of the flag state under the first clause of recent United States treaty provisions on the subject or involves the "execution of contracts" which is within the primary jurisdiction of the local authorities.[293] There is a strong argument that a dispute concerning union representation, right to picket *etc.* is within the primary jurisdiction of the local authorities, since such activity of necessity raises questions of the obligations of the seamen under the employment contract. However, the further question of whether a statute should be construed as controlling a dispute of that type on board a foreign flag ship is another matter.

In *Sandberg v. McDonald,*[294] the court determined that a statute of the United States [295] was inapplicable to invalidate advances of wages to seamen on foreign vessels in foreign ports. The Court said, "when the contract and payment were made in a foreign country where the law sanctioned such contract and payment .... Had Congress intended to make void such contracts and payments a few words would have stated that intention, not leaving such an important regulation to be gathered from implication." [296]

[293] See *Empresa Hondurena de Vapores, S.A. v. McLeod,* 300 F. 2d 222, 236 (2d Cir. 1962).
[294] 248 U.S. 185 (1918).
[295] The Seamen's Act of 1915, ch. 153, § 11, 38 Stat. 1168.
[296] *Supra* note 294 at 195.

In 1928, the Court in *Jackson v. S.S. Archimedes*,[297] came to the same conclusion when construing the same statute with its present wording: "This section shall apply as well to foreign vessels while in waters of the United States ...." [298] Thereafter, Congress had under consideration an extension of the statute to cover even those situations where the contract was entered into in a foreign country and the contested payments made abroad. This proposal caused such a rash of diplomatic protest [299] that it was never passed.

In *Benz v. Compania Naviera Hidalgo*,[300] the Supreme Court held the Labor Management Relations Act of 1947 [301] inapplicable to a controversy concerning union representation on board a Liberian flag vessel in a United States port. The crew struck and got the support of several American unions which successively picketed the ship, effectively keeping it inoperative at the dock for about two and a half months. The action was against the unions and their officers for damages for unlawful picketing under Oregon law; the defense, that the 1947 Act had pre-empted the field from the states, and therefore that Oregon law could not be applied. The defendants were held liable for substantial damages. A contrary holding would by implication have extended the jurisdiction of the National Labor Relations Board to control of the labor relations on board foreign vessels which were transiently within the United States. The Court cited the history of the Seamen's Act of 1915 and the international controversy caused by the proposal to extend its operation to foreign seamen's contracts entered into abroad, and went on to say:

> And so here such a "sweeping provision" as to foreign applicability was not specified in the Act. The seamen agreed in Germany to work on the foreign ship under British articles. We cannot read into the Labor Management Relations Act an intent to change the contractual provisions made by these parties. For us to run interference in such a delicate field of international relations there must be present the affirmative intention of the Congress clearly expressed. It alone has the facilities necessary to make fairly such an important policy decision where the possibilities of international discord are so evident and retaliative action so certain. We therefore conclude that any such appeal should be directed to the Congress rather than the Courts.[302]

[297] 275 U.S. 463 (1928).

[298] 46 U.S.C. 599(e), 1920, 41 Stat. 1006.

[299] U.S. For. Rel.: 1928 at 830–838 (State Dept. 1942); *id.:* 1929 at 1005–1009 (State Dept. 1943); *id.:* 1932 at 959–960 (State Dept. 1948).

[300] 353 U.S. 138 (1956).

[301] 29 U.S.C. 141–188, 61 Stat. 136–160.

[302] 353 U.S. 138, 146–147 (1956). It should perhaps be noted at this point that since the executive has been Constitutionally delegated the power to control international relations,

Mr. Justice Douglas, in his dissent in the decision under consideration, was concerned with the interference with the free flow of commerce, inconsistent with the expressed intent of Congress,[303] which would result if the various states' laws were permitted to have effect upon commerce as permitted by the majority decision. What he neglected to consider, it is submitted, was that the operation of state law in this case did not tend to burden international commerce, but on the contrary, made it more free. There was no suggestion in the majority opinion that state law would be permitted to interfere with the employer-employee relationship on board foreign vessels within their waters any more than would the federal statute be so construed. In this case, the state law merely granted damages in tort for illegally interfering with the rights of the foreign shipowner while his ship was within the state. The right which was being interfered with was the right to have his ship come and go freely and without interference with its internal management – in this case, the management of employee relations. If the state law purported to control intra-ship relationships, it is submitted, this would be clearly beyond state competence, since there is a federal statute on that subject, held by the majority not to be applicable to foreign vessels. The federal statute has, by acting in that area but excepting foreign vessels from its effect, implicitly preempted the states from controlling the activity. This does not mean that all state remedies are excluded, however, as in *San Diego Building Trades Council v. Garmon*.[303a] Those remedies, only, which interfere with the exercise by the flag state of exclusive jurisdiction over labor relations on board would be excluded. And, of course, damages for and injunction against interference with the operation of a foreign flag vessel by picketing of United States labor unions attempting to organize its crew members tends to facilitate rather than interfere with flag state jurisdiction.[303b] The federal courts have by statute been deprived of jurisdiction to enjoin such conduct,[303c] but there is no such impediment to State action.

In *Empresa Hondurena de Vapores, S. A. v. McCleod*,[304] the Court

Congress too should not interfere. It is, however, too late to question the competence of Congress to domestically neutralize by statute the efforts of the executive in international relations.

[303] 29 U.S.C. 141, 61 Stat. 136. "It is the purpose and policy of this chapter, in order to promote the full flow of commerce ...."

[303a] 359 U.S. 236 (1959).

[303b] See *Incres S.S. Co. v. International Maritime Workers*, 372 U.S. 24 (1963).

[303c] *Marine Cooks & Stewards v. Panama* S.S. Co., 362 U.S. 365 (1960), *rehearing denied*, 363 U.S. 809 (1960).

[304] 300 F. 2d 222 (2d Cir. 1962).

of Appeals extended the *Benz* case to preclude the National Labor Relations Board from taking jurisdiction and conducting a representation election on board foreign flag vessels wholly beneficially owned by nationals of the United States and operating substantially exclusively in trade to and from United States ports. The Court stated in conclusion:

> In order to avoid any possible misunderstanding in this controversial area, we emphasize that we are deciding only the case before us; what the result should be when the contacts with the country of the flag are weaker relative to those of the United States than here, we do not say.[305]

A possible inference is that an application of something like the "center of gravity" theory in conflict of laws problems is operating in this area. It is submitted that there is no scope for the operation of any such theory. This is not a choice of laws problem, but a question of jurisdiction. Either Congress intended to intervene into this area of foreign flag operation (improperly, I suggest) or they did not. The only question should therefore be whether the ship is a vessel of foreign nationality or one of the United States. On review, the Supreme Court rejected the theory objected to and sustained the holding of inapplicability of the Act. Their reasoning was based upon the prima facie exclusiveness of the jurisdiction of the flag state in matters concerning the internal economy of the vessel.[305a] The inapplicability of the National Labor Relations Act in such a situation was also established, in *Incres S.S. Co. v. International Maritime Workers Union.*[305b]

The United Nations Convention on the High Seas [306] would seem to preclude interference with the internal administration of foreign vessels on any theory that there is a stronger contact with the forum than with the flag state. Article 5, section 1, states:

> Each State shall fix the conditions for the grant of its nationality to ships, for the registration of ships in its territory, and for the right to fly its flag. Ships have the nationality of the State whose flag they are entitled to fly. There must exist a genuine link between the State and the ship; in particular, the State must effectively exercise its jurisdiction and control in administrative, technical and social matters over ships flying its flag.[307]

[305] *Id.* at 236.
[305a] *McCulloch v. Sociedad de Marineros de Honduras*, 372. U.S. 10, 19 (1963).
[305b] 372 U.S. 24 (1963.
[306] (1958) TIAS 5200, 13 USTIAS 2312.
[307] 13 USTIAS 2315

Even assuming that this article implicitly admits of other states' refusing to recognize a ship nationality conferral absent a "genuine link" with the conferring state, it is submitted that the inference is clear that they may not refuse it if there is one. Therefore, any application of the "center of gravity" theory which resulted in ignoring a conferred nationality supported by a "genuine link" would constitute a violation of international law.[308] No court should contrue a statute susceptible of another interpretation in such a manner as to be inconsistent with international law.[309]

Even in absence of a "genuine link" between the flag state and the ship, most bilateral treaties of the United States which treat the subject of vessel nationality require the United States to recognize a vessel nationality conferred by the other state – without reference to any contacts with the state.

Evidence of the policy which dictates a construction, where possible, of the labor laws of the United States as inapplicable to seamen's employment contracts on foreign vessels signed abroad may be found in the construction of United States patent laws by the courts. These laws, although not expressly inapplicable to foreign flag vessels in United States ports have been so construed. An action based upon an infringing device fitted on the vessel abroad was dismissed in *Brown v. Duchesne*.[310] The language of the Court in that case is particularly interesting:

> The construction claimed by the plaintiff [that such use infringed his legal rights in the United States when the vessel was there] would confer on patenteess not only rights of property ,but also political power, and enable them to embarras the treaty making power in its negotiations with foreign nations, and also to interfere with the legislation of Congress when exercising its constitutional power to regulate commerce. And if a treaty should be negotiated with a foreign nation, by which the vessels of each party were to be freely admitted into the ports of the other, upon equal terms with its own, upon the payment of the ordinary port charges, and the foreign Government faithfully carried it into execution, yet the Government of the United States would find itself unable to fulfill its obligations if the foreign ship had about her, in her construction or equipment, anything for which a patent had been granted. And after paying the port and other charges to which she was subject by the treaty, the master

[308] The convention under consideration has been ratified by the United States but has not yet come into force. However, it does represent a consensus among the representativef of nearly all maritime states as to what the law is or should be. See Dissenting Opion os Judge Quintana in *Constitution of the Maritime Safety Committee of the Inter-Governmental Maritime Consultative Organization*, 1960 I. C. J. 150, 178.

[309] *Supra* at p. 65. Of course, Congress can intentionally and explicitly pass such a statute, but we do not have that problem here.

[310] 60 U.S. 183 (1856).

would be met with a further demand, the amount of which was not even regulated by law, but depended upon the will of a private individual.[311]

> Congress may unquestionably, under its power to regulate commerce, prohibit any foreign ship from entering our ports, which, in its construction or equipment, uses any improvement patented in this country, or may prescribe the terms and regulations upon which such vessel shall be allowed to enter. Yet it may be doubted whether Congress could by law confer on an individual, or individuals, a right which would in any degree impair the constitutional powers of the legislative or executive departments of the Government, or which might put it in their power to embarrass our commerce and intercourse with foreign nations, or endanger our amicable relations.[312]

> the use of such [patented] improvement, in the construction, fitting out, or equipment of such vessel, while she is coming into or going out of a port of the United States, is not an infringement of the rights of an American patentee, provided it was placed upon her in a foreign port, and authorized by the laws of the country to which she belongs.[313]

It is apparent that the policy implemented in the construction of this statute is the prevention of any intolerable burden upon international commerce unless Congress clearly evinces such an intent. This same policy has been implemented in the multilateral Convention for the Protection of Industrial Property to which the United States is a party.[314]

> The use on board ships of other countries of the Union of any article forming the subject matter of his patent in the body of the ship, in the machinery, tackle, rigging, and other accessories, when such ships shall enter temporarily or accidentally the waters of the country, provided that such article is used there exclusively for the needs of the vessel [shall not be considered as infringing the rights of the patentee].[315]

United States statutory law is consistent with the treaty provisions discussed.[316]

It is submitted that the same interests which were protected by holding the patent laws of the United States inapplicable to foreign vessels entering the United States for the purposes of commerce are equally involved when the question is the applicability of the labor laws. In both situations, there is a relationship established under and protected by the laws of another state; in both, an interposition of American law would unnecessarily burden a vessel only casually within

[311] *Id.* at 197.
[312] *Id.* at 198.
[313] *Id.* at 198–199.
[314] Concluded in 1883, revised 1900, 1911, 1925, 1934, 53 Stat. 1768.
[315] Article 5 ter., 53 Stat. 1768, 1776.
[316] "The use of any invention in any vessel ... of any country which affords similar privi-

the jurisdiction without conferring any particular benefit upon the United States; in both, the international aspects of the problem have been and are being regulated by treaty; and in both, the only reasonably certain result would be retaliation by other states' exercising similar restraints upon American vessels within their waters, with a resultant intolerable burden on international commerce. There seems to be no reasonable alternative to continuing the policy of imposing restraints upon foreign vessels in port only to the extent necessary to protect some vital local interest; and, of course, only under circumstances where we are prepared to concede the same competence *vis-à-vis* American vessels abroad.

The United States has actually applied the Shipping Act of 1916 to foreign flag vessels. There, the vital domestic policy was the control of monopoly in the foreign trade ocean shipping of the United States.[317] In *Compagnie Générale Transatlantique v. American Tobacco Co.*,[318] the statute was applied to a bill of lading issued in France by a foreign flag ship. In this situation, of course, the activity subjected to regulation has a more direct effect upon persons within the United States than does a problem concerning labor relations on board the vessel or even the use of American patents on foreign ships.[319] The establishment of monopoly and the following of discriminatory practises in the foreign commerce of a state certainly has potentially far more serious impact domestically than the other activities under discussion. This result is consistent with the policy of conceding by treaty exclusive control to foreign consuls only where the activity is restricted in its effects to the vessel. The labor relations on board the vessel are unlikely to have serious repercussions ashore, as is also true in the case of patent infringement; but where cargo is shipped into and out of the United States, an American national will nearly always have an interest in the freight charged and the other terms of carriage.

leges to vessels ... of the United States, entering the United States temporarily or accidentally, shall not constitute infringement of any patent, if the invention is used exclusively for the needs of the vessel ... and is not sold in or used for the manufacture of anything to be sold in or exported from the United States." 35 U.S.C. 272, 66 Stat. 812 (1952).

[317] 46 U.S.C. 801–842, 40 Stat. 900–903.

[318] 31 F. 2d 663 (2d Cir. 1929), *cert.* denied, 280 U.S. 555 (1929).

[319] The employment relationship is wholly internal to the vessel, whereas in the patent situation, an American national has a direct interest.

PERSONAL INJURY TORT CLAIMS INVOLVING FOREIGN VESSELS

In a situation occurring on a vessel of a state with which the United States has a treaty conferring exclusive cognizance over internal matters upon the consul of the flag state, a controversy concerning a personal injury to a seaman on board is one which should be within his cognizance. It certainly is a controversy the effects of which do not reach beyond the ship and her company, whether the claim be against the ship or another member of the crew.

In *Gerradin v. United Fruit*,[320] the court rejected a claim that the treaty between the United States and Honduras, which contained a clause conferring exclusive jurisdiction upon the consul in matters concerning the internal economy of the ship,[321] barred the court from determining the issues. The decision was based upon a construction of the treaty provision, the court stating that an action in negligence against the (American) owner did not arise out of the internal order of the ship.[322] The court also said that "Honduras is not concerned",[323] apparently meaning that the law of international claims gives Honduras no valid complaint if an American court holds an American shipowner liable in a tort action.[324] However, the very fact that the action interferes with a right arising under a treaty forecloses that problem. The complaint of Honduras would be based upon an infringement of her own sovereign rights under the treaty. The *I'm Alone* case [325] involving the United States and Canada demonstrates that fact very clearly. There, an American owned Canadian flag ship was wrongfully sunk by United States vessels. It was held to be a violation of Canada's rights notwithstanding the fact that the injury was sustained by an American national through his ownership of the vessel. It is submitted that the court's construction of the convention as not including actions in tort against a vessel's owner is not supportable in logic, nor is its finding that the treaty did not apply because of the nationality of the defendant.

It is also difficult to maintain that a personal injury dispute is an issue concerning the contract of service, thus placing it within the

[320] 60 F. 2d 927 (2d Cir. 1932).
[321] (1927) Art. XXII, 45 Stat. 2618, 2634–2635.
[322] *Supra* note 320 at 930.
[323] *Id.* at 929.
[324] See V Hackworth, *Digest of International* 802, which describes common nationality of the claimant and the plaintiff state as a prerequisite to a valid international claim.
[325] II Hackworth, *Digest of International Law* 703–708.

primary jurisdiction of the local authorities under recent treaty provisions; [326] nor is it a wage claim, likewise coming within that jurisdiction. Of course, it frequently happens that a clause is incorporated in the employment contract making the law of the flag in the employment contract making the law of the flag applicable to any internal disputes, including those arising out of personal injury,[327] but it would be a bizarre result if the presence of a clause designed to assure application of the law of the flag changed a problem which would otherwise have been within the exclusive jurisdiction of the consul, who would apply that law pursuant to its direction, into one within the primary jurisdiction of the local authorities applying their own law-albeit a choice of laws rule which may result in the application of the law of the flag.

Under the general maritime law as applied in the United States, it frequently transpires that a seaman may choose to pursue his remedy for personal injuries under a contract theory. One such theory is referred to as "maintenance and cure".[328] The other is an action for breach of the "warranty of seaworthiness". The theory of this action is that there is an implied warranty of seaworthiness included in every seaman's employment contract, the breach of which, resulting in injury, gives rise to an action for indemnity.[329] The proposition that it is a term of the contract is derived from *Carlisle Packing Co. v. Sandanger,*[330] in which the Court held the plaintiff-seaman entitled to recover for personal injuries even in absence of negligence if they were caused by an unseaworthy condition. The Court cited as authority for this conclusion two cases involving damage to cargo caused by unseaworthiness.[331] The warranty of seaworthiness in cargo cases is clearly contractual.[332]

The question then is whether the foreign seaman, by bringing an action for either maintenance and cure or unseaworthiness thereby

[326] *Supra* at p. 170.
[327] See *Lauritzen v. Larsen,* 345 U.S. 571 (1953).
[328] See *The Federal No.* 2, 21 F.2d 313 (2d Cir. 1927); *Jones v. Waterman* S.S. Corp., 155 F.2d 992 (3d Cir. 1946). It is not pertinent to discuss the dimensions of the remedy at this point. At any rate, all elements of recovery could be had under a tort theory in most situations, although not all elements of tort damages may be recovered under the theory.
[329] For a discussion of the origin of the theory, see *Dixon v. United States,* 219 F.2d 10 (2d Cir. 1955). Dixon leaves open the question whether the remedy is one in tort or contract, but the logic of the reasoning would seem to indicate contract. See also *Le Gate v. The Panamolga,* 221 F.2d 689 (2d Cir. 1955), also leaving the question open. This theory too results in a recovery of tort damages for personal injuries.
[330] 259 U.S. 255 (1922).
[331] *The Silvia,* 171 U.S. 462 (1898), and *The Southwark,* 191 U.S. 1 (1903).
[332] *Work v. Leathers,* 97 U.S. 379 (1878); *The Caledonia,* 157 U.S. 124 (1895).

deprives the consul of his exclusive jurisdiction because, by virtue of the form of action, it now is an issue concerning the contract of employment. In a sense, of course, all tort actions by an employee against his employer concern the contract of employment, since that contract helps to define the standards of care owed by the employer to the employee. However, it is submitted that the more rational construction of the treaty provision being considered is that only disputes essentially concerning questions of performance under the contract are intended to be within the primary jurisdiction of the local authorities. Those which are essentially tortious in nature are reserved for the exclusive jurisdiction of the consul. If the claim is for damages for personal injuries, it is tort regardless of the contract theory of recovery; if for wages or other benefits arising directly from an obligation of the contract, it will be within the primary jurisdiction of the local authorities under those treaties.

In absence of a controlling treaty between the United States and the flag state allocating jurisdiction between the local authorities and the consular officer, the problem is customarily treated by the United States courts as a choice of laws problem [333] or a question of *forum non conveniens*.[334]

As a first step in making a determination as to whether the law of the flag is to be considered at all in these matters, it will be necessary to determine whether the ship *bona fide* carried those colors.[335] In *Lauritzen v. Larsen*,[336] the Court recognized this problem and implied that a purely formal registration would not be recognized:

> But it is common knowledge that in recent years a practice has grown, particularly among American shipowners, to avoid stringent shipping laws by seeking foreign registration eagerly offered by some countries. Confronted with such operations, our courts on occasion have pressed beyond the formalities of more or less nominal foreign registration to enforce against American shipowners the obligations which our law places upon them.[337]

Some courts have treated the fact of American ownership practically unalloyed with other contacts with the United States as sufficient cause for applying American law.[338] To the extent that these cases imply that

[333] See *Lauritzen v. Larsen*, 345 U.S. 571 (1953).

[334] See *Conte v. Flota Mercante Del Estado*, 277 F.2d 664 (2d Cir 1960) and *Brillis v. Chandris (U.S.A.) .Inc*, 215 F. Supp. 520 (S.D. N.D. 1963).

[335] See *Southern Cross Steamship Co. v. Firipis*, 285 F. 2d 651, 653 (4th Cir. 1960).

[336] 345 U.S. 571 (1952).

[337] *Id.* at 587. *Cf. Central Vermont Co. v. Durning*, 294 U.S. 33 (1935).

[338] *Zielinski v. Empresa Hondurena de Vapores*, 113 F. Supp. 93 (S.D. N.Y. 1953); *Gerradin v. United Fruit Co.*, 60 F.2d 927 (2d Cir. 1932); *cert.* denied, 287 U.S. 642 (1932).

the flag state can have no legitimate complaint because the vessel is not owned by its nationals, they should not be accepted.[339] The flag state has an interest in the vessel based purely upon the fact of registration under its laws. However, it is true that some distinction could be drawn between an *in rem* proceeding against the vessel conferring a right to attach the vessel at the outset, and an *in personum* action against the owner not accompanied by an attachment. No doubt, the *in rem* proceeding has a more detrimental effect on the flow of commerce, but in view of the fact that an attachment would lie at some point in time if the seaman was successful, and that witnesses from the vessel would be required, the distinction is of minimal consequence. If the action were by the seaman against another member of the ship's company, there would be less reason to fear an adverse effect on the commerce of the flag state.

It is true that Article 5, section 1, of the United Nations Convention on the High Seas [340] implies that a registration may be defective under international law if there is no "genuine link" between the vessel and the state. However, it by no means makes ownership the only possible link which is genuine. In fact, the inference is clear that a vessel may be foreign owned and still have a "genuine link" with the state. The last sentence of the section says: "There must exist a genuine link between the State and the ship; in particular, the State must effectively exercise its jurisdiction and control in administrative, technical and social matters over ships flying its flag." It would appear, therefore, that the possibility of a genuine registration for nationality purposes exists, provided, as a minimum contact, sufficient control is exercised by the state. With regard to those countries with which the United States has treaties obligating her to recognize the nationality of a vessel purely on the basis of registration within the state, not even a minimum "genuine link" would be required.[341]

Although there can be no doubt of the fact that a state has an interest in vessels because they fly its flag, and certainly have such an interest if the vessel has its nationality (either by special treaty or by the U.N. Convention on the High Seas), it does not necessarily follow that the exercise of jurisdiction over a tort claim by a seaman against the vessel or owner violates the rights of the state. We have seen that such exercise probably violates the treaty rights of a state party to a

[339] See the discussion of the *I'm Alone case, supra* at pp. 194–195.
[340] *Supra* at p. 190.
[341] See *e.g.*, Article X, Treaty of 1937 with Honduras, 45 Stat. 2618, 2625–2626.

treaty like the one with Honduras,[342] and that customary international law too probably reserves this type of claim to the flag state.[343] However, United States courts, at least in absence of treaty, treat the matter as purely a choice of laws and *forum non conveniens* question. Both *Lauritzen v. Larsen* [344] and *Romero v. International Terminal Operating Co.*[345] assumed the jurisdiction of American courts to hear and decide this type of claim. In *Lauritzen*, the Court said: "A cause of action under our law was asserted here, and the court had power to determine whether it was or was not well founded in law and in fact." [346] The entire decision was predicated upon the assumption that if there were enough contracts with the United States, the matter would be properly determined in the local courts. The same is true of *Romero*. The only question is what contacts will be sufficient to justify its exercise. In *McCulloch v. Sociedad Nacional de Marinerros de Honduras*, the balancing of contacts method of resolving even the choice of laws problem in personal injury suits was questioned, the court citing the "cardinal importance to the law of the flag."

On the question of the necessary minimum contacts which would justify United States courts taking jurisdiction, the *Romero* Court said:

> We are not here dealing with the sovereign power of the United States to apply its law to situations involving one or more foreign contacts. But in the absence of a contrary congressional direction, we must apply those principles of choice of law that are consonant with the needs of a general federal maritime law and with due recognition of our self-regarding respect for the relevant interests of foreign nations in the regulation of maritime commerce as part of the legitimate concern of the international community .... The controlling considerations are the interacting interests of the United St ates and of foreign countries, and in assessing them we must move with the circumspection appropriate when this Court is adjudicating issues inevitably entangled in the conduct of our international relations.

Romero was injured while temporarily in American territorial waters. This difference does not call for a difference in result [from Lauritzen] ... To impose on ships the duty of shifting from one standard of compensation to another as the vessel passes the boundaries of territorial waters would be not only an onerous but also an unduly speculative burden, disruptive of international commerce and without basis in the expressed policies of this country. The amount and type of recovery which a foreign seaman may receive from his foreign employer while sailing on a foreign ship should not depend upon the wholly fortuitous circumstance of the place of injury.[347]

[342] *Supra* at pp. 194–195.
[343] *Supra* at p. 152 *et seq.*
[344] 345 U.S. 571 (1952).
[345] 358 U.S. 354 (1958).
[346] p. 575.
[346a] 372 U.S. 10, 19 n. (1963).
[347] 358 U.S. 354, 382–384.

In *Lauritzen*, the Court disposed of the locus of the tort as a basis for applying American law in preference to the law of the flag as follows:

> But the territorial standard is so unfitted to an enterprise conducted under many territorial rules and under none that it usually is modified by the more constant law of the flag.[348]

It appears from the foregoing that almost no weight at all can be afforded the fact that the tort occurred in the United States rather than somewhere else. That is an entirely satisfactory conclusion. The fact that a ship may have crossed the line dividing the high seas from the territorial waters of a state or between the territorial waters of the two states should have no significance on the question of the law applicable to the controversy.[349]

At the other extreme, insofar as significant contacts are concerned, is the nationality or domicile of the injured seamen. Previously, this question was not much of a problem, since a seaman, by signing on a vessel of foreign registry was deemed to have acquired her nationality for legal purposes incidental to the employment.[350] Thus, the mere fact of an actual difference between the nationality of the ship and that of the seaman was immaterial. However, the Court in *Lauritzen* said, after citing *In re Ross:* "each nation has a legitimate interest that its nationals and permanent inhabitants be not maimed or disabled from self support. In some later American cases, courts have been prompted to apply the Jones Act by the fact that the wrongful act or omission alleged caused injury to an American citizen or domiciliary." [351] This is certainly an endorsement of the position that the law of the flag will not necessarily be applied if a national is suing in a court of the United States. It gives weight to some lower court decisions which have exercised jurisdiction primarily on the ground of the nationality or domicile of the plaintiff-seaman.[352] However, this isolated statement should not be taken to require an application of local law in such a situation. It is still only one factor, albeit a weighty one, to be considered in deciding which law is applicable.

[348] 345 U.S. 571, 584 (1952).

[349] The place of contracting too is purely fortuitous and should have no bearing on the choice of governing law. *Id.* at 588.

[350] *In re Ross*, 140 U.S. 453 (1891); *Rainey v. New York & P.S.S. Co., Ltd.*, 216 Fed. 449 (9th Cir. 1914).

[351] 345 U.S. 586.

[352] *Gambera v. Bergoty*, 132 F.2d 414 (2d Cir. 1942); *Bolden v. Jensen*, 70 Fed. 505 (D. Wash. N.D. 1895). It should be pointed out that this does not affect the constitutional argument discussed previously. *Supra* at pp. 169 *et seq.*

Another rather substantial contact which would tend to justify the application of American law is the nationality of the shipowner, who generally will be the employer and defendant in the personal injury suit.[353] This ties in with the question of nominal registration, which the Court discussed. In fact, the implication is raised that if the foreign registration is not a nominal one, the fact of United States national ownership would not justify application of local law.[354]

If the employment contract includes a designation of controlling law, this should be given great weight, provided that there is some substantial contact between the transaction and the law chosen as controlling. For example, a designation of the law of the flag state as controlling would be a provision which should be enforced, at least assuming that the question of nominal registration does not arise.[355] The Court in *Lauritzen* made the comment that "a quite different result would follow if the contract attempted to avoid applicable law, for example, so as to apply foreign law to an American ship." [356] This statement surely should not be construed to mean that the contractual designation of a controlling law is only valid if that law would have been controlling in absence of such designation. Such a construction would make the contract clause utterly without significance and the Court's discussion of it meaningless. There is an implication that American law must be applied to seamen on board American owned vessels regardless of contacts with other states. However, in the context of the rest of the decision, the probable meaning is that a designation of the law of a jurisdiction with which there are no substantial contacts would be invalid, at least if the vessel were American. This statement also leaves open the question of what ships are to be considered American.

Having determined that a particular foreign law controls the resolution of a controversy, the next question a court will have to determine will be whether the local action should be dismissed. It does not necessarily follow that because foreign law applies that a court of that state must apply the law.[357] Frequently, the claim will be that it is

[353] See *Lauritzen v. Larsen*, 345 U.S. 571, 587 (1952).

[354] As a matter of cutomary international law, there can be no question of the right of the United States to prescribe rules of conduct binding on its own nationals anywhere in the world and to apply these rules to them at will. *Supra* at p. 108. See *Skiriotes v. Florida*, 313 U.S. 69, 73 (1940); *Steele v. Bulova Watch Co.*, 344 U.S. 280, 282 (1952).

[355] See *Lauritzen v. Larsen*, 345 U.S. 571, 588–589 (1952); *cf. Pinney v. Nelson*, 183 U.S. 144 (1901); *Hatzoglou v. Asturias Shipping Co.*, 193 F. Supp. 195 (S.D. N.Y. 1961).

[356] 345 U.S. 589.

[357] See *Kontos v. The S.S. Sophie C.*, 184 F. Supp. 835. 837 (E.D. Pa. 1960).

part of the applicable foreign law that a consular officer of that state resolve the dispute. Evidence of this plus the fact that, under that law, he stands ready to grant effective remedy – possibly even pay an indemnity – has weighed heavily in convincing American courts to dismiss actions and relegate the man to action by the consul of the flag state.[358] The cases cited all indicated a willingness to dismiss an action governed by foreign law provided there is an adequate remedy locally available through the consul of the flag state. This is certainly an appropriate way to dispose of this type of situation. It would be utterly irrational to conclude that foreign law is applicable, that that law provides for consular jurisdiction and administration of an effective remedy, and then to persist in making a final decision. It should perhaps be pointed out that all these cases were decided without reference to any treaty which may or may not have pertained to the problem.

It is, of course, true to say that suits of this kind are sometimes dismissed without reference to the question of an effective remedy in a local consul. This would happen if the seaman pleaded a cause of action peculiar to United States law. For example, if a court determined that Danish law applied to a particular transaction; and the seaman had only pleaded a cause of action under the Jones Act, his action must of necessity be dismissed.[359] He would have to have pleaded a right under Danish law in order for the court ever to reach the question of a possible discretionary dismissal for *forum non conveniens*.

In the situation where the applicable foreign law either provides no consular authority in the premises or gives him merely interim authority, a final remedy to await the seaman's return to the flag state, the local courts then must decide whether the local forum chosen by the plaintiff is an appropriate one under all the circumstances. As a starting point in making this determination, a quotation from a decision of the United States Court of Appeals for the Second Circuit is appropriate:

[358] *The Paula*, 91 F.2d 1001 (2d Cir. 1937), *cert.* denied, 302 U.S. 750 (1937) ;*Berendson v. Rederiaktiebolaget Volo*, 257 F.2d 136 (2d Cir. 1958); *The Ivaran*, 121 F. 2d 445 (2d Cir. 1941); *The Knappingsborg*, 26 F2d 935 (E.D. N.Y. 1928); *The Ferm*, 15 F.2d 887 (E.D. N.Y. 1926); *Radovcic v. The Princ Pavle*, 45 F. Supp. 15 (S.D. N.Y. 1942) – in a prior decision in the same matter, the court had declined to dismiss the action because there was no showing that the remedy by the Yugoslav official in New York would result in getting mony into the hands of the seaman. That defect was corrected before this decision. See 43 F. Supp. 1013. *The Lynhaug*, 42 F. Supp. 713 (E.D. Pa. 1941); *The Astra*, 34 F. Supp. 152 (D. Md. 1940).

[359] See *Lauritzen v. Larsen*, 345 U.S. 571 (1953).

It is *prima facie* undesirable that an overburdened District Court should conduct a trial in a personal injury action between foreigners, with all the evidence on the issue of liability and much of the evidence on damages given in a foreign tongue by witnesses equally or more available in the foreign forum, and with reliance having to be placed on expert testimony as to the governing law, when, as here, an adequate remedy is available in the country where both parties reside and to which the plaintiff will return. Moreover, try as we may to apply the foreign law as it comes to us through the lips of experts, there is an inevitable hazard that, in those areas, perhaps interstitial but far from inconsequential, where we have no clear guides, our labors, moulded by our own habits of mind as they necessarily must be, may produce a result whose conformity with that of the foreign court may be greater in theory that it is in fact.[360]

The most significant idea expressed here is that there might be a remedy available to the plaintiff which is adequate even though not effective immidiately and in the United States. Tending to fortify this position is the common sense proposition that a United States court is not as competent to apply foreign law as would be a court of that state. In other words, it could result in an unjust result, and the court should take that into account in determining whether to exercise its jurisdiction. The question which the court must determine, then, is whether, notwithstanding that the seaman's remedy is deferred until it can be sought in another land, it is nevertheless justified to relegate him to that forum.

It is submitted that the fact that the applicable foreign law provides no remedy is absolutely irrelevant on the question of whether the local court should retain jurisdiction. In *The Apurimac.*[361] the court mentioned this as a reason for retaining jurisdiction. A commentator on the subject has said: "Starting with the proposition, which follows from the existence of jurisdiction in the first place, that a case will be retained whenever it is not perfectly clear that a plaintiff can recover elsewhere if the facts he alleges are true ...." [362] The implication is that, if American law provides a remedy in a particular fact situation and the applicable foreign law (If American law applied, the case *certainly* would not be dismissed for trial in a foreign country.) does not, jurisdiction should be retained. This, it is submitted, is a *non sequitur*, since if the matter were retained for decision under those circumstances, the most the court could do would be to dismiss on the merits instead of for *forum non conveniens*. If the argument is that where the applicable

[360] *Conte v. Flota Mercante Del Estado*, 277 F.2d 664, 667 (2d Cir. 1960).

[361] 7 F.2d 741 (E.D. Va. 1925), aff'd, 12 F.2d 500 (4th Cir. 1926).

[362] Bickel, Alexander M., "Forum Non Conveniens in Admiralty," 35 Cornell L.Q. 12, 28 (1950).

foreign law provides a remedy which for some collateral reason might be barred if the seaman were relegated to the courts of that state – such as the impending expiration of the period of limitation under that law [363] – the local court should retain jurisdiction, that would be a more logical position. It is fair to say, however, that if the bar under foreign law had already arisen when the local action was commenced, since that law is by hypothesis applicable to the controversy, the action should be dismissed either for *forum non conveniens* or upon the merits. In other words, it is only where the dismissal will legally prejudice a claim otherwise tenable under the controlling law that the court should retain it for decision on the merits.

On the question of whether plaintiff will be factually prejudiced (as distinguished from legal prejudice) by a dismissal (assuming a theoretical cause of action on the alleged facts under the applicable foreign law), perhaps the most significant factor which the courts should consider is the probability that the plaintiff would, but for the pending local action, in the normal course of events go to the state the law of which is applicable.[364] If the man is an American national who has not taken up a permanent residence in the foreign state, the chances are negligible that he would go there for any other reason than to pursue his remedy. Under such circumstances, it would be an unconscionable result to relegate him to such a forum. The same is true of a foreign national who has taken up permanent residence in the United States.[365] Of course, if United States immigration laws preclude the probability of his remaining in the United States, that would make it much more reasonable for the court to dismiss the action.

On the question of whether the plaintiff should be relegated to the

[363] See *Kontos v. The S.S. Sophie C.*, 184 F. Supp. 835, 837 (E.D. Pa. 1960).

[364] In *Kontos v. The S.S. Sophie C.*, *id.*, the court retained jurisdiction notwithstanding that the plaintiffs had returned to Greece, the country claimed to constitute a more convenient forum to resolve the dispute. However, in that case, the vessel was registered in Liberia, owned by a British corporation, the beneficial interest in which was held by an Argentine national. It was therefore by no means clear that the Greek court would not be applying Liberian law which incorporates the non-statutory maritime law of the United States, a law which United States courts are more competent to apply. *Id.* at 837. At any rate, there was no forum common to plaintiff and defendant, which would have been a much more persuasive argument for dismissal. See *The Belgenland*, 114 U.S. 355, 368–369 (1884).

[365] *The S.S. Emmy*, 39 F. Supp. 871 (S.D. N.Y. 1940); *The Seirstad*, 12 F.2d 133 (E.D. N.Y. 1926). In the latter case, the motion to dismiss was originally granted upon a showing that the Norwegian consul was prepared to provide the plaintiff with free transportation to Norway where an effective remedy for his injuries existed. However, on reargument, the court was satisfied that the seaman had taken out "first papers" for American citizenship and would in all probability because of the seriousness of his injuries be unable to return to the United States. The court felt that it would be an undue hardship under these circumstances to relegate him to his remedy in Norway.

foreign forum, the seriousness of his injuries – which may effectively prevent recourse to that forum –[366] should be considered. Additionally, it is important to determine whether he can economically travel to the foreign state within a reasonable time. If the ship or the consul stands ready to provide prompt and free transportation to that country, the court should be much more prepared to permit the action to be litigated there.[367] On the other hand, if he is not to actually return with the vessel which caused the injury, it might be an injustice to relegate him to the foreign forum.[368] The vessel might not herself be returning there, and he may never again have both the vessel and the witnesses together in the same jurisdiction.[369] That problem might be partially overcome by requiring the defendant to put up a bond to the extent of the amount of the claim. There might be circumstances where it would be manifestly unjust to insist that the seaman be repatriated on the vessel on which he was injured. If the master or officers have demonstrated already such a depraved mentality as to justify the inference that the seaman would not be safe or accorded ordinary human dignity on that ship,[370] he certainly should not be expected to return on her.

CONCLUSION

Whenever a vessel of one state is transiently within the waters of another, a conflict potentially exists between them as to which will control the incidents of various activities in and around the ship, and which will resolve controversies concerning the vessel and her company.

Inherent in the jurisdictional conflict problem is the question of what state is entitled to claim the vessel as its own. In United States practice, that problem has generally been resolved by looking to the registration. The courts, on occassion, have toyed with ideas of purely nominal registrations not entitled to recognition for that reason, but on the whole, there has been surprising consistency in accepting the registration as conclusive on the question. The only slight deviation, other than some isolated court decisions in personal injury actions, has

[366] See *The City of Carlisle*, 39 Fed. 807 (D. Ore. 1889); *The Seirstad, id; c.f. O'Neill v. Cunard White Star, Ltd.*, 160 F.2d 446 (2d Cir. 1947).

[367] See *The Seirstad*, 12 F.2d 133 (E.D. N.Y. 1926); *The Troop*, 128 Fed. 856, 862–863 (9th Cir. 1904).

[368] *Cf. The Walter D. Wallet*, 66 Fed. 1011 (S.D. Ala. 1895).

[369] *The Noodleburn*, 30 Fed. 142 (D. Ore. 1887); *The Troop*, *supra* note 367.

[370] See *The City of Carlisle*, 39 Fed. 807 (D. Ore. 1889).

been the conclusion of the United Nations Convention on the High Seas with its clause requiring a "genuine link" between a ship and the state which registers her. The ultimate jurisdictional consequences of that provision are as yet unpredictable with any degree of certainty; but because of the great number of bilateral treaties of the United States expressly resolving the question in favor of conclusiveness of the registration – which agreements are expressly preserved by the High Seas Convention – it can have little effect in United States foreign relations.

The country to which the vessel belongs has a well defined and internationally recognized interest in the vessel, her crew and activities. The interests of that state are best served by the least possible interference by local authorities in the operations of the ship. Even the slightest interposition of local authority sows the seed of complication and potential detention of the vessel, with its resultant harm to the foreign commerce of the flag state.

Maritime commerce being an internationally shared enterprise, most states which receive vessels of other nations in turn send ships abroad which there create similar problems. Additionally, the purpose of vessel movement being primarily the international transport of merchandise and passengers, receiving states have an interest in expediting ship activities for the resultant beneficial effect upon the flow of goods and people across their boarders. The interest, then, in non-interference with vessel movements is one which can be said to be international in scope. However, the institution of national sovereignty with its concomitant and largely emotional dedication to domestic administrative control of all incidents of human activity within the state is deeply ingrained in the minds of men. Thus, each state finds itself always in an ambivalent position. Its long term economic interests are best served by permitting vessel movements to be unimpeded to the greatest extent possible, but this of necessity involves the exercise of alien authority within the state, and that offends the national pride. In opposition to the common international interest in expediting vessel movements by limiting the exercise of local jurisdiction is the purely local interest in protection of the public and its individual members against the adverse effects of these same operations. In any particular situation, this interest is exclusive to the territorial authorities where the vessel happens to be, but the same general problem is common to all maritime states. The balancing, then, of this interest against the interest in a free flowing maritime commerce is of importance to any state engaged in that commerce.

In the very earliest history of an international maritime commerce, the tendency was to solve the jurisdictional conflict by agreement, express or tacit, excluding not only vessels and crews, but also foreign merchants generally, from the exercise of local authority. Also symptomatic of the same problem, and extending even further back into history, was the development of a special, largely uniform, body of commercial law applicable to merchants and mariners everywhere in the then known world of commerce. Doubtlessly, widely divergent social and legal philosophies contributed to these results.

As the countries of Europe gradually moved towards a common culture, the consensus arose that it was no longer necessary to exclude the foreign merchants from local authority. This attitude was reinforced by the rising tide of nationalist sentiment which held it undesirable that an alien authority should hold away, even to such restricted extent within the national territory. The exceptions in favor of ships and seamen, however, continued for the same reasons which brought them into existence.

The Arabic and other non-European peoples neither developed common social and legal assumptions nor nationalist sentiments as early as the European states. As a result, the broad jurisdictional exclusionary rules continued in favor of nationals of states of the European heritage in those areas. Ultimately, as was to be expected, demands for equality of treatment as sovereign nations, coupled with changing attitudes towards the rights of individuals and the state, produced an end of the "capitularies". There remained only the residuum of special rules applicable universally to ships and their crews.

The dispersal of governmental authority in the United States has confused the question of defining the American viewpoint concerning consular authority. Of course, to the extent that primary local jurisdiction is asserted, it constitutes a denial of consular authority, with the concomitant recognition of a like reciprocal right of denial. Although it it impossible to delineate exactly the line of demarkation between relevant activities of the three branches of government, it is possible to determine generally the differences which exist in certain specific areas.

The main tensions in underlying policy between governmental authorities which can be discerned exist between Congress and the Executive. As a general statement, it appears that Congress is more jealous of territorial sovereign rights of administration, whereas the

Executive is more prepared to admit of restrictions upon local competence where the interests of commerce will thereby be subserved. The courts maintain an uneasy balance between assertions of unlimited local sovereign powers and recognition of international legal or comity restrictions on that power.

The State Department position on the question of jurisdictional exclusionary rules for foreign maritime interests has not in itself really been consistent. Abstract statements have always insisted that any such rights are rooted in the consent of the local sovereign. This is consistent with the theory that all international law, including customary rules, grows out of the consent of sovereign states. However, an additional element has been introduced in this area by the United States by equating assent with formal treaty commitments, denying that there is any binding customary law on the subject.

On the other hand, both the State Department and the courts have rather consistently handled controversies in the area as if tacitly assuming that there are governing rules even absent controlling treaty provisions. These assumptions follow generally the pattern set by the similar provisions of the numerous bilateral agreements to which the United States is party.

From the time of independence, the treaty line of demarkation between local and flag state jurisdiction was drawn between situations which were restricted in their effect to the ship and its company and those which were not. They were framed in terms of "exclusive jurisdiction" in the flag state authorities – usually the consul – over those problems, controversies and activities which had no direct effect external to the vessel. The "peace of the port" provisions were used to aid in defining those situations where it was an alleged criminal act which had occurred. Special provisions were adopted to dispose of problems raised by desertions from foreign vessels, the consul being accorded the right to require arrest and surrender of the seaman to him or the vessel. Wages and employment contract problems were especially reserved for his jurisdiction.

Until 1915, the only marked tension between Congress and the State Department positions, and one which raised little atcual controversy, was in the area of criminal law. Statutory provisions, which are still extant, purported to attach penal consequences to conduct on board vessels, wherever they might be, owned in whole or in part by American nationals. Treaty provisions at the same time, and also continuing to date, made registration conclusive on the question of ship nationality.

This was implicit recognition of the prescriptive jurisdictional competence of that state, raising the possibility of a conflict of jurisdiction on foreign flag vessels owned by American nationals when they are outside the United States.

In 1915, special statutes were passed intended to nullify any possible consular right to reclaim deserters, and imposing certain wage controls upon foreign vessels in United States ports. This action ran counter to treaty obligations of the United States, requiring, as a result, a change in the pattern of related international agreements. Since that time, there has been no provision for arrest of deserters, and local jurisdiction has been made primary in cases of wage and employment contract disputes.

More to be deplored than the treaty provisions concerning wage and employment contract disputes is the modern tendency in United States treaty practice of leaving the extent of consular maritime authority intentionally ambiguous by use of terminology which might possibly be construed to permit local legal nullification of consular authority recognized by other provisions of the same treaty. If the purpose of this type of clause is in fact to make local jurisdiction primary in all situations – as has been the case in wage and contract disputes since 1915 – more felicitous phrases could have been adopted to accomplish that goal. It is submitted that there is no particular virtue in leaving such a question to be resolved by future disputes.

It is not suggested that the United States should aim to make local jurisdiction primary in those situations where it is not already dictated by federal statutes – as it is in wage disputes. In fact, it is impossible to find rational justification for any interference by the territorial authorities in activities or controversies wholly confined in their immediate effects to the ship.

So long as an offender is confined securely on board the ship, there should be no question of local prosecution for a crime involving only members of the ship's company. The "peace of the port" doctrine which dictates otherwise in cases of more severe crimes, it is submitted, should be remodeled to restrict the exercise of local authority in such cases to assuring that the accused is not a threat to local security. It is difficult to imagine what philosophic principle is vindicated by imprisoning or executing an offender who is not a resident and therefore not a menace to the local populace. Not only would this approach save the expense of trial and execution of punishment locally, at no sacrifice of a domestic interest, but it would expedite the ship's departure by interposing the minimum amount of interference with the activities and people on board. If the consular officer had already adequately secured the offender, there would be negligible expense to the local authorities and negligible interference with international commerce.

In the area of civil controversies, too, there appears to be no sufficient justification for local interference so long as it is wholly confined in effect to the vessel. Of course, in view of the wage statutes which are by their terms applicable to foreign ships, that type of controversy must be decided by the courts when brought before them. However, the original purpose in the passage of those statutes has long since been accomplished to the extent that these acts are capable of affecting the problems which brought them into being. It was, perhaps, naive to imagine that these laws could effect an equalization of wages and conditions between American and foreign crews. They may have had some such tendency, but there are so many other economic factors which influence the problem that their influence would be minimal. At any rate, Congress has long since given up encouragement of foreign seamen to desert their vessels in the United States. Today, they are even discouraged by rather stringent immigration laws from leaving their employment. It is clearly time that Congress reviewed this whole area with the idea of rendering it consistent with policies expressed elsewhere. There does not seem to be any good reason today for United States courts to resolve labor disputes between foreigners on foreign vessels by application of American law.

If the desire is to apply American law to American owners of foreign flag vessels, this can be accomplished without making the law applicable to all foreign flag shipping. When the problem involves "runaway shipping" the United States may well have an interest sufficient to justify the additional burden upon international commerce incidental to the application of certain American laws on board. There are, however, more efficient ways of discouraging "flags of convenience", if that is the intent, than exercising civil or criminal jurisdiction over internal matters while they are in United States ports. In fact, such application of authority would at best have a purely nominal effect, and that possibly at the expense of retaliatory measures abroad the cumulative effect of which could constitute an onerous burden on commerce. Thus, the most desirable course would be a repeal of those laws which are by their terms applicable to foreign flag ships in United States harbors and the execution of treaties which recognize the primacy of the flag state jurisdiction and law in all situations where the direct effects of the activity or controversy are limited to the vessel and her company.

An exception which legitimately might be engrafted upon the rule espoused in the preceding paragraph, it is submitted, should be for the benefit of an American national or permanent resident upon whom the application of the foreign law would work an injustice. For example, if an American seaman on a foreign flag vessel were discriminatorily left without an effective remedy for personal injury under the foreign law, it would be rational to provide him with one. This does not mean that a mere lack of remedy or the apparent inadequacy of an existing remedy would justify interference; but if the reason was his alien status, the courts should intervene. Similarly, if the punishment under foreign law for an act on board were, for example, mutilation, a local court would be wholly justified in "rescuing" an American national from such a possible fate by asserting jurisdiction over the act.

Finally, in a situation where the foreign law provides a remedy, but which remedy, because of the peculiar circumstances, is ineffective unless enforced locally, it should be possible to accomplish that end. This would, of course, not be true in any case where the consul was empowered by the foreign law to effectuate the remedy. This type of situation, as well as the one envisaged in the preceding paragraph, could be anticipated by appropriate treaty provision.

In summation, it is time that the United States began revamping their foreign policy in the maritime jurisdiction area so that law and practice are consistent one with the other and with the real interests of the United States. Jurisdiction should only be exercised over foreign flag vessels when there is some genuine interest of the United States to be served, and that interest justifies interfering with the flow of commerce in all such future situations at home and abroad. This might well be the case where the act or activity has a direct effect upon the rights and interests of people outside the ship, but it is unlikely to be justified otherwise. Certainly the sole fact of physical presence within the country, regardless of the nature of the problem, is not sufficient justification for interfering in the internal economy of a foreign vessel over the protests of her consul. It is absurd to attempt to justify any such acts by reliance upon some such archaic doctrine as that of the "peace of the port" or by claiming that the sovereign dignity requires that the act be punished.

APPENDIX A

TREATIES OF THE UNITED STATES

1.	1778	France, Amity and Commerce	8 Stat.	12
2.	1782	The Netherlands, Amity and Commerce	8 Stat.	32
3.	1783	Sweden, Amity and Commerce	8 Stat.	60
4.	1785	Prussia, Amity and Commerce	8 Stat.	84
5.	1787	Morocco, Peace and Friendship	8 Stat.	100
6.	1788	France, Consular Convention	8 Stat.	106
7.	1794	Great Britain, Amity, Commerce and Navigation	8 Stat.	116
8.	1795	Algiers, Peace and Amity	8 Stat.	133
9.	1796	Tripoli, Peace and Friendship	8 Stat.	154
10.	1797–1799	Tunis, Peace and Friendship	8 Stat.	157
11.	1800	France, Convention for Terminating Differences	8 Stat.	178
12.	1805	Tripoli, Peace and Amity	8 Stat.	214
13.	1815	Algiers, Peace and Amity	8 Stat.	224
14.	1815	Great Britain, Commerce and Navigation	8 Stat.	228
15.	1816	Sweden, Friendship and Commerce	8 Stat.	232
16.	1816	Algiers, Peace and Amity	8 Stat.	244
17.	1822	France, Navigation and Commerce	8 Stat.	278
18.	1824	Tunis, Peace and Friendship	8 Stat.	298
19.	1824	Colombia, Peace, Amity, Navigation and Commerce	8 Stat.	306
20.	1825	Federation of the Centre of America, Peace, Amity, Commerce, and Navigation	8 Stat.	322
21.	1826	Denmark, Friendship, Commerce, and Navigation	8 Stat.	340
22.	1827	Sweden and Norway, Commerce and Navigation	8 Stat.	346
23.	1827	Lubeck, Bremen and Hamburg, Friendship, Commerce and Navigation	8 Stat.	366
24.	1828	Prussia, Commerce and Navigation	8 Stat.	378
25.	1828	Brazil, Peace and Friendship	8 Stat.	390
26.	1829	Austria, Commerce and Navigation	8 Stat.	398
27.	1830	Ottoman Porte, Friendship	8 Stat.	408
28.	1831	Mexico, Amity, Commerce, and Navigation	8 Stat.	410
29.	1832	Chile, Peace, Amity, Commerce, and Navigation	8 Stat.	434
30.	1832	Russia, Navigation and Commerce	8 Stat.	444

31.	1833	Siam, Amity and Commerce	8 Stat. 454
32.	1833	Muscat, Amity and Commerce	8 Stat. 458
33.	1836	Venezuela, Peace, Friendship, Navigation and Commerce	8 Stat. 466
34.	1836	Morocco, Peace and Friendship	8 Stat. 484
35.	1836	Peru – Bolivia, Peace, Friendship, Commerce and Navigation	8 Stat. 487
36.	1837	Greece, Commerce and Navigation	8 Stat. 498
37.	1838	Sardinia, Commerce and Navigation	8 Stat. 512
38.	1839	The Netherlands	8 Stat. 524
39.	1839	Equador, Friendship, Commerce and Navigation	8 Stat. 534
40.	1840	Hanover, Commerce and Navigation	8 Stat. 552
41.	1840	Portugal, Commerce and Navigation	8 Stat. 560
42.	1844	China, Peace, Amity, and Commerce	8 Stat. 592
43.	1845	Belgium, Commerce and Navigation	8 Stat. 606
44.	1846	Hanover, Commerce and Navigation	9 Stat. 55
45.	1846	New Granada, Peace, Amity, Navigation, and Commerce	9 Stat. 79
46.	1848	Austria, Commerce and Navigation	9 Stat. 152 [944]
47.	1849	Hawaiian Islands, Friendship, Commerce, and Navigation	9 Stat. 178
48.	1849	Guatemala, Peace, Amity, Commerce, and Navigation	10 Stat. 1 [873]
49.	1850	San Salvador, Amity, Navigation, and Commerce	10 Stat. 71 [891]
50.	1850	New Granada, Consular Convention	10 Stat. 80 [900]
51.	1850	Borneo, Peace and Friendship	10 Stat. 89 [909]
52.	1850	Swiss Confederation, Friendship, Reciprocal Establishments, Commerce, and Surrender of Fugitive Criminals	11 Stat. 1 [587]
53.	1851	Costarica, Friendship, Commerce, and Navigation	10 Stat. 18 [916]
54.	1851	Peru, Friendship, Commerce, and Navigation	10 Stat. 28 [926]
55.	1852	Hanseatic Republic, Consular Convention	10 Stat. 95 [961]
56.	1853	France. Consular Convention	10 Stat. 114 [992]
57.	1853	Argentine Confederation, Friendship, Commerce, and Navigation	10 Stat. 233 [1001]
58.	1853	Argentine Confederation, Free Navigation of Rivers Parana and Uruguay	10 Stat. 237 [1101]
59.	1854	Lew Chew, Compact	10 Stat. 211 [597]

60.	1854	Japan, Peace and Amity	11 Stat. 11 [639]
61.	1855	The Two Sicilies, Peace, Friendship, Commerce, etc.	11 Stat. 89 [709]
62.	1856	Persia, Friendship, Commerce, etc.	11 Stat. 115 [683]
63.	1856	Siam, Amity and Commerce	11 Stat. 149
64.	1857	Japan, Regulation of Intercourse	11 Stat. 723
65.	1858	Bolivia, Peace, Friendship, Commerce, and Navigation	12 Stat. 1003
66.	1858	China, Peace, Amity, and Commerce	12 Stat. 1023
67.	1858	Belgium, Commerce and Navigation	12 Stat. 1043
68.	1858	Japan, Amity and Commerce	12 Stat. 1051
69.	1859	Paraguay, Friendship, Commerce and Navigation	12 Stat. 1091
70.	1860	Venezuela, Amity, Commerce, Navigation, and Surrender of Fugitives	12 Stat. 1143
71.	1861	Denmark, Friendship, Commerce, and Navigation	13 Stat. 605
72.	1862	Ottoman Empire, Commerce and Navigation	12 Stat. 1213
73.	1862	Liberia, Commerce and Navigation	12 Stat. 1245
74.	1864	Honduras, Friendship, Commerce, and Navigation	13 Stat. 699
75.	1864	Hayti, Amity, Commerce, and Navigation etc.	13 Stat. 711
76.	1867	Dominican Republic, Amity, Commerce, and Navigation	15 Stat. 473
77.	1867	Madagascar, Commerce	15 Stat. 491
78.	1867	Nicaragua, Friendship, Commerce and Navigation	15 Stat. 549
79.	1868	Italy, Consular Convention	15 Stat. 605
80.	1868	China, Additional Articles to Treaty of 1858	16 Stat. 739
81.	1868	Belgium, Consular Convention	16 Stat. 757
82.	1870	Austria-Hungary, Consular Convention	17 Stat. 821
83.	1870	Peru, Friendship, Commerce, and Navigation	18 Stat. 698
84.	1870	Salvador, Amity, Commerce, and Consular Privileges	18 Stat. 725
85.	1871	Italy, Commerce and Navigation	17 Stat. 845
86.	1871	Germany, Consuls and Trademarks	17 Stat. 921
87.	1871	Orange Free State, Friendship, Commerce, and Extradition	18 Stat. 749
88.	1875	Belgium, Commerce and Navigation	19 Stat. 628 [72]
89.	1878	The Netherlands, Consular Convention	21 Stat. 662
90.	1878	Samoa, Friendship and Commerce	20 Stat. 704
91.	1878	Italy, Consular Convention	20 Stat. 725
92.	1880	Belgium, Consular Convention	21 Stat. 776
93.	1881	Italy, Consular Convention	22 Stat. 831
94.	1881	Madagascar, Friendship and Commerce	22 Stat. 952
95.	1881	Serbia, Commerce and Navigation	22 Stat. 963
96.	1881	Roumania, Consular Convention	23 Stat. 711
97.	1882	Corea, Peace, Amity, Commerce and Navi-	

		gation	23 Stat. 720
98.	1884	Multilateral Convention for the Protection of Submarine Cables	24 Stat. 989
99.	1884	Egypt, Commerce and Customs	24 Stat. 1004
100.	1886	Zanzibar, Amendments to Treaty of 1833	25 Stat. 1438
101.	1886	Tonga, Amity, Commerce, and Navigation	25 Stat. 1440
102.	1887	Peru, Friendship, Commerce, and Navigation	25 Stat. 1444
103.	1891	Congo, Amity, Commerce, and Navigation	27 Stat. 926
104.	1892	United Kingdom, Recovery of Deserters from Merchant Vessels	27 Stat. 961
105.	1894	Japan, Commerce and Navigation	29 Stat. 848
106.	1899	Great Britain and Germany, Samoan Islands Relations	31 Stat. 1878
107.	1902	Spain, Friendship and General Relations	33 Stat. 2105
108.	1902	Greece, Consular Convention	33 Stat. 2122
109.	1903	China, Commercial Relations	33 Stat. 2208
110.	1904	France, Relations in Tunis	33 Stat. 2263
111.	1905	Great Britain, Relinquishment of Extraterritorial Rights in Zanzibar	34 Stat. 2870
111.a	1906	Multilateral, Act of Algeciras	34 Stat. 2905
112.	1910	Sweden, Consular Convention	37 Stat. 1479
113.	1911	Japan, Commerce and Navigation	37 Stat. 1504
114.	1919	Multilateral, International Labor Organization	49 Stat. 2712
115.	1920	Siam, Amity, Commerce and Navigation	42 Stat. 1928
116.	1923	Germany, Friendship, Commerce and Consular Rights	44 Stat. 2132
117.	1924	France, Rights in Syria and Lebanon	43 Stat. 1821
118.	1924	United Kingdom, Rights in Palestine	44 Stat. 2184
119.	1925	Esthonia, Friendship, Commerce and Consular Rights	44 Stat. 2379
120.	1925	United Kingdom, Rights in Togoland	44 Stat. 2433
121.	1926	Cuba, Consular Convention	44 Stat. 2471
122.	1926	El Salvador, Friendship, Commerce and Consular Rights	46 Stat. 2817
123.	1927	Honduras, Friendship, Commerce and Consular Rights	45 Stat. 2608
124.	1928	Latvia, Friendship, Commerce and Consular Rights	45 Stat. 2641
125.	1928	Multilateral, Pan American Consular Convention	47 Stat. 1976
126.	1928	Norway, Friendship, Commerce and Consular Rights etc.	47 Stat. 2135
127.	1930	Great Britain, Rights in Iraq	47 Stat. 1817
128.	1931	Multilateral, Convention on Narcotic Drugs	48 Stat. 1543
129.	1931	Turkey, Establishment and Sojourn	47 Stat. 2432
130.	1931	Poland, Friendship, Commerce and Consular Rights etc.	48 Stat. 1507
131.	1934	Finland, Friendship, Commerce and Consular Rights	49 Stat. 2659
132.	1934	Multilateral, Protection of Industrial Property	53 Stat. 1748
133.	1936	Multilateral, Liability of the Shipowner in Case of Sickness, Injury or Death of Seamen	54 Stat. 1693
133.a	1936	Multilateral, Officers' Competency Certificates	54 Stat. 1683

134.	1937	Multilateral, Abolition of Capitulation in Egypt	53 Stat. 1645
135.	1937	Siam, Friendship, Commerce and Navigation	53 Stat. 1731
136.	1938	Liberia, Friendship, Commerce and Navigation	54 Stat. 1739
137.	1938	Iraq, Commerce and Navigation	54 Stat. 1790
138.	1942	Mexico, Consular Convention	57 Stat. 800
140.	1943	China, Relinquishment of Extraterritorial Rights	57 Stat. 767
141.	1944	Syria and Lebanon, Rights of American Nationals	58 Stat. 1491
142.	1946	Yemen, Friendship and Commerce	60 Stat. 1782
142.a	1946	China, Friendship, Commerce and Navigation	63 Stat. 1300
143.	1947	Nepal, Friendship and Commerce	61 Stat. 2566
144.	1947	Multilateral, General Agreement on Tariffs and Trade	61 Stat. Pt. 5, A 21
145.	1947	Phillipines, Consular Convention	62 Stat. 1593
146.	1948	Costa Rica, Consular Convention	TIAS 2045, 1 USTIAS 247
149.	1950	Ireland, Friendship, Commerce and Navigation	TIAS 2155, 1 USTIAS 785
150.	1950–1952	Ireland, Consular Officers	TIAS 2984, 5 USTIAS 949
151.	1951	Denmark, Friendship, Commerce and Navigation	TIAS 4797, 12 USTIAS 908
152.	1951	United Kingdom, Consular Officers	TIAS 2494, 3 USTIAS 3426
153.	1951	Multilateral, North Atlantic Treaty, Status of Forces	TIAS 2846, 4 USTIAS 1792
154.	1951	Ethiopia, Amity and Economic Relations	TIAS 2864, 4 USTIAS 2134
155.	1951	Israel, Friendship, Commerce and Navigation	TIAS 2948, 5 USTIAS 550
156.	1951	Greece, Friendship, Commerce and Navigation	TIAS 3057, 5 USTIAS 1829
156.a	1951	Multilateral, W.H.O., International Sanitary Regulations	TIAS 3625, 7 USTIAS 2255
157.	1953	Japan, Friendship, Commerce and Navigation	TIAS 2863, 4 USTIAS 2063
158.	1954	Federal Republic of Germany, Friendship, Commerce and Navigation	TIAS 3593, 7 USTIAS 1839
159.	1955	Iran, Amity, Economic Relations, and Consular Rights	TIAS 3853, 8 USTIAS 899
160.	1956	Multilateral, Status of Tangier	TIAS 3680, 7 USTIAS 3035
161.	1956	The Netherlands, Frienship, Commerce and Navigation	TIAS 3942, 8 USTIAS 2043

162.	1956	Republic of Korea, Friendship, Commerce and Navigation	TIAS 3947, 8 USTIAS 2217
163.	1956	Nicaragua, Friendship, Commerce and Navigation	TIAS 4024, 9 USTIAS 449
164.	1958	Muscat and Oman and Dependencies, Amity, Economic Relations and Consular Rights	TIAS 4530, 11 USTIAS 1835
165.	1958	Multilateral, Protection of Industrial Property	TIAS 4931, 13 USTIAS 1
166.	1958	Multilateral, Law of the Sea (Convention on the High Seas)	TIAS 5200, 13 USTIAS 2312
167.	1958	Multilateral, Law of the Sea (Convention on the Continental Shelf)	TIAS 5578, 15 USTIAS 471
167.a	1958	Multilateral, Law of the Sea (Convention on the Territorial Sea and the Contiguous Zone)	U.N. Doc. A/CONF. 13/L. 52
167.b	1958	Multilateral, Law of the Sea (Convention on Fishing and Conservation of the Living Resources of the High Seas)	U.N. Doc. A/CONF. 13/L. 54
168.	1960	Pakistan, Friendship and Commerce	TIAS 4683, 12 USTIAS 110
168.a	1961	Denmark, Friendship, Commerce and Navigation	TIAS 4797, 12 USTIAS 908
169.	1954–1961	Multilateral, Oil Pollution of the Sea, Prevention	TIAS 4900, 12 USTIAS 2989
170.	1961	Viet-Nam, Amity and Economic Relations	TIAS 4890, 12 USTIAS 1711
171.	1961	Belgium, Friendship, Establishment and Navigortion	TIAS 5432, 14 USTIAS 1285
172.	1962	Luxembourg, Friendship, Establishment and Navigation	TIAS 5306, 14 USTIAS 251
173.	1963	Korea, Republic of, Consular Convention	TIAS 5469, 14 USTIAS 1637
174.	1963	Japan, Consular Convention and Protocol	TIAS 5602, 15 USTIAS 768
175.	1963	Multilateral, Vienna Convention on Consular Relations	U.N. Doc. A/CONF. 25/12, 57 AJIL 995 (1963)

BIBLIOGRAPHY

Académie-Diplomatique Internationale, *Dictionnaire Diplomatique*. Paris, A-D I, 1933.

Adair, Edward Robert. *The Extraterritoriality of Ambassadors in the Sixteenth and Seventeenth Centuries*. London. Longmans, Green, 1929.

Albrecht, Arthur Emil. *International Seamen's Union of America, A Study of its History and Problems*. U.S. Bureau of Labor Statistics, Bulletin No. 342, June, 1923. Washington, D.C. Government Printing Office, 1923.

American Law Institute. Restatement of the Law – Conflict of Laws. St. Paul, Minn. A.L.I., 1934.

American Law Institute. Restatement of the Law – Judgments. St. Paul, Minn. A.L.I., 1942.

American Law Institute. Restatement of the Law – The Foreign Relations Law of the United States, Proposed Official Draft. Philadelphia, Pa. A.L.I. Executive Office, 1962.

American Law Institute. Restatement of the Law Second, Tentative Draft No. 4, Conflict of Laws. Philadelphia, Pa. A.L.I. Executive Office, 1957.

Amos, Andrew. *Roman Civil Law*. London. Stevens and Sons, 1883.

Ashburner, Walter. *The Rhodian Sea-Law*. London. Oxford University Press, 1909.

Barnes, William, and John Heath Morgan. *The Foreign Service of the United States*. Washington, D.C. Government Printing Office, 1961.

Benedict, Erastus Cornelius. *The Law of American Admiralty*. 7 volumes, 6th revised edition by Arnold Whitman Knauth. New York, N.Y., Baker, Voorhis, 1940.

Bickel, Alexander M. "Forum Non Conveniens in Admiralty." 35 *Cornell Law Quarterly* 12, 1950.

Block, Louis. "The Seamen's Right to Strike." XXXII *The American Labor Legislation Review* No. 2, 73. American Ass'n for Labor Legislation, June 1942.

Boczek, Boleslaw Adam. *Flags of Convenience*. Cambridge, Mass. Harvard University Press, 1962.

Boggs, S. Whittemore. "National Claims in Adjacent Seas." 41 *Geographical Review* 183–209, 1951.

Borchard, Edwin. "The Relation Between International Law and Municipal Law." 27 *Virginia Law Review* 137, 1940.

Bowett, D. W. *The Law of International Institutions*. New York, N.Y. F.A. Praeger, 1963.

Briggs, Herbert W. *The Law of Nations*. Second Edition. New York, N.Y. Appleton-Century-Crofts, 1952.

British Foreign Office. Treaties, etc. of Commerce and Navigation between Great Britain and Foreign Powers Wholly or Partially in Force on January 1, 1907. London. Harrison and Sons, 1907.

Bryce, James. *The Holy Roman Empire*. London. Macmillan and Co., 1889.

Burdick, Charles Kellogg. *The Law of the American Constitution*. New York, N.Y. G. P. Putnam's sons, 1922.

Burke, William T., and Myers S. McDougal. "Crisis in the Law of the Sea: Community Perspectives Versus National Egoism." 67 *Yale Law Journal* 539–589, 1958.

Cadwalader, John T. *Digest of the Published Opinions of the Attorneys-General, and of the Leading Decisions of the Federal Courts, with Reference to International Law, Treaties and Kindred Subjects*. Washington, D.C. Government Printing Office, 1877.

Cahn, Edmond Nathaniel. *Supreme Court and Supreme Law*. Bloomington, Ind. Indiana University Press, 1954.

Carr, W. J. "The American Consular Service." 1 *A.J.I.L.* 891, 1907.

Catudal, Honoré Marcel. "The Most-Favored-Nation Clause and the Courts." 35 *A.J.I.L.* 41–54, 1941.

Charteris, A. H. "Habeas Corpus in Respect of Detention on a Foreign Merchantman." 8 *Journal of Comparative Legislation and International Law* 246, 1926.

Charteris, A.H. "The Legal Position of Merchantmen in Foreign Ports and National Waters." I *British Yearbook of International Law* 45, 1920–21.

Cheng, Bin. *General Principles of Law as Applied by International Courts and Tribunals*. London. Stevens and Sons, 1953.

Childs, James Rives. *American Foreign Service*. New York, N.Y. H. Holt, 1948.

Colombos, Constantine John. *The International Law of the Sea*. Fifth revised edition. London. Longmans, 1962.

Columbia Law Review. Comment, Panlibhon Registration of American-Owned Merchant Ships: Government Policy and the Problem of the Courts. 60 *Columbia Law Review* 711, 1960.

Corbett, Percy E. "The Search for General Principles of Law." 47 *Virginia Law Review* 811, 1961.

Corwin, Edward Samuel. *The Constitution and World Organization*. Princeton, N.J. Princeton University Press, 1944.

Crandall, Samuel B. *Treaties, Their Making and Enforcement*. Washington, D.C. John Byrne & Co., 1916.

Cutler, John Ward. "The Treatment of Foreigners." 27 *A.J.I.L.* 225, 1933.

Davis, Kenneth Culp. *Administrative Law Treatise*. 4 volumes. St. Paul, Minn. West Publishing Co., 1958.

Devlin, Robert T. *The Treaty Power under the Constitution of the United States*. San Francisco, Calif. Bancroft-Whitney Co., 1908.

Dickinson, Edwin D. "The Law of Nations as National Law: 'Political Question.'" 104 *University of Pennsylvania Law Review* 451, 1956.

Dickinson Edwin D. "The Law of Nations as Part of the National Law of the United States." 101 *University of Pennsylvania Law Review* 26, 1953.

Domke, Martin. *International Trade Arbitration: A Road to World-Wide Cooperation*. New York, N.Y. American Arbitration Association, 1958.

Encyclopaedia Britannica. Chicago, 111.
Encyclopaedia Britannica, 1950.

Fachiri, Alexander P. "Interpretation of Treaties." 23 *A.J.I.L.* 745–752, 1929.

Fatouros, A. A. *Government Guarantees to Foreign Investors*. New York, N.Y. Columbia University Press, 1962.

Fenwick, Charles Chequiere. *International Law*. Third Edition. New York, N.Y. Appleton-Century-Crofts, 1948.
Finch, George A. "Editorial Comment, The Eisler Extradition Case." 43 *A.J.I.L.* 487, 1949.
Fitzmaurice, Sir Gerald. "Some Results of the Geneva Conference on the Law of the Sea." 8 *International and Comparative Law Quarterly* 73, 1959.
Franklin. *Protection of Foreign Interests*. Washington, D.C. Government Printing Office, 1946.
Goodenough, Erwin Ramsdell. *The Jurisprudence of the Jewish Courts in Egypt*. New Haven, Conn. Yale University Press, 1929.
Gorter, Wytze. *United States Shipping Policy*. New York, N.Y. Published for the Council on Foreign Relations by Harper, 1956.
Gregory, Charles Noble. "Jurisdiction over Foreign Ships in Territorial Waters." 2 *Michigan Law Review* 333, 1904.
Hackworth, Green H. *A Digest of International Law*. 8 volumes. Washington D.C. Government Printing Office, 1940–1944.
Hall, William Edward. *International Law*. Eighth Edition by Higgins. Oxford, Clarendon Press, 1924.
Harvard Law School. "Developments in the Law – Res Judicata." 65 *Harvard Law Review* 818, 1952.
Harvard Law School. "Research in International Law, Draft Convention on Responsibility of States." 23 *A.J.I.L. Special Supplement* 131, 1929.
Hawkins, Harry C. *Commercial Treaties and Agreements*. New York, N.Y. Rinehart, 1951.
Hawthorne, Nathaniel. *Hawthorne's Works*, Vol. VII, Our Old Home, and English Note-Books, Vol. I. Boston, Mass. Boughton, Mifflin & Co., 1863.
Hawthorne, Nathaniel. *Hawthorne's Works*, Vol. VII, Passages from the English Note-Books, Vol. I. Boston, Mass Fields, Osgood, 1870.
Hendry, James McLeod. *Treaties and Federal Constitutions*. Washington, D.C. Public Affairs Press, 1955.
Hertslet, Lewis (Compiler). *Hertslet's Commercial Treaties*. Volume 2. London. Henry Butterworth, 1840.
Higgins and Colombos. *The International Law of the Sea*. Second revised Edition by Colombos. London, 1951.
Hohman, Elmo Paul. "Maritime Labour in the United States: I: The Seamen's Act and its Historical Background." 38 *International Labour Review* 190. Geneva, 1938.
— "Maritime Labour in the United States: II: Since the Seamen's Act." 38 *International Labour Review* 396. Geneva, 1938.
— "Merchant Seamen in the United States, 1937–1952." 67 *International Labour Review* 1. Geneva, 1953.
Hudson, Manley O. "Aviation and International Law." 24 *A.J.I.L.* 228–240, 1930.
Hudson, Manley O. *Cases and Other Materials on International Law*. Third Edition. St. Paul, Minn. West Publishing Co., 1951.
Hudson, Manley O. *International Legislation*. Washington D.C. Carnegie Endowment for International Peace, 1931.
Hudson, Manley O. "The Development of International Law Since the War." 22 *A.J.I.L.* 330, 1928.
Hudson, Manley O. "The Factor Case and Double Criminality in Extradition." 28 *A.J.I.L.* 274–306, 1934.
Hunt, Harry E. "How the Great lakes Became 'High Seas,'" and their Status Viewed from the Standpoint of International Law. 4 *A.J.I.L.* 285–313, 1919.

Hunt, Gaillard *The Department of State of the United States, Its History and Function.* New Haven, Conn. Yale University Press, 1914.
Hyde, Charles. *International Law Chiefly as Interpreted and Applied by the United States.* 3 volumes. Second revised Edition. Boston, Mass. Little, Brown & Co., 1945.
Hyde, Charles Cheney. "The Interpretation of Treaties by the Permanent Court of International Justice." 24 *A.J.I.L.* 1–19, 1930.
International Labour Organization. Conditions in Ships Flying the Panama Flag, Studies and Reports, New Series, No. 20–23. Geneva, 1950.
International Labour Organization. Conference Documents, 41st. Session (1958) Geneva. International Labour Organization, 1957.
Jennings, Robert Y. "Comment." 26 *British Yearbook of International Law* 468, 1949.
Jessup, Philip Caryl. *A Modern Law of Nations.* NewYork, N.Y. Macmillan, 1948.
Jessup, Philip Caryl. "The Anti-Smuggling Act of 1935." 31 *A.J.I.L.* 101, 1937.
Jessup, Philip, Caryl. *The Law of Territorial Waters and Maritime Jurisdiction.* New York, N.Y. G. A. Jennings Co., 1927.
Jones, Burr W. *The Law of Evidence, Civil and Criminal.* 4 volumes. Fifth Edition. San Francisco, Calif. Bancroft-Whitney, 1958.
Johnson, Emory R. "The Early History of the United States Consular Service, 1776–1792." 13 *Political Science Quarterly* 19–40, March 1898.
Keim, De. B. Randolph. *The Consular Service of the United States of America.* Report, Special and General. Washinton, D.C. Government Printing Office, 1873.
Kent, James. *Commentary on International Law,* J.T. Abdy (Editor). Second Edition. Cambridge. Dreighton, Bell, and Co., 1878.
Ladas, Stephen Pericles. *The International Protection of Industrial Property.* Cambridge, Mass. Harvard University Press, 1930.
Law Notes. The Origin of Consuls. Volume 30, page 17. April, 1926.
Law Times. The Rights, Duties, and Wrongs of Foreign Consuls. Volume 172, page 410. London, Field Press, 1931.
Lay, Tracy Hollingsworth. *The Foreign Service of the United States.* New York, N.Y. Prentice-Hall, 1925.
Lee, Luke T. *Consular Law and Practice.* London. Stevens & Sons, 1961.
Lee, Luke T. "Jurisdiction over Foreign Merchant Ships in the Territorial Sea." 55 *A.J.I.L.* 77, 1961.
Lee, Robert Warden. *Elements of Roman Law.* Second Edition. London. Sweet & Maxwell, 1949.
McDougal, Myres S., and William T. Burke and Ivan A. Vlassic. "The Maintenance of Public Order at Sea and the Nationality of Ships." 54 *Yale Law Journal* 25–116, 1960.
McNair, Arnold Duncan. *The Law of Treaties.* New York, N.Y. Columbia University Press, 1938.
McNair, Arnold Duncan. *The Law of Treaties.* Oxford. Clarendon Press, 1961..
Mann, F. A. "Reflection on a Commercial Law of Nations." 33 *British Yearbook of International Law* 34, 1959.
Manning, Charles Anthony Woodward. *The Nature of International Society.* London. London School of Economics and Political Science, 1962.
Miller, Arthur S. "The Corporation as a Private Government in the World Community." 46 *Virginia Law Review* 1959, 1960.
Mitchell, William. *An Essay on the Early History of the Law Merchant.* Cambridge. University Press, 1904.

Monro, C. H. *The Digest of Justinian.* 2 volumes. Cambridge. University Press, 1904.
Moore, John Bassett. *A Digest of International Law.* Washington, D.C. Government Printing Office, 1906.
Morgenstern, Felice. "Judicial Practice and the Supremacy of International Law." 27 *British Yearbook of International Law* 42, 1950.
Moss, H. St. L. B. *The Birth of the Middle Ages.* London. Oxford University Press, 1959.
Nielsen, Fred. K. "The Lack of Uniformity in the Law and Practice of States with Regard to Merchant Vessels." 13 *A.J.I.L.* 1–21, 1919.
Oppenheim, Lassa F.L. *International Law.* Sixth Edition, Lauterpacht, Longmans, Green and Co. Eighth Edition, Lauterpacht. New York, N.Y. David McKay, 1955.
Paetow, Louis John. *A Guide to the Study of Medieval History.* New York, N.Y. Kraus Reprint Corp., 1959.
Peaslee, Amos Jenkins. *Constitutions of Nations.* Second Edition. The Hague. M. Nijhoff, 1956.
Pergler, Charles. *Judicial Interpretation of International Law.* New York, N.Y. Macmillan, 1928.
Phillimore, Sir Robert Joseph. *Commentaries on International Law.* Four volumes. Philadelphia, Pa. T. & J. W. Johnson, 1854–1857.
Phillipson, Coleman. *The International Law and Custom of Ancient Greece and Rome.* Two volumes. London. Macmillan, 1911.
Piggott, Sir Francis. *Exterritoriality: The Law Relating to Consular Jurisdiction in Oriental Countries.* Hongkong. Kelly & Walsh, 1907.
Pirenne, Henri. *Mohammed and Charlemagne.* Bernard Miall (Translator). London. G. Allen & Unwin, 1956.
Pollock, Sir Frederick, and Maitland, Frederic William. *The History of English Law Before the Time of Edward I.* Two volumes. Cambridge, University Press, 1895.
Post, Charles Gordon. *The Supreme Court and Political Questions.* Baltimore, Md. The Johns Hopkins Press, 1936.
Potter, Harold. *An Historical Introduction to English Law and Its Institutions.* Second Edition. London. Street & Maxwell, 1943.
Powicke, Sir Frederick Maurice. *The Thirteenth Century 1216–1307.* Oxford. Clarendon Press, 1953.
Preuss, Lawrence. "Current Notes, Kidnapping of Fugitives from Justice in Foreign Territory." 29 *A.J.I.L.* 502, 1935.
Preuss, Lawrence. "On Amending the Treaty-Making Power: A Comparative Study of the Problem of Self-Executing Treaties." 51 *Michigan Law Review* 1117, 1953.
Puente, Julius I. "Extraterritorial Powers of the Consular Office." 19 *California Law Review* 111, 1931.
Puente, J. Irizarry y. "Functions and Powers of the Foreign Consulate – A Study in Medieval Legal History." 20 *New York University Law Quarterly Review* 57, 1945.
Puente, Julius I. "The Nature of the Consular Establishment." 78 *University of Pennsylvania Law Review* 321, 1930.
Radin, Max. *Handbook on Roman Law.* St. Paul, Minn. West Publishing, 1927.
Reiff, Henry. "The Enforcement of Multipartite Administrative Treaties in the United States." 34 *A.J.I.L.* 661–679, 1940.
Reiff, Henry. "The Proclaiming of Treaties in the United States." 30 *A.J.I.L.* 63–79, 1936.

Reiff, Henry. *The United States and the Treaty Law of the Sea*. Minneapolis, Minn. University of Minnesota, 1959.

Rienow, Robert. *The Test of Nationality of a Merchant Vessel*. New York, N.Y. Columbia University Press, 1937.

Robertson, James H. Comment, Anti-Smuggling Bill, Jurisdiction on the High Seas. 35 *Michigan Law Review* 1146, 1937.

Sack, Alexander N. "The Doctrine of Quasi-Territoriality of Vessels and the Admiralty Jurisdiction over Crimes Committed on Board National Vessels in Foreign Ports." 12 *New York University Law Quarterly Review* 628, 1935.

Sanborn, Frederic Rockwell. *Origins of the Early English Maritime and Commercial Law*. New York, N.Y. The Century Co., 1930.

Savigny, Carl von. *The History of the Roman Law during the Middle Ages*. Volume 1. E. Cathcart (Translator). Edinburgh. Adam Black, 1829.

Savigny, Friedrich Carl von. *Private International Law and the Retrospective Operation of Statutes: A Treatise on the Conflict of Laws and the Limits of their Operation in Respect of Place and Time*. Wm. Guthrie (Translator). Edinburgh. T. & T. Clark, 1880.

Schopflocker, Ernst H. "The Doctrine of Res Judicata in Administrative Law." *Wisconsin Law Review* 198, 1942.

Schuyler, Eugene. *American Diplomacy and the Furtherance of Commerce*. New York, N.Y. C. Scribner's sons, 1886.

Schwartz, Bernard. *An Introduction to American Administrative Law*. Second Edition. Dobbs Ferry, N.Y. Oceana Publications, 1962.

Schwarzenberger, Georg. "The Most-Favored-Nation Standard in British State Practice." XXII *British Yearbook of International Law* 96, 1945.

Scott, James Brown (Editor). *The International Conferences of American States 1889–1928*. New York, N.Y. Oxford University Press, 1931.

Sherman, Charles P., and Robinson, T. R. *Roman Readings in Roman Law*. New York, N.Y. Baker, Voorhis, 1933.

Simmonds, K. R. "The 'Rationale' of Diplomatic Immunity." 11 *International and Comparative Law Quarterly* 1204, 1962.

Snyder, Richard Carlton. *The Most-Favored-Nation Clause*. Mew York, N.Y. Kings Crown Press, 1948.

Strachan - Davidson, James Leigh. *Problems of the Roman Criminal*. Oxford. Clarendom Press, 1912

Treaties, etc. of Commerce and Navigation Between Great Britain and Foreign Powers Wholly or Partly in Force on January 1, 1907. London. Henry Butterworth and Sons, 1907.

Twiss, Sir Travers (Editor). *The Blackbook of Admiralty*. Four volumes. London. Longmans & Co., 1871–1876.

Twiss, Sir Travers. *The Law of Nations*. Second revised Edition. Oxford. Clarendon Press, 1884.

United States, Department of State. Commercial Treaty Program of the United States (Department of State Publication 6565). Washington, D.C. Government Printing Office, 1958.

United States, Department of State. Foreign Affairs Manual. Washington, D.C. Government Printing Office, 1961.

United States House of Representatives. Study of Vessel Transfer, Trade-in and Reserve Fleet Policies, Part I. Washington, D.C. Government Printing Office, 1957.

Verzijl, J. H. W. "The United Nations Conference on the Law of the Sea," Geneva, 1958. 6 *Nederlands Tijdschrift voor Internationaal Recht* 115, 1959.

Walker, Herman Jr. "Modern Treaties of Friendship, Commerce and Navigation." 42 *Minnesota Law Review* 805, 1958.

Walker, T. A. *A History of the Law of Nations*. Cambridge. University Press, 1899.

Warden, David Baillie. *On the Origin, Nature, Progress and Influence of Consular Establishments*. Paris. Smith, 1813.

Wharton, Francis. *A Digest of the International Law of the United States*. Washington, D.C. Government Printing Office, 1887.

Wheaton, Henry. *Elements of International Law*. Third Edition. Philadelphia, Pa. Lea & Blanchard, 1846.

Wheaton, Henry. *Elements of International Law*. Eight Edition by R. H. Dana, Jr. Boston, Mass. Little, Brown & Co., 1866.

White, Lyman Cromwell. *International Non-Governmental Organizations*. New Brunswick, N.J. Rutgers University Press, 1951.

Wigmore, John Henry. *A Treatise on the Anglo-American System of Evidence in Trials at Common Law*. Ten volumes. Third Edition. Boston, Mass. Little, Brown & Co., 1940.

Wilson, Robert R. "A Decade of New Commercial Treaties." 50 *A.J.I.L.* 927, 1956.

Wilson, Robert R. "Postwar Commercial Treaties of the United States." 43 *A.J.I.L.* 262, 1949.

Wilson, Robert R. *The International Law Standard in Treaties of the United States*. Cambridge, Mass. Harvard University Press, 1953.

Wilson, Robert R. Editorial Comment. " 'Treaty-Merchant' Clauses in Commercial Treaties of the United States." 44 *A.J.I.L.* 145, 1950.

Wilson, Robert R. *United States Commercial Treaties and International Law*. New Orleans, La. Hauser Press, 1960.

Woolf, Leonard Sidney. *International Government* Westminster. Fabian Society, 1916.

Yale Law Review. Comment. The Difficult Quest for a Uniform Maritime Law: Failure of the Brussels Conventions to Achieve International Agreement on Collision Liability, Liens and Mortgages. 64 *Yale Law Journal* 878, 1955.

INDEX

GPSR Compliance

The European Union's (EU) General Product Safety Regulation (GPSR) is a set of rules that requires consumer products to be safe and our obligations to ensure this.

If you have any concerns about our products, you can contact us on ProductSafety@springernature.com

In case Publisher is established outside the EU, the EU authorized representative is:

Springer Nature Customer Service Center GmbH
Europaplatz 3
69115 Heidelberg, Germany

Batch number: 10830943

Printed by Printforce, the Netherlands